Augustine's World

An Introduction to His Speculative Philosophy

Donald X. Burt, O.S.A.

University Press of America, Inc.

B
655
. Z 7
B 85
1996

Copyright © 1996 by
University Press of America,® Inc.
4720 Boston Way
Lanham, Maryland 20706

3 Henrietta Street
London, WC2E 8LU England

Library of Congress Cataloging-in-Publication Data

Burt, Donald X.
Augustine's world : an introduction to his speculative philosophy /
Donald X. Burt.
p.   cm.
Includes bibliographical references and index.
1. Augustine, Saint, Bishop of Hippo. I. Title.
B655.Z7B85   1996   189'.2--dc20   96-10254 CIP

ISBN 0-7618-0294-0 (cloth: alk. ppr.)
ISBN 0-7618-0295-9 (pbk: alk. ppr.)

⊖™The paper used in this publication meets the minimum
requirements of American National Standard for information
Sciences—Permanence of Paper for Printed Library Materials,
ANSI Z39.48—1984

Dedication

To
Robert P. Russell, O.S.A.,
teacher, mentor, and friend
Requiescat in Pace

Contents

Abbreviations of the Works of Augustine

In order to conserve space I have taken the liberty of abbreviating references to Augustine's works. The following list gives (a) the abbreviation of the work, (b) the Latin title of the work, (c) an English translation of the title, and (d) where the work can be found in the *Patrologia Latina* (Migne ed.) for example, PL 32, 659-868 in reference to the work *The Confessions* means that the Latin text can be found in volume 32, columns 659 through 868.

C. Confessiones (The Confessions) PL 32, 659-868.

CA. Contra academicos (Against the Academics) PL 32, 905-958.

CEM. Contra epistolam Manichaei quam vocant Fundamenti (Against the Letter of the Manicheans Called "Fundamental") PL 42, 173-206.

CEP. Contra duas epistulas Pelagianorum ad Bonifacium Papam, IV (Against Two Pelagian Letters) PL 44, 549-638.

CFM. Contra Faustum Manichaeum (Against Faustus the Manichaean), PL 42, 207-518.

CJH. Contra Julianum haeresis Pelagianae defensorem (Against Julian the Heretic) PL 44, 641-874.

CLP. Contra adversarium Legis et Prophetarum (Against Opponents of the Law and Prophets) PL 42, 603-66.

CPO. Contra Priscillianistas et Origenistas ad Orosium (Against the Priscillianists and Origenists to Orosius) PL 42, 669-678.

CSM. Contra Secundinum Manichaeum (Against Secundinus the Manichean) PL 42, 577-602.

DA. De anima et ejus origine (On the Soul and Its Origin) PL 44, 475-548.

DAC. De agone Christiano (The Christian Combat) PL 40, 289-310.

DB. De beata vita (On the Happy Life) PL 32, 959-976.

DBC. De bono conugali (On the Good of Marriage) PL 40, 373-96.

DBV. De bono viduitatis ad Julianum (On the Good of Widowhood) PL 40, 429-50.

DC. De continentia (On Continence) PL 40, 348-72.

DCD. De civitate Dei (The City of God) PL 41, 13-804.

DCE. De consensu Evangelistarum (On the Harmony of the Gospels) PL 34, 1041-1230.

DCG. De correptione et gratia (On Rebuke and Grace), PL 44, 915-958.

DCM. De cura pro mortuis gerenda (On the Care of the Dead), PL 40, 591-610.

DCR. De catechizandis rudibus (On Catechizing the Uninstructed) PL 40, 309-348.

DDA. De duabus animabus contra Manichaeos (On Two Souls against the Manichaeans) PL 42, 93-112.

DDC. De doctrina Christiana (On Christian Doctrine) PL 34, 15-122.

DDP. De dono perseverantiae (On the Gift of Perseverance) PL 45, 993-1034.

DDQ. De diversis quaestionibus 83 (On 83 Diverse Questions) PL 40, 11-100.

DFS. De fide et symbolo (On Faith and the Creed) PL 40, 181-196.

DGA. De gratia et libero arbitrio ad Valentinum (On Grace and Free Will to Valentine) PL 44, 881-912.

DGC. De gratia Christi et peccato originali (On the Grace of Christ and Original Sin) PL 44, 359-410.

DGI. De Genesi ad litteram, liber imperfectus (An Incomplete Literal Commentary on Genesis) PL 35, 219-246.

DGL. De Genesi ad Litteram (A Literal Commentary on Genesis) PL 34, 245-486.

DGM. De Genesi contra Manichaeos (On Genesis against the Manicheans) PL 34, 173-220.

DGP. De gestis Pelagii (On the Deeds of Pelagius) PL 44, 319-60.

DIA. De immortalitate animae (On the Immortality of the Soul) PL 32, 1021-34.

DFO. De fide et operibus (On Faith and Works) PL 40, 197-230.

DLA. De libero arbitrio (On Free Choice) PL 32, 1221-1310.

DMA. De Magistro (On the Teacher) PL 32, 1193-1220.

DMC. De moribus ecclesiae Catholicae et de moribus Manichaeorum (The Morals of the Catholic Church and the Morals of the Manichaeans) PL 32, 1309-78.

DMU. De musica (On Music) PL 32, 1081-1194.

DNB. De natura boni contra Manichaeos (On the Nature of the Good Against the Manicheans) PL 42, 551-72.

DNC. De nuptiis et concupiscentia (On Marriage and Concupiscence) PL 44, 413-74.

DNG. De natura et gratia contra Pelagium (On Nature and Grace against Pelagius) PL 44, 247-90.

DO. De ordine (On Order) PL 32, 977-1020.

DOD. De octo Dulcitii quaestionibus (On the Eight Questions of Dulcitius) PL 40, 147-70.

DOM. De opere monachorum (On the Work of Monks) PL 40, 547-82.

DPM. De peccatorum meritis et remissione et de baptismo parvulorum (On Merits and the Remission of Sins and on Infant Baptism) PL 44, 109-200.

DPS. De praedestinatione sanctorum (On the Predestination of the Saints) PL 44, 959-92.

DQA. De quantitate animae (On the Magnitude of the Soul) PL 32, 1035-80.

DQS. De diversis quaestionibus VII ad Simplicianum (On Seven Various Questions to Simplicianus) PL 40, 101-148.

DSL. De spiritu et littera (On the Spirit and the Letter) PL 44, 201-246.

DSM. De sermone Domini in monte (On the Lord's Sermon on the Mount) PL 34, 1229-1308.

DT. De trinitate (On the Trinity) PL 42, 819-1098.

DUC. De utilitate credendi (On the Usefulness of Believing) PL 42, 63-92.

DUJ. De utilitate jejunii (On the Usefulness of Fasting) PL 40, 707-716.

DVR. De vera religione (On the True Religion) PL 34, 121-172.

E. Epistolae (Letters) PL 33, 61-1162.

E*. Epistolae ex duobus condicibus nuper in lucem prolatae (New Letters Recently Discovered) *Corpus Scriptorum Ecclesiasticorum Latinorum*, volume 88.

EEG. Expositio epistulae ad Galatas (A Commentary on the Epistle to the Galatians) PL 35, 2105-2148.

EER. Expositio quarumdam propositionum ex Epistola ad Romanos (Commentary on Some Propositions from the Epistle to the Romans) PL 35, 2063-2088.

ENC. Enchiridion ad Laurentium de fide, spe, charitate (The Enchiridion on Faith, Hope, and Charity) PL 40, 231-290.

ENN. Enarrationes in Psalmos (Commentaries on the Psalms) PL 36, 67-1028; PL 37, 1033-1968.

IEJ. In Epistolam Joannis ad Parthos (On the Letter of John to the Parthians) PL 35, 1977-2062.

IJE. In Joannis Evangelium (On the Gospel of John) PL 35, 1379-1976.

OIJ. Opus imperfectum contra Julianum (Incomplete Work against Julian) PL 45, 1049-1608.

QE. Quaestionum Evangeliorum (Questions on the Gospels [Matthew And Luke]) PL 35, 1321-1364.

QH. Quaestiones in Heptateuchum (Questions on the Heptateuch) PL 34, 547-824.

R. Regula sancti Augustini (The Rule of Saint Augustine). A manuscript of Augustine's "Rule for Monasteries" can be found in Letter 211, 5-16 (PL 33, 960-65). However the critical edition is contained in the work of Luc Verheijen, O.S.A, *La Règle De Saint Augustin*, Études Augustiniennes: Paris, 1967, pp. 417-37.

RET. Retractationum (Retractions) PL 32, 583-656.

SER. Sermones (Sermons) PL 38, 23-1484; PL 39, 1493-1736.

SO. Soliloquia (The Soliloquies) PL 32, 869-904.

Preface

Kant once remarked that all of the interests of the human mind come down to three questions:

1. What can I know?
2. What can I hope for?
3. What should I to do?

(*Critique of Pure Reason,* A 805, B 833)

The first two questions reflect our desire to understand the past, comprehend the present, and predict the future. All of us want to know what our world is like: its origins, present status, and future possibilities. "If only we could know this [we say], we could then perhaps answer the next question: 'What should I do?'"

St. Augustine spent most of his life trying to answer such questions. He was driven by an over-powering desire for happiness and he was convinced that if happiness was ever to be achieved, it could come only by possession of some "good" that existed in the real world. The first step in his search for happiness had to be a discovery process whereby he would come to understand those aspects of reality most relevant to his quest: namely, God and himself.

Augustine wanted to understand the condition of the world in which he lived and to understand his instruments for coping with such a world: his powers of knowledge and choice. He wanted to get an accurate picture of where he was, where he came from, and where he was going. Finally, he wanted to know if there was a really existing "good" which had the potentiality for slaking his infinite thirsts. Was there an infinite being, a God, who could be possessed? What were the characteristics of such a God? Was this God indifferent or caring, distant or near? His "self" and his God set the parameters for his investigation of reality and as he began his search for happiness he prayed for only two things: "O God, let me know myself; let me know you." (*Soliloquies,* 2.1.1.)

The pages that follow are an attempt to lay out as clearly as possible the answers Augustine received to this prayer. It is an exploration of his speculative thought, his answer to the question "What is my world like?" The other questions that he would ask ("How should I govern my life?" "How should I deal with others in society?") are issues for another time and another book.

Acknowledgements

Speciel thanks are due to the staff of Augustinian Press
and the Augustinian Historical Institute for their kind assistance
in the preparation of the manuscript for publication.

Introduction

The Environment[1]

The Place

Augustine was born in the town of Thagaste in the Roman province of Numidia in North Africa in the year 354. At that time Rome's influence stretched along the coastline of present day Algeria and Tunisia, extending inland with diminishing power to the borders of the Sahara desert. These coastal regions were a fertile land, producing great crops of grain and vegetables in the river valleys and huge forests or olive trees on the hillsides and arid high plains.

The town of Thagaste (the present Souk-Ahras in Algeria) was situated in the northeast highlands of Numidia, some sixty miles from Hippo Regius (the present Annaba [Bone]), the seaside city where Augustine was to spend the last forty years of his life. It was about fifteen miles from Madaura (the present M'Daourouch, Algeria) where he went to "prep" school and about one hundred and fifty miles from Carthage on the coast of present day Tunisia, where he was to go for higher education and where he was to spend the early years of his teaching career. Carthage was the grand metropolis of the land. Founded by the Phoenicians nine centuries before the coming of Christ, destroyed by Rome in 146 BC, reestablished by the Emperor Augustus in 29 BC, it had become in Augustine's day the second largest city in the Western Empire. Only Rome itself was larger.

Thagaste had no such pretensions to grandeur. Though it had already existed for three hundred years before Augustine was born (and was to last even till today), it was nothing more than a somewhat pleasant county-seat for farms and great estates. It is likely that its population was never more than a few thousand people, if that. It was situated in the river valley of the Medjerda, a fertile land filled with corn and pastures and gardens. The hills (where they were not cultivated with olive trees) were heavily forested with oak and pine and in these natural habitats lived lions and bears and panthers, animals frequently captured to be sold for the Roman amphitheater games. Wildflowers were sprinkled through the open ground and flocks of various birds coursed through the clear skies. It was a land of four seasons with a climate not unlike that of southern Spain. The winters were short, of course, but snow was not unknown. The summers were long and very hot. In sum it was a land full of life, pungent smells, and violent colors. It is no wonder that Augustine's writings are filled with analogies from the land and that he so often speaks about the beauty of this world. He grew up and lived most of his life in a beautiful land.

The People

This vitality was reflected in the people of the land. The native North Africans were Berbers, and these were still the dominant population in the rural areas (for example, Thagaste) in the fourth century. Added to these roots was that of the Phoenicians who had founded Carthage nine centuries before the coming of Christ. There was also some Roman blood intermixed, coming from the army veterans who had been given land as a reward for their services some two hundred years before. Roman settlement had ceased when Augustine was born, though many of the great estates were owned by absentee Roman landlords. The flow of immigrants would increase later on as the barbarians swept down on Rome in the early fifth century.

The people had a taste for wine, women, and song. They were sociable and gregarious but given to violent anger when they felt abused. Augustine in 420 gave the following sympathetic description of the typical North African Christian who was serious about salvation. He was like a husband who did good works from time to time, who was faithful to his wife and enjoyed having sex with her, who was very serious about his honor and who thought seriously about taking revenge on anyone who sullied that honor. He valued his property without being especially greedy or grasping. He would give some of his goods to those in need but would fight vigorously anyone who dared to steal from him. He did not pretend to be a saint nor did he think he was God. He was ready to admit his failings and in all humility recognized that without the grace of God they were likely to occur again.[2]

The society was characterized by defined social strata. At the very top were the landowners, high government officials, and rich expatriates from Italy. The landowners lived like feudal kings supported by the annual fees paid by tenant farmers for the use of the land. Many of them were absentee landlords, taking little interest in the products or the people that provided their income. At the second level were minor bureaucrats, merchants, lawyers, and teachers. If the great estate owners were the noble rich, these were the noble poor. They were noble in that they lived by their wits more than by their sweat, but they were poor because any extra funds from gainful employment were quickly absorbed by high taxes. The problems that this middle class had in "making ends meet" is exemplified in the difficulty Patricius had in keeping his son in school much beyond the elementary level. It was only through the kindness of the wealthy Romanianus that Augustine was able to continue his education and career in Carthage.

At the third level in society were the peasants, poor fishermen, and day-laborers of the city. These lived a hard life, glad on any given day to find a warm bed and adequate food. Their only equity was their physical strength and when this ran out they faced disaster. It was not unknown for them to sell their children into slavery so that both they and the children could get enough to live. Sometimes they turned to crime, attacking any person foolish enough to travel far from the towns without military escort. People of the land, they had a healthy suspicion of any alien people or alien ideas that threatened their historic culture. The peasants owned little but themselves. The very lowest class in society, the slaves, owned not even that. Still, from a material point of view their lot was sometimes better than that of the poor freeman. If their master was kind, they could at least be sure of daily meals and evening shelter. In truth they were not free, but at least their owner was a human being who could just possibly take pity on them. The peasant was chained by a harsher master . . . an economic condition which could not feel pity or any other emotion and which destroyed the very possibility of a truly human, secure, comfortable existence.

The Political Environment

When Augustine was born in the middle of the fourth century, the western Roman Empire was still a force to be reckoned with. Though rebellions of border tribes in Northern Europe were a continuing aggravation, Rome could still claim control over most of the civilized world in Europe and North Africa. When Augustine died seventy-six years later, all this had changed. The western Empire was under siege from the barbarians from the north. They had invaded France and Spain. In 410 they captured the city of Rome itself. They moved on into North Africa and by 430 were laying siege to Hippo where Augustine lay dying. They were to rule in North Africa for a hundred years thereafter.

During most of Augustine's life, Rome held uneasy control of its North African provinces. Its influence was quite strong in the cities and larger towns, but lost its vigor the further one moved out into the country. There the native North African people held sway, suspicious of any foreign challenge to their historic practices and filled with hatred for the "aliens" from across the sea who took their crops and imposed impossible levies on their possessions. Symptomatic of the power of this native spirit was the success of Donatism, a vigorous faction within North African Christianity. Part of its strength, it would seem, came from its identification as a "North African" thing . . . an ultra-conservative interpretation of salvation doctrine that struck a resonant chord in the rigid native mind.

The life of Augustine thus spanned a tumultuous time in the history of the western Empire and the western Church. In the late fourth century it seemed that the North African Church would be torn apart by religious civil war. In the early fifth century it seemed possible that western civilization itself would come to an end. It is no wonder that in 398 Augustine would observe to a friend that on every border and in every province peace depended on the sworn oaths of barbarians.[3] As he lay dying listening to the Vandals attacking his beloved Hippo, he looked back over the violence of his times and ruefully observed that one could not be called particularly wise if they were overcome with amazement when things of wood and stone fell apart and people who are mortal eventually died.[4]

The Religious Environment

The North African people were greatly attracted by mystery. The world of the unseen was just as real to them as the world of the seen. Few if any had a problem with whether God (or gods) existed. The only question was what the divine was like. Daily life was a continuing ritual aimed at placating and worshiping innumerable unseen spirits. Magic to control the present and astrology to learn the future were accepted tools for protecting one's existence. It is no great wonder that mystery cults such as Manichaeism found a fertile field among the North Africans. There was special veneration of the dead, a veneration which in Christian times was converted to a deep reverence for those who had died for the faith. The border between the living and the dead was very thin and in the perilous times of the fourth and fifth century it was a line that was easily crossed.

At the same time there was a pessimism about what one could do to make life better. Fate and chance ultimately ruled one's life.

When Augustine was born Christianity was a major force in the Roman provinces of North Africa. Yet there still remained a healthy residue of the native mystery cults as well as the pagan rites imported with Rome. Christianity had appeared in North Africa by the second century. It had survived the persecutions of the third century and had produced such giants as Tertullian and Cyprian. By the time of Augustine Christianity was the approved religion of the Empire, but in North Africa it was split into two factions: the Roman Catholic and the Donatist. The Donatist faction represented a conservative, rigorist element in Christianity. They claimed to be the only "pure" Christianity since none of their group came from the despised "Traitors" (*Traditores*) who had denied their faith in the midst of the persecutions. They followed the Cyprian principle that there can be no salvation outside the Church and the Church was for those who remained faithful after baptism. Augustine, who was of the liberal faction, was to spend much of his early years as a bishop in battle with the Donatists, ultimately winning the day by getting their position rejected by the Pope and proscribed by the Emperor.

In dealing with his own congregation over forty years Augustine had to take into account their passion for the mysterious and their tendency toward fatalism. He spoke frequently against such practices as astrology and magic. He preached Divine Providence, rather than fate and chance, as the ruling force in life. He complained about their superstitious worship of the martyrs and their tendency to use the feast days as an excuse for debauchery. He attempted to center their enthusiasm on Christ and to channel their passionate nature into a warm and enduring love for God and all humans, even enemies. In this he was not completely successful, on one occasion having to remonstrate with them for participating in the lynching of an unpopular public official.[5] He could not change the hard conditions of their life nor their passionate nature nor their exuberant taste for life. But he did have some success in calling on their generosity to help the poor, in substituting hope in providence for fear of fate, and in encouraging them not to stop loving but only to love in some sort of orderly fashion.

Life

Augustine was born in 354, the third child of Monica and Patricius. He had an older brother, Navigius, and at least one sister. Monica his mother was almost certainly a Berber and his father was probably a mixture of Berber and Roman ancestry. Monica was a fervent Catholic Christian while Patricius remained a good-natured pagan for most of his life, perfectly willing to let Monica take care of the religious training of the children. From her Augustine learned about Christianity as a child. He was, however, never baptized. This was in accord with the normal practice of the day of putting off baptism until the adolescent days of sowing wild oats were over. There is some indication that Augustine was still intermittently going to Christian exercises in his late teens, but it seems clear that he was far from serious about any religion in those days, consumed more by ambition and bodily desires.

Augustine grew up in middle class surroundings. Patricius had a small family estate and worked as a minor government bureaucrat, a position of some respect but little income. He was able to provide the necessities of life for his family but he had trouble providing funds for the education of the children. It would seem that Augustine was the only one provided with much of a formal education. Patricius and Monica shared a common dream that their precocious child would bring honor to the family by being successful in some noble career.

The child gave promise of such success. He was very bright and ambitious and headstrong. As a child he wanted to have his own way and cried loudly when he did not get it. He did well at his studies but did not like school all that much. He had an insatiable desire to know things but he also liked to play ball and to go to shows and for these last ventures he was beaten often. He did not seem to relish being a child. When he was in his forties he was able to look back and thank God for the good things he experienced in his growing up[6] but he also ruefully observed that any sensible person, given the choice between doing it over again or dying, would surely choose death.[7]

Since the boy Augustine had strong Berber roots, he may have been of swarthy complexion (although O'Meara is of the opinion that it is unlikely that he was any darker than the average Roman of the day).[8] We do know from his physical remains that he was not very tall. It seems that he was somewhat physically frail. A stomach ailment almost killed him when he was a boy and a terrible fever (perhaps malaria) brought him close to death again when he was in his twenties. He did survive for seventy-six years but throughout his life he was plagued with asthma, a bad stomach, insomnia, and recurrent fevers. His weak lungs were a factor in his decision to give up teaching when he was still a young man (though this did not stop him from preaching at length without benefit of microphone for forty years in his cathedral church at Hippo). When he was fifty-six exhaustion did force him to take time off in the country, but he continued with his preaching and teaching and writing thereafter till shortly before his death twenty years later. Perhaps because of his ailments, Augustine did not have much faith in the medical practice of his day.[9] Little wonder that he had so much to say about facing up to death. Its possibility was his constant companion, especially as he grew older.

Still, his sometime physical disability did not lessen the vigor of his mind. The young Augustine quickly outgrew the schools in Thagaste and, with the financial support of a family friend (Romanianus), he was shipped off to the neighboring town of Madauros to study grammar and literature. He was in his early teens, away from home for the first time, and he went a little crazy. He lied to his teachers, stole small things to bribe his way into classmate games, and then cheated and quarreled so that he could win. For all of that he learned easily and was pronounced "a boy of great promise."[10]

When he was sixteen the money for his education ran out and he was forced to spend a year at home in idleness while his father tried to scrape together the funds to send him on to higher studies in Carthage. Neither his father nor his mother seemed terribly upset by his adolescent frivolity during the idle year. Patricius saw it as a sign of his son's growing "macho" manhood and Monica hoped that it was a way of "getting evil vapors out of his system." She did warn him about any actions (for example, fornication and adultery) that might jeopardize his future, but there is some hint that he listened politely and then did what he wanted to do. Certainly he traveled with a bad crowd. Augustine admits that he was not the worst of them but he pretended to be the worst with lying boasts about fictional exploits.[11] All in all it was a bad year. Augustine wasted his time, Patricius worked overtime, and Monica worried each day about the possible disasters that could destroy her son. The whole family sighed with relief when the funds were accumulated to send Augustine off to Carthage for his "higher education."

At Carthage the seventeen year old Augustine continued his education and his wild behavior. He came in contact with another gang of rowdies (the "Wreckers") dedicated to disrupting classrooms and making life unpleasant for new students. Though Augustine did not approve nor participate in all of the gang's activities, he did value their friendship and lived with them.[12] He made good progress in his studies while indulging his passion as much as he could. He describes himself at this time in his life as being "in love with loving and it was even more delicious when I was able to enjoy the flesh of my love."[13] He did carry on the pretense of religion by going to church sometimes but (as he suggests) his main reason for going was to see girls.[14] He was in fact leading a double life, trying to act in a refined and sophisticated manner while being driven by his physical needs.[15] In this pretense he was eminently successful. He was perceived as a young man guaranteed a fine future in public service as long as he did not make some terrible mistake.

It seemed to those around him that he made such a mistake when he fell truly in love. There is no record of the woman's name but apparently she was the daughter of a freed slave. Formal marriage would thus have been an obstacle to Augustine's career plans. But Augustine apparently truly loved her. He lived with her for eleven years (an extraordinary commitment for those days) and by her had a son, Adeodatus. This ended his leisurely academic life. Now he had to find work to support his family while still pursuing his studies. He was nineteen.

It was about this time that the direction of his academic interests changed. While still pursuing his career in rhetoric, he now (through the influence of Cicero's book *Hortensius*) became excited about philosophy and its claim to wisdom. From being a manipulator of words he now dreamed of understanding reality. At first he turned to the Bible for answers but found that the stories and language that had so entranced him as a child at the knee of Monica seemed crude and unsophisticated now that he was a student of literature. Like many of his compatriots among the intelligentsia of Carthage he turned to Manichaeism, that mysterious cult from the East that promised an easy explanation for both the wild passions of humans and the phenomena of nature. Augustine was to remain connected with this sect for nine years, at the very end attached more by its political advantage than by any deep-seated conviction.

In 375 Augustine was forced to leave Carthage and return to Thagaste to find work. He was by this time a truly dedicated and proselytizing Manichaean and Monica initially refused to have anything to do with him. Eventually she relented, but Augustine was not destined to stay long in Thagaste under any circumstances. A friend of his died and so overcome was he with grief that he fled back to Carthage to escape the places of Thagaste that brought back painful memories of shared experiences.[16]

For eight years (376-84) he tried to support his family and further his career in Carthage. It was a difficult period in his life. He was becoming increasingly disenchanted with the teachings of Manichaeism. For a time he was intrigued by astrology and the writings of magicians but turned away from them also. At twenty-six he wrote his first book, but no one bought it . . . a truly depressing experience for one who believes that he has discovered the nature of truth. He was always able to get enough students to support his family, but he found the Carthaginian scholars disruptive. With his weak voice and his tendency to be distracted, Augustine was fair game for young stalwarts more interested in love and wine than logic and wisdom. Indeed, Augustine discovered that there were very few denizens of Carthage with whom he could hold an intelligent conversation. The leaders of the Manichaeans were no better than the novices in providing answers. All in all it was not a propitious place to be, either to pursue his career or to develop his mind. He decided to leave North Africa and go to Rome. Monica was dead-set against his plan. By this time Patricius had died and she had taken as her remaining life-work the conversion of her wandering son. She was certain (considering his past history) that to be alone in a pagan city without the protection of family and friends would destroy him. But Augustine had made up his mind (he had always been stubborn) and tricked his mother into believing that he would stay while he instead sailed away on the evening tide.

Augustine arrived in Rome without money or a job in 383. He became deathly ill and only survived through the kindness of Manichaean friends. While he had begged for baptism when he was near death as a boy, now as a young man the thought never entered his mind. He thought as a Manichaean, not as a Christian, and was dependent financially and emotionally on his Manichaean companions. Indeed, it was through the recommendation of the Manichaean Symmachus, Prefect of Rome, that in 384 Augustine achieved the pinnacle of his secular career. He was appointed professor of rhetoric for the city of Milan, the city of the Imperial Court.

By this time he had given up all belief in the Manichaean doctrines. For a time he lived as a skeptic but found that unsatisfactory too. He still had a residual belief in Christ and an intuition that there was something more to being human than being a body. This intuition was confirmed through the influence of the Neoplatonist, Plotinus. Through his reading of these "Platonists" he was able to perceive the intellectual validity of asserting the existence of a world of spirit and of a human soul within which one could possibly even survive death. However, his belief in spirit still did not mean that the spirit controlled his earthy passions. He seemed to have all other aspects of his life under control. His new position in

Milan gave him the assured income necessary to support his family. Soon he was joined in Milan by his wife, his son, his mother Monica, his brother Navigius, and assorted cousins and friends.

Meanwhile Augustine was faced with a difficult personal decision. He had reached a point where his career demanded a proper marriage into a respected Roman family. Such a marriage would bring both added finances and added influence at the imperial court. Augustine's love of eleven years was an obstacle. She consented to return to Africa (leaving Adeodatus with Augustine), and Augustine, with the encouragement of his mother (who hoped that the stability of marriage might be a step toward her son's baptism) became engaged to a young daughter of a noble family. However the girl was too young for an immediate marriage and Augustine was unable to wait. He himself describes what happened:

> I could not wait patiently for the required two years. I was not a lover of marriage. I was a slave of my lust. And thus I began an affair with another woman.[17]

Both intellectually and morally he was still a distance from conversion to Christianity. He was in a period of vacuum. The only thing he knew for sure was that he was unhappy. He had nothing to substitute for his long-held Manichaeism but the dream of going off somewhere to seek wisdom with like-minded people. He and some friends took steps to form such a philosophic community but the plan fell apart when they suddenly realized that those who were married would never get the necessary permissions from their wives.[18]

Looking at Augustine's life from the outside it seemed that he was about to achieve his goals. But as his professional life became more ordered, his spiritual life had become more and more torn. Under the influence of Ambrose's preaching he was coming to see that the spiritual meaning of the Sacred Scriptures was not as simplistic as he had thought. However the moral challenge of Christianity to change his life was still beyond him. It took almost thirty years for him to come to believe in Catholic Christianity. It took him three more years before he could muster the strength to act on it. Finally, when he was thirty-three the conversion of his will occurred. He made the decision to give up his bad habits and try to live a moral life. In the spring of 387 he and his son Adeodatus were baptized by Ambrose in Milan. The first part of his restless journey was over.

Augustine spent the last forty years of his life trying to be true to his baptism. He returned to North Africa in 388 and set up a small commu-

nity of dedicated Christian laymen in Thagaste. Its purpose was the study
of Scripture and mutual service while living a life somewhat withdrawn
from the hurly-burly of the world. This peace and quiet was not to last
very long. In 391 he made the "mistake" (as he calls it) of going to Hippo
to interview a candidate for his little community. Seeing him in the
church one day, the people demanded that he be ordained their priest. He
accepted on the condition that he could continue his community there in
Hippo. This he did and from that community he began his service of the
people of Hippo. In 395 he was consecrated their bishop and in that position he spent the last thirty-five years of his life.

They were years of intense activity filled with preaching to his own
people every day and teaching through his writings the world of western
Christianity. In the course of those thirty years he combated (more or less
in succession) the powerful challenges of Manichaeism, Donatism, Pelagianism and (at the very end of his life) Arianism. He tried to describe
how God works in the individual soul through his *Confessions* and how
God works in history through his *City of God*. In his voluminous correspondence and smaller books he commented on the events of the day and
how a human is meant to cope with them. He tried to understand the
origin of the universe through his commentaries on Genesis and the destiny of humans through his commentaries on the writings of St. Paul and
St. John.

In the midst of these intellectual battles, Augustine witnessed the
growing spread of the barbarian invasions which seemed to threaten civilization itself. Rome fell in 410 and soon afterward the Vandals invaded
North Africa. Augustine lived with their threat through the last years of
his life, and as he lay dying he could hear the pounding of the barbarian
armies at the gates of his beloved Hippo. To a person without faith it
could easily have seemed that a lifetime of effort had been wasted. But
Augustine was a person of faith and hope and with such support he was
able to die happily despite the turmoil in the world outside. His death
occurred in 430 in his monastery at Hippo. His contemporary biographer,
Possidius, describes the scene as follows:

> He died with his body intact. He could still see and hear and his mind
> was clear to the very end. As we looked on and prayed for him he
> passed in sleep into the land of his ancestors, well-nourished in good
> old age.[19]

Notes

1. My summary of the environment in which Augustine lived and worked is heavily dependent on the excellent treatment given in such works as the following: Peter Brown, *Augustine of Hippo* (Los Angeles, Cal.: University of California Press, 1967); Gerald Bonner, *St. Augustine of Hippo* (Philadelphia, Pa.: Westminster Press, 1963); W. H. C. Frend, *The Donatist Church* (London: Oxford Univ. Press, 1952); John J. O'Meara, *The Young Augustine* (New York, N.Y.: Longman, 1980); F. Van Der Meer, *Augustine the Bishop*, trans. Brian Battershaw & G. R. Lamb (New York, N.Y., Sheed & Ward: 1961). The very readable popular work *The Restless Heart* by Michael Marshall (Grand Rapids, Mich.: Eerdmans, 1987) was also helpful.

2. *CEP*, 3.5.14: PL 44, 598. For the sake of brevity, abbreviations will be used for the works of Augustine cited. A list of abbreviations used is contained in the Preface. If the particular work contains several books, each having chapters and paragraph numbers, the first number in the citation will give the book, the second will give the chapter and the third (when used) will give paragraph numbers in the Latin edition. If there are no chapters in the book, the second number will give paragraph numbers. All citations to the Latin text are taken from Migne's *Patrologia Latina* abbreviated as follows "PL (vol. numb.), (column numb.)" Thus the unabbreviated citation above would read, *Contra duas epistulas Pelagianorum ad Bonifacium Papam, IV*, book 3, chapter 5, paragraph 14, in *Patrologia Latina*, volume 44, column 598. The advisability of using abbreviations is evident.

3. *E 47*, 2, PL 33, 185.

4. Possidius, *Vita S. Augustini Episcopi*, chapter 28, PL 32, 58.

5. See *SER 302*, PL 38, 1385-93. See F. Van Der Meer, *op. cit.* p. 142.

6. *C*, 1.20, PL 32, 675-76.

7. *DCD*, 21.14, PL 41, 728.

8. O'Meara, *op. cit.*, p. 29.

9. See *ENN 102*, 5, PL 37, 1319-20.

10. See *C*, l.19 & 16, PL 32, 674 & 672.

11. *C*, 2.3, PL 32, 678.

12. *C*, 3.3, PL 32, 685.

13. *C*, 3.1, PL 32, 683.

14. See *C*, 3.3, PL 32, 685.

15. *C*, 3.1, PL 32, 683.

16. *C*, 4.4, PL 32, 696-98.

17. *C*, 6.15, PL 32, 732.

18. *C*, 6.14, PL 32, 731.

19. Possidius, *op. cit.*, chapter 31, PL 32, 64.

Chapter 1
The Human Condition

Introduction

It will be helpful to begin an examination of Augustine's thought with a general overview of the universe as he saw it. Such a summary description will set the context in which he seeks to answer such questions as:

1. Who or what am I?
2. How do I fit into the world in which I live?

The first sort of question is about the human microcosm, the facts that are true of the individual as an individual. The second question is about the human macrocosm, the place the individual holds in the universe and its relationship to other existing things. The first question is thus about nature; the second is about environment. Here a very general description of both will be given. Examination of specific aspects of this broad picture will be addressed in later chapters.

The Human Microcosm

The first truth about humans is that they are *mysteries* both to themselves and to others. In his *Confessions* Augustine remarks that in looking at himself he saw only a life of many facets, impossible to measure.[1] The human conscience, that deep where the individual decides between good and evil, is more profound than any ocean.[2] When Augustine tried to plumb these unfathomed depths, he found a complex world that could be unpacked only with difficulty and much sweat. The understanding of himself became his major task in life, a task that would occupy him till the day he died. After many years of thinking about the problem of self-discovery, he reached the conclusion that it was easier for a person to count the comings and goings of the hairs on his head than to keep track of the surging feelings coursing through their hearts day after day.[3]

A mystery to ourselves, we are even more of a mystery to others. If my heart is an abyss hidden even to myself, how can another know my depth?[4] I am made for friendship but I must face the somber truth that:

> Every human is a stranger in this life because every one of us is clothed with a flesh that hides our heart. . . . As we pass by each other day after day, each one carries his heart within, and every heart is hidden from every other heart.[5]

To begin to solve the mystery of being human we must start deep inside ourselves. There we shall find that great solitude that is the core of each one of us. It is a personal hermitage closed off from every other human, but if we have the patience to dwell there for a time in silence, we shall find that we are not alone . . . that indeed we have a window on the universe, a universe illuminated by the light of the Divine Teacher who dwells within. This is the Teacher who can help us know ourselves. Through that Teacher we will even come to understand something of the secret counsels hidden in the hearts of others.[6]

A second fact about being human is that we are *composite*. After some early ambivalence,[7] Augustine became convinced that the human being is constituted not by the body alone nor by the soul alone. The human being is rather the substantial composite of the two.[8] The human has an essential material component but is more than pure matter. The human's existence is "enlivened" by the presence of a non-material principle of life. While sharing with other animals actions characteristic of material being, the human is also capable of actions proper to spirit, actions such as abstract knowledge and free decision. The individual is by nature a "dusty angel," both earthy and spirit. This sets up a tension at the root of our being, drawn both to the world of pure spirit above and the world of pure matter below. In an ideal world this tension would be under control. We would not live by "fits and starts," now reaching for the stars, now plummeting to the depths. Since the world is not ideal, our lives become tangled bundles of knots as we race from the heights to the depths and back again. We cry with Augustine: "Who can untie such a tortured and complicated knot?"[9]

A third fact about being human is that we are *contingent*. Augustine expressed this fact in one of his sermons where he said to his people:

> Do you wish to know what you are when left to yourself, what you can accomplish on your own? Well, listen to the psalmist: "His spirit left him and he went back into the earth. On that day all thought of him perished." [Ps. 146, 4] Behold! This is what you are when there is nothing in you but yourself![10]

The message that he was trying to convey was simply this: every existing human being is a "something" pulled toward nothingness. In a word, we are contingent. As the song from the musical *Porgy and Bess* reminds us: "We ain't necessarily so." We don't have to exist. We may in fact exist now, but there is evidence that at one time we did not. Creation is a free act of an infinite being and the continuation of the support of that being is essential for our continuing in existence. As Paul told the Greeks: "In him we live and move and have our being."[11]

Augustine uses various analogies to explain our fragility in being and action. We are not like a house that can remain even after the builder departs. If God should blink and "lose sight of us," we would instantly cease to be.[12] We are not like a field that can support life once it has been plowed and fertilized. We are more like shining air, fighting to retain the light. We cannot remain luminous on our own. We escape the darkness of non-being only so long as the light-support of Infinite Being stays with us and in us.[13] We share the fragility of the spider and its web. Like them, we can be destroyed by even the slightest unfriendly touch. Like them, we cannot even maintain our existence without a little help from our Divine Friend.[14] Perhaps the balloon is the best image for our existence. The delicate air of being would easily escape if it were not maintained within our person by the gentle pressure of God's hand. Our spirit makes us desire eternal existence but in fact we live on the edge of annihilation. It is this tension that is at the root of our continuing anxiety. We want to be something (at times pretending to be everything) but are in fact always on the verge of being nothing.

Fragile as we are it is no wonder that we need others in order to be fulfilled as human beings. We are *social animals*; "by the laws of nature itself we humans are driven toward fellowship with our kind."[15] By reason of our common heritage, the "life of the wise man both here and hereafter must be social."[16] We humans may be able to "live" by ourselves but we need the help of others to live well. It is for this reason that Augustine will say that in this life only two things are really necessary:

good health and good friends. We receive life and health from God but if we are not to live as a hermit, we must make friends ourselves. Friendship may begin at home with one's family, but from there it must reach out to embrace even strangers.[17]

Humans are driven to live in society . . . family, state, the heavenly city . . . and ideally the glue that holds humans together will be the glue of friendship. Happiness depends on friendship. Without friends in this life there is no place on earth that is friendly.[18] Without friends in eternal life there is only hell. When temporal societies rest on friendship, the subordination of ruled to ruler required for complex associations of free beings is neither forced nor denigrating. To rule a friend does not mean to "master" him nor to pretend to be "greater" than he is.[19] Indeed, to base one's rule on fear or power or pretended superiority vitiates the love that should be the "glue" binding ruler and ruled. When love is the energy that drives the members of a society together and allocates to each his proper place, there is no coercion. This is so because the force comes from within, not from without.[20]

We are meant to live in society and we need the society of other humans to fulfill ourselves, but at the same time we are superior to any society in matters affecting our eternal destiny. We do not have worth because we are in society. Our value as humans comes from our being loved into life by an Infinite Being and from our destiny of being united to that Being for all eternity. The human race is divided into two societies that extend beyond time, but our membership in one or the other is not based on a difference in our value as individuals but rather on the difference in what we value as individuals. If we cherish earthly values more than God then we are citizens of the earthly city. If we cherish God more than the things of earth, then we are citizens of the city of God. Both societies rest on love but in the case of "heavenly love" we are driven outside ourselves to love others as ourselves and God above all. In the case of "earthy love" (the inordinate desire for the goods of earth) we are driven back upon ourselves in selfish self-absorption.

Which love shall dominate our lives is the most important decision any of us can make and there is no society that can take precedence over our right to make our decision for ourselves and to take the consequences. There is a paradox of sorts here. Although we are social beings (whose love has eternal implications), we are always more important than any temporal society; because we are social beings (who cannot ignore the needs of others and be true to ourselves), we must sometimes subordinate our own needs and desires in the temporal order for the common good.

Augustine was convinced that, despite all that seems to be wrong with human beings, they are still have the *highest value* of all creation. He writes:

> All the miracles done in this world are less wonderful than the world itself. . . . But of all the miracles that God works through the human being, the human being itself is the greatest miracle.[21]

All creation is in some sense a reflection of God. The Infinite Being contains the plan according to which every created being was made. Every created being is thus a mirror reflecting in its own peculiar way the Divine Image. The human soul is the most complete reflection of God and it is only because of our superior ability to mirror God that we humans have been given dominion over those less perfect reflections that are earth and plant and animal.[22] It is also because each of us "images" God in our own special individual way in accordance with God's plan that no human can be called "junk." As Augustine writes:

> In view of the encompassing network of the universe and the whole creation, a network that is perfectly ordered in time and place, where not even one leaf of a tree is superfluous, it is not possible to create a useless human being.[23]

The reflection of God in the human being finds its most powerful expression in its *human powers*, especially the powers of knowledge and choice. Though many animals can "know," only the human animal (as far as we know) "knows that it knows," that is, is self-conscious. The human can reflect on the past, plan for the future, and live in a present composed of realities that can be sensed (for example, this page) and realities beyond the comprehension of senses (for example, the virtue of justice). Though limited in time and place, the human in some mysterious way can comprehend the meaning of the eternal and infinite.

The human shares with all reality the tendency to be drawn in one direction or another by the physical forces of the universe. Also, like other animals, the human being has the power to be drawn toward certain goods perceived to be good by the sense powers. People can and should feel the powerful emotions of desire/abhorrence, love/hate, joy/sadness, fear etc. which make them more than cold automatons. But above and beyond these "earthy" movements, the human is drawn by a desire to live forever, a desire to have meaning, a desire to be loved, a desire to know everything about everything. There is even a greater wonder in this: people have the power to choose freely the direction of choice, and thereby to choose their destiny, to make their history. Just as God freely chose to create this world of time and place, so individuals have the power (with God's help) to choose the nature of their eternal world. In their infinite thirst to "know" and in their freedom to choose, people give evidence that they are indeed the reflection of the Infinite Being.

The glory of human beings is that we carry within us the image of the Divine. Our burden is that we carry that precious image in a vessel that is *cracked*. God made humans to be healthy images of Divinity but over time we have made ourselves to be somewhat wounded and imperfect.[24] Our powers of knowledge have been dulled. Our control over our desires is inconsistent. Though we have a natural tendency to seek the good and the beautiful, this is often overcome by distraction or less noble desires. We have great gifts and great powers, great hopes and great ideals, but our actions are sputtering. We are engines that are somewhat "out of tune." We may not be "junk" but we do need repair. All of us race through life with a slight limp. How this happened and what can be done about it are perhaps the most important questions about human life this side of death.

The Human Macrocosm

To fully know oneself it is not enough to know what is going on "inside." One must also know the world in which one lives and how one fits into it. If we spend our lives like a bug plodding across a mosaic floor with our attention buried in this one tile that defines our inner self, we will miss the beauty of the whole and make terrible mistakes about the nature of our lives. Indeed, if we do not get beyond ourselves to realities above and around us, we cannot truly say that we know ourselves. Self-knowledge demands that we go beyond the information gained from sensation, that we plunge into ourselves to ponder our lives, but this does not mean that we can afford to ignore the world beyond us.[25]

At the highest level of reality is Infinite Being, that Being who is the "best" in all possible worlds. This is the world of God, the world of the everlasting. In God are found the *"rationes aeternae,"* those unchanging "exemplars" on which every created being is modeled. God's world is also the "place" of eternal truths, truths that are unchanging and true in every possible world. When a changing human somehow comes to recognize such eternal truths, it is almost as though the world of "God" is touched. This too is a great mystery, one which Augustine will try to unravel in this theory of knowledge.

Augustine's Christian faith filled out his knowledge of this Infinite Being by telling him that this God is a personal God. He knows all that there was, is, or will be. He is capable of doing anything that is possible. He is perfectly good and he cares about all that exists. He is both the creator of and the model for the universe. God "made" the universe from nothing and he made each part to be some sort of likeness to himself.

The universe outside God is not infinite. It is not necessary. It is contingent and thus has a natural tendency toward dissolution. Having been created from nothing, it has a natural tendency to return to nothing. This fragility is not the sign of some primordial wound but a natural characteristic of being created. As created by God, the universe is necessarily limited but good. Even now, "the world is a smiling place" and easy to be loved.[26] God cared enough about it to "make it" and continues to care for it by "guiding it." Divine action began creation history and divine providence continues to guide its unraveling. Nothing happens in time and space that is not foreseen and at least allowed by God.

The great mystery of the universe is that it is a mixture of good and bad.[27] God made the world good but it seems to be not so good now. The universe seems to be slightly disordered, sputtering. Each being has a natural drive to perfection and conscious being has a natural desire for happiness but few seem to achieve it perfectly. Few seem to become "as good as they could be" and for none is existence an unmixed blessing. We have great joys and experience great wonders, but still we and the universe seem to have gone wrong. How to explain this "wrongness" and overcome it was a question that would come to dominate most of Augustine's life.

> No sea (he says) is as deep as the riddle of why God permits the good to suffer while the wicked flourish. . . . Only holding onto Christ allows the believer to sail this abyss.[28]

For one who (like Augustine) believes in a God who cares, the nagging question must be: "If God is good, why do I feel so bad? If God made me good, why can't I do better?" The presence of evil as part of the human condition is a problem that needs to be addressed at more length. It will introduce the first great ideological battle that Augustine faced after his conversion: the Manichaean controversy.

Notes

1. *C*, 10.17.26, PL 32, 790.
2. *ENN 76*, 18, PL 36, 980.
3. *C*, 10.16.25, PL 32, 789.
4. *ENN 41*, 13, PL 36, 473.
5. *ENN 55*, 9, PL 36, 652.
6. *SER 47*, 14.23, PL 38, 312.
7. See *DMC*, 1.5.7 & 1.27.52, PL 32, 1313 & 1332.
8. *DCD*, 13.24.2, PL 41, 399; *DT*, 7.4.7; 15,7.11, PL 42, 939 & 1065.
9. *C*, 2.10.18, PL 32, 682.
10. *SER 335B* [Guelferb. 31]), 4, *Miscellanea Agostiniana,* G. Morin (ed.) (Rome: Vatican Press, 1930), vol. I, p. 561
11. Acts 17:28. See *DGL*, 4.12.23 & 5.16.34, PL 34, 304 & 333.
12. *DGL*, 4.12.22, PL 34, 304.
13. *DGL*, 8.12.26, PL 34, 383.
14. *ENN 38*, 18, PL 36, 427.
15. *DCD*, 19.12.2, PL 41, 639.
16. *DBC*, 1.1, PL 40, 373; *DCD*, 19.5, PL 41, 631.
17. *SER 299D* (Denis, 16), # 1, *Miscellanea Agostiniana*, vol. 1, p. 75.
18. *E 130*, 2.4, PL 33, 495.
19. *IEJ*, 8.8 & 8.14, PL 35, 2040 & 2044; *DDC*, 1.23.23, PL 34, 27; *DCD*, 19.15, PL 41, 643-44.
20. *IJE*, 26.4-5, PL 35, 1608-09; *SER 131*, 2.2, PL 38, 730.
21. *DCD*, 10.12, PL 41, 291.
22. See *Ser 265F* [C. Lambot 25], in *Revue Benedictine*, 62 (1952) 97-100.
23. ". . . non posse superfluo creari qualemcumque hominem, ubi folium arboris nullum superfluo creatur": *DLA*, 3.23.66, PL 32, 1303.

24. "Multi enim sibi promiserunt quod impleturi essent illam vitam sanctam, in commune habentem omnia, ubi nemo dicit aliquid suum, quibus est una anima et cor unum in Deo [Acts 4:32.33]: missi sunt in fornacem, et crepuerunt." *ENN 99*, 11, PL 37, 1277.

25. See *DO*, 1.1.2-3, PL 32, 979.

26. *SER 158*, 7, PL 38, 866.

27. *DCD,* 22, 22-24, PL 41, 784-92.

28. *ENN 91*, 8, PL 37, 1176.

Chapter 2
The Problem of Evil

Introduction

Any discussion of the problem of evil must begin with an answer to the question: "What shall we mean by the term 'evil'?" A simple answer would be to say: "Evil is whatever humans dislike, whatever makes them unhappy or dissatisfied." Such a response is attractive but both narrow and vague. Do we really wish to define evil simply by human attitudes? Is the pain of animals, the disease of plants, the pollution of the air to be called "good" if humans "desire" it? History testifies to the unhappy fact that we humans have some macabre pleasures. Sometimes we create "needs" which, if fulfilled, would destroy us and others. We create frivolous "needs" and then make happiness depend upon their satisfaction. Human happiness is a vague norm for measuring good and evil because of the difficulty in distinguishing ephemeral joy from a happiness that is lasting and truly fulfilling.

Identifying evil with imperfection seems a more productive course to take if pursued cautiously. It must be pursued cautiously because not every limit is a sign of imperfection. Some limits are natural, setting a being in its particular place in reality. One cannot be shocked that bright balloons someday lose their air nor that a contingent, changing universe does not stay the same forever. That a rock cannot propagate, a tree cannot run, an earthworm cannot see, a human cannot fly, is bothersome only to the simple-minded. No one or no thing can be reasonably expected to be capable of every act, only those acts that are proper to its nature. The beauty of the universe comes from the ordered diversity of its parts and this diversity flows from the different ways in which the parts are empowered.

The absence of every perfection is the sign of limited perfection, not imperfection. A tree that cannot think is not diseased. It is just being a tree. Properly "imperfection" is used to designate the absence of a perfection that is due, a perfection that can be reasonably expected to be present at a particular level of being. The absence of such perfection means that the being is "less than it could be" and that its "unhappiness" (if it is capable of such feeling) with its imperfect situation is a legitimate sign that truly "something is wrong."

Such reasoning leads to the conclusion that evil is the lack of a due perfection. Using a human being as an example, "death" is evil because to be human is to have life. Ignorance is evil for a particular individual only if it is an absence of knowledge that should be present, taking into account that person's station in life. "Maliciousness" is evil for every human since it stands for an absence of correspondence between what is willed and what should be willed.

This lack of correspondence between choice and obligation in free beings is called moral evil. The absence of a perfection that should be present in the "being" of the various things that actually exist is called natural evil. Cruelty, deceit, selfishness, pride, sloth are moral evils proper only to beings who could do otherwise. Disease, pain, disfigurement, disability are natural in that they point to a gap in "being" in a reality, a gap which may be caused by the malice, stupidity, or simply the natural movement in a changeable being. The causes (for example, malice/stupidity) may not be in accord with nature but the gap itself is a natural effect.

Evil is a personal trial for anyone who is sensitive to its existence. It is an intellectual problem for anyone who wishes to understand it. Faced with this problem, one may react in various ways:

> 1) One may choose to deny that evil exists, to say (for example,) that "evil is in the eye of the beholder," that it is a problem of human attitude rather than a true warp in reality;

> 2) One may admit the existence of evil but give up hope of ever making sense of it, saying: "Evil is not something to be explained; it can only be endured."

3) One may admit the existence of evil and blame it on some positive force in the universe, a force so powerful as to be beyond the control of any human or any "divine" principle.

4) One may admit the existence of evil and blame it on the action of a Supreme Being who, though infinitely good, for some unfathomable reason wants evil to be part of the universe.

5) One can blame oneself and other free beings for the existence of evil in a world created good by an infinitely good Supreme Being.

Evil in any universe is a tragedy. It becomes an intellectual problem when the universe is dependent on the will of a perfect God. The dilemma can be stated as follows:

A. It is impossible that both of the following propositions be true:

(1) An omniscient, omnipotent, all-good God exists; (2) evil exists.

B. But evil exists.

C. Therefore God does not exist.

The second assertion is beyond doubt. Even the worst Pollyanna would be hard-pressed to prove that some lack of due perfection is not present in the real world. We can try to make the best of bad situations but this does not make them good. Thus, if there is weakness in the argument, it must be centered in the first statement. But here too the logic seems persuasive:

(1) A world which contains free beings inferior to God and which contains no evil is possible.

(2) God, since he is omnipotent, can make actual any possible world.

(3) God, since he is all-good, should want to make actual the possible world containing free beings inferior to God and yet containing no evil.

(4) The fact that the actual world contains evil means that if a "God" exists, this "God" is not infinite in its perfection.

The dilemma posed by a universe in which both God and evil existed was a serious problem for Augustine. He needed and wanted God, convinced that he could never achieve happiness in a God-less world. But at the same time he could not deny the sometimes overpowering presence of evil in himself and the world. God and evil: how to explain such apparently contradictory realities? Augustine's first attempt at understanding was through the teaching of Manichaeism.

The World-View of Manichaeism

One way of avoiding the apparent contradiction implied in the con-current existence of the All-Good and some evil is to limit the power of the good. This was the solution offered by the mystical world-view pro-posed by Mani in the third century.

Mani agreed that there was indeed an eternal principle of good at the root of the universe but it was neither infinite nor supreme over all other beings. It was matched by a coequal and coeternal principle of evil. From all eternity these principles of good and evil, light and darkness, existed in a state of fragile truce, neither able to totally overcome and conquer the other. Each had its own territory and as long as the boundaries were re-spected there was peace.

Eventually the violent turbulence characteristic of the kingdom of evil spilled over into the domain of the good and conflict began. At first passive, the principle of good rose to repel the invader and in the process of battles won and lost, good became mixed with evil. The final victory will occur only when the particles of light are free of the confining walls of darkness that entrap them. We now witness in ourselves and in others the struggle of the good to escape the prison of matter which is the place of evil in this world.

The individual human is part of this cosmic battleground. Humans were in fact made by the principle of darkness as a device for continuing to entrap light in body. Procreation is thus not a blessing but a curse. It is another victory of darkness over light through the creation of a new body-prison holding back bits of light from rising up to rejoin their source. Still, humans are not all bad. In their minds and wills they show that they con-tain elements of the good, parts of the divine light. They are "pieces" of God trapped in vessels of evil.

Our task as humans is to work to free the light within us so that it can rejoin its eternal source. To do this we must listen diligently for the illu-minating instruction that comes directly to each person through the power of Jesus (himself an emanation of the good) and the words of the proph-ets, especially the greatest and last, Mani himself. This special hidden knowledge will allow the chosen elect to know the universe and them-selves. It will reveal to them the noble ascetic practices by which they can free the good from the prison of evil created by their body. The destiny of each human is to have what is best in them finally reunited with the sub-stance of the eternal good. Those who live at the highest level of asceti-cism (the *electi*) can achieve the release of the good in themselves in one lifetime. Those who are unable to reach that exalted level of virtue (the *auditores*) can accomplish the same end but only after a series of recurrent lifetimes.

At the end of time Good will finally conquer. Evil will once again be confined to its own separate kingdom, nevermore to encroach upon the good. Time will end as it began: with peaceful coexistence of two eternal principles. Humans will be no more, but they will have achieved a noble purpose if they have lived such a life as to permit the "pieces of light" trapped in their matter to escape and become one again in the eternal principle of good.

Augustine spent nine years of his early life as an auditor in the Manichaean religion. He was attracted to it for a number of reasons, some negative and some positive. First of all, it seemed like a more perfect form of the Christianity that he had become accustomed to in his youth. It respected Jesus Christ and St. Paul as great prophets and the writings of the latter (read from a Manichaean perspective) were seen as valuable instruments of illumination for the chosen soul. This respectful acceptance of Christ and Paul appealed to Augustine. He also liked their criticism of the Old Testament. Himself an accomplished writer and speaker, the young teacher was influenced by style as much as by substance. The literal interpretation of the Old Testament was simply too much to bear. The style was far from Ciceronian and the content was too crass for a truly sacred book.

Manichaeism also appealed to the young Augustine's ego. Excited by the quest for wisdom, Augustine was ready for a teacher who claimed to bring an understanding of the universe through reason alone. Manichaeism did precisely that, promising that the illumination that would come would be personal and overpowering. It promised its disciples that they would not need to "believe." They would know things beyond the powers of ordinary folks. Though not bound to a terribly ascetic life, they would be comrades with those who were . . . the "Elect," those "better" people smart enough to understand difficult truths and brave enough to commit to a noble way of life.

Augustine also found parts of the doctrine personally satisfying. It did not demand a belief in spirit. All reality was material, differing only in density. Evil was substantial, a positive force coequal and coeternal with the good. The turmoil that humans see in themselves and in the world is but one phase of a cosmic battle. The principle of good and light is not the cause of evil but its victim. So too is every imperfect human being. At the same time humans are called to a truly noble task of being foot-soldiers on the side of good. Only a few can reach the higher ranks but even the least can be "illuminated" by the teaching of Mani and can play a part in the contest by being a "listener" to the truth and a servant of the "elect." Even the humble can be confident that they are servants of the good even though the power of evil seems to dominate their lives.

It was a comforting ethic. It promised the elect that they could discover the truth and finally take control of their lives by a rational choice. It gave consolation to those who were too weak to be noble by assuring them that their weakness was not their fault. This combination of intellectual snobbery and moral absolution was very attractive to Augustine. He was encouraged to develop his mind and was given an excuse for indulging his passions. In the midst of his less than perfect life, he could repeat the comforting words used by many before and since: "This dastardly deed is not my fault; it is the evil force within me that did it."

Eventually Augustine became disenchanted with Manichaeism. He discovered that they were better at criticism of others than defense of themselves.[1] Their fantastic vision of the universe simply did not agree with the facts revealed by science.[2] Their supposedly "rational" descriptions of humanity, divinity, and reality in general foundered on the hard rock of ordinary experience. Moreover their vision of God was simply incomprehensible to Augustine, a "shadowy being" impossible to trust.[3] The idea that a good God could be at the mercy of some coequal power was simply too antithetical to the vision of God as supreme being that he still retained from his early training. Still, he had no conception of spirit and was unable to understand how a material God could be either infinite or unchangeable.[4] He was left in an intellectual vacuum and for a time gave up hope of ever finding a satisfying solution.[5]

In truth, he was somewhat afraid of finding a solution if this meant that he would need to admit that the evil in his life was his own fault. In his late twenties, Augustine still prided himself on being better than the rest of humanity, "a youthful mind seeking truth who was proud and opinionated in his academic debates with learned men."[6] How could it be that his childish self-centeredness, his animal lust, his passion for obviously trivial honors and ephemeral passing things, could be his own fault? His spirit cried: "I am a true seeker of wisdom! I am devoted to truth! My destiny is nobler than that of common folk! How then can it be that I cannot control my passion?"

Two events, one intellectual and one moral, moved him beyond this impasse. First, his reading of the Platonists brought him to an understanding of "spirit" as true being and "evil" as an absence of being. Second, he developed the humble realization that he was no better than the rest of humanity, that he could not blame his evil deeds on anyone but himself. The reason why he could not move beyond his passions by a truly converting choice was because he did not "want" to and the reason why he did not "want to" was because he was "cracked." Augustine finally came to the conclusion that, despite his pretending to be superior, he was wounded in mind and will and needed help to know the true and to choose the good. With this new beginning, he returned to the problem of evil and gradually developed the answer that was to be his final position on the matter.

Augustine's Final Position

Augustine had too much sensitivity to the human condition to attempt to deny the reality of evil.[7] And, despite his youthful bout with skepticism, he had too much faith in the reasonableness of reality to give up the hope that some day he would understand how and why evil exists. This passion for finding a sensible answer eventually drove him out of Manichaeism and brought him to the explanation that he would defend for the rest of his life. The following presentation of his final explanation will be centered around these themes:

1. the nature of evil

2. natural evil

3. moral evil

4. the best possible world

The Nature of Evil

Augustine at last came to realize that evil is not a substance as the Manichaeans claimed. It is not a "thing" at all. Quite the opposite, it is a "no-thing," an absence of being. "Whatever is must be good; and hence evil . . . cannot be a substance. If it were, it would be good."[8] What Augustine is saying is that disease in animals is an absence of health. Vice in humans is an absence of virtue. When a disease is cured, this does not entail that it has gone somewhere else. I do not rid myself of a cold by giving it to someone else. My return to health means only that my malady has disappeared from me. Similarly, overcoming my vice does not impose it upon another. My lack of virtue is not a "demon" which must be cast out. It is a gap in my moral life that needs to be filled.[9]

Augustine agrees with the common sense notion that evil is not properly attributed to every lack in a being but only to that lack of measure, form, or order that should be present in a particular nature.[10] In proportion as things are better measured, formed, and ordered they reach a higher level of goodness; but this does not mean that beings with less measure, form, and order thereby suffer evil. "These three things, where they are great, are great goods; where they are small, they are small goods."[11] It is only when there is an absence of the measure, form, and order that is due the nature of a being that evil is present. Evil, in fact, is constituted by "not being in accord with nature."[12] Since this is so, evil is truly present only in the human mind and will, the only created powers able to act against nature.[13]

Evil is rooted in the reality of being. Human likes and dislikes have little to do with its definition. Indeed, those without wisdom are very likely to praise lesser creatures over higher if they are more relevant to their personal pleasure. A farmer will prefer that all the stars should fall rather than one of his cows be lost. A child would rather see a passing human die than a pet bird. Humans without wisdom would like to improve on God's plan by favoring their own comfort and will blame God bitterly when their whims are not fulfilled. Such foolishness should be corrected if possible but more often than not it can only be tolerated by those who are wiser.[14] Humans may sometimes be silly beasts but it would be even more silly to define "evil" in terms of their likes and dislikes. Evil is constituted by disorder in nature . . . not by the distress of a fool.

Natural Evil

Evans remarks that Augustine had little interest in natural evil.[15] This is certainly true if she means Augustine's theoretical interest. For him the so-called problem of natural evil (death, suffering, natural disasters, etc.) was never as "real" or as mysterious as the problem of moral evil. No natural reality is evil. To the extent that it is a real part of the created world it is good. The only proper use of the word "evil" is to refer to an absence of some reality, not a presence.[16]

However, Augustine was very much affected by natural evil as a practical problem. He was very much moved by the troubles endured by himself, his loved ones, and the universe in general. For example, he had an aversion to death for as long as he lived. He recognized that "first" death of the body was incomparably less terrible than the "second" death of eternal damnation, but this did not make it desirable. He did not believe that anyone, not even the suicide, could embrace death as a good.[17] Indeed, he goes so far as to say that anyone who seems to have lost the fear of death is probably already dead.[18] Like so many other unpleasant things in life, death can be tolerated but never loved.[19] When he was thirty-three Augustine wrote that he had three great fears in this life: the fear of losing his loves, the fear of pain, and the fear of death.[20] These fears stayed with him through his life. He never considered illness to be a good and he feared the pain of the treatment even more. At the very end of his life he was still praying for the strength to endure.[21]

Throughout his life, Augustine was upset by the trials of those he loved. Friendship and loving are necessities of human life but they have a "down" side. The more loves we have, the more we have to worry about. We worry that our loves will leave us. We worry that something bad will happen to them. Augustine never mastered a calm acceptance of the death of his loves. As a young man he was almost destroyed by the death of a friend. In his mature years he bore the death of his mother badly. As an old man he described the burden of having all one's loves die first.

Having said this, it should not be assumed that Augustine had a somber personality. He in fact rejoiced in the pleasant things of this life.[22] But at the same time he never made light of the calamities of ordinary life, calamities which sometimes are so dreadful that we begin to doubt whether "a life so full of such great ills can properly be called a life at all."[23]

When he came to consider natural evil as a theoretical issue, Augustine was guided by the information supplied by his Christian faith and by his own personal experience. His faith told him that all created things were particular reflections of God's perfections and thus could be nothing else than good.[24] His experience of the actually existing world told him that:

1. All things are corruptible, deteriorate, and eventually cease to exist. Earth wears away and living things eventually die.

2. Some of these beings are sensitive to this process of corruption in themselves. Some are also sensitive to this process happening to others that they care about. As a result there is distress and pain and unhappiness.

The theoretical issue raised by these facts is whether such wasting away is not a sign of defect. If we and the world are not defective in some way, why do we weep so much? How can one explain this corruption and distress in a creation coming from a supposedly omnipotent and good God?

Augustine says of himself that he began his study of the origin of evil, that is, the origin of corruption, "with the conviction that to be corrupted is not a desirable prospect, that the incorruptible is superior to the corruptible.[25] But if a corruptible being is a lesser good than the incorruptible, is its lesser existence therefore a defect that can be deplored and blamed? Can we reasonably cry: "Oh, that's too bad!" and blame the creator for having made damaged goods?

The first answer to such questions is to argue that God could not have created otherwise. The corruptibility and eventual corruption of created things is but the natural effect of having come from nothing.[26] God was free to create or not create, but he was not free to create incorruptible being. This would be equivalent to having God create God, another nature supreme in being. But to have two "supremes" is contradictory and therefore impossible. God made created beings good but they were goods less than God because they were corruptible.

Augustine was not disturbed intellectually by the corruption that comes as a part of nature. He would not have been upset if he had known about entropy . . . that tendency in nature to come to a halt. There is a loss of measure and form in nature but the process is not due to nature lacking something that it should have. It is due rather to its not-being something that it could not be: that is, a being that did not come from nothingness. Nature must fade toward nothingness but even in its dissolution a certain order is maintained. It is not disorderly that living things die nor that complex nature breaks apart into simpler forms. Such corruption is an expression of nature; it is not a defect.

This distinction between a corruption that comes from nature and a corruption which goes against nature is crucial in Augustine's analysis of "natural" evil. He argues that only imperfection is worthy of blame and that the only reason why an imperfection is called evil is because it is opposed to the very nature of which it is an imperfection.[27] Not every corruption or deterioration in created being is blamable. "It does not make sense (he writes) to blame what is as it ought to be."[28] Only corruption which is opposed to the nature corrupted should be called evil. Thus, death is not properly speaking an imperfection in a living, contingent, changeable thing. It is not contrary to that nature; it is an expression of it. It may be woeful but it is not wicked.

There is of course an element of wickedness in death and destruction when it occurs "out of due time" because of disordered choices of free beings. It may be natural for animals to die but their death is disorderly when it is caused by the cruelty of humans. The changes in the environment follow a natural pattern, but when these changes are transformed by human "trashing" then they are disorderly. The earth shall naturally come to the day when it shall no longer support life. By good choices humans can push that day farther into the future . . . maintaining the fragile biosphere beyond its expected time. By bad choices humans can reverse the process, disturbing the order of nature so as to bring about its early death. Nature like a brutalized child is at the mercy of its masters. That it should perish someday is natural. That it should perish at an unnecessarily young age because of bad choices is a true evil, but the evil is centered in the human choice rather than in the being's demise.

Just as the corruption of corruptible beings is an expression of their nature, so too is the suffering of sentient beings going through the process. The metaphysical root of suffering is in the soul's drive toward unity, a drive which allows it to reflect in a unique way the unity of God. The special distress of the sentient soul is to experience the corruption in transient unity that is its being. The special distress of the rational soul is to be frustrated by error and ignorance in its search for the unity of truth. The special agony of the human being is to be frustrated in its desire to be joined as one with all good. Spreading out from itself the human soul is battered by the immensity of the task and like a beggar is worn down by the natural need to seek for that which is one while being buffeted by the multitude of things which cry for its attention and stand in the way of achieving unity.[29]

Like other sensitive souls, the human spirit has a horror of "falling apart," of seeing its friend the body gradually grow old and deteriorate. This natural tendency of soul (or form) to seek unity, to "keep it all together," is the source of its pain when it perceives its "falling apart." In the words of Augustine:

> Pain is a sign of resistance to "falling apart" and corruption. This shows clearly how eager the soul is for unity and how strongly it tries to maintain the completeness of the body. It is not indifferent to the suffering of the body because it sees that the bodily unity is sadly in the process of being shattered.[30]

In souls with the burden of consciousness there is a distress that comes with the awareness of corruption and the loss of unity that it portends. Form in general and soul in particular seek an unchanging "one-ness." They treasure stability, preservation of the "status quo." They are hostile toward any movement. This hostility or pain may be described as useful if the movement is toward something better. It may be useful, but is never enjoyable. The unpleasant pain of change testifies to the pleasure of the previous condition. Pain is a resistance toward giving up what it was because what it was is seen as good.[31] Perhaps this is the reason why it is a "a pain" to grow up, why it is "a pain" to develop the mind, why it is "a pain" to die. The fact that the new state may be better does not take away the distress at losing the good of the old . . . the innocence of child-hood, the simplicity of ignorance, the glory of even a brief existence.

The special distress that humans (and, perhaps, other higher ani-mals) experience when others die is likewise a sign of something good in them, an expression of their nature rather than a defect in nature. As social animals, we are driven to care for others, to desire unity with special loved ones, to become one with our loves in spirit and body. This being so, it is only natural that we weep at their passing. One who condemns us for such tears must first show us how we can avoid loving others.[32] We must weep because if we have loved another deeply, that person's passing must leave a hole in our lives.[33]

Some suffering can be explained by the nature of things but the ex-tent and intensity of suffering need further explanation. It is here that the fact of sin plays a part in understanding. Some suffering is punishment and such suffering is in accord with the order of a universe in which sin cries out for penalty. No one can complain about suffering brought down upon oneself because of perverse choices. However the argument that suffering is to some extent a penalty is less satisfying when applied to the suffering of animals and children incapable of personal choice of evil or good.

Of course there is an element of truth in saying that animal suffering is not comparable to the suffering of humans. Though their moment of present pain may be unpleasant, they are not plagued by its memory or frightened by its future possibility. In sickness they cannot make unhappy comparisons with their days of health. In their days of flourishing they do not worry about disabling old age. Whether their dissolution comes from an inevitable natural process or from an unlucky meeting with a more powerful predator, sentient creation cannot cry "unfair." Their demise is simply part of the order which demands that lesser beings serve the needs of the greater and which dictates that all created being should eventually return to its source in nothingness.

The words "reward" and "punishment" have no place in the explanation of suffering in non-rational beings.[34] The suffering of animals may be caused by the sin of others, for example, the indifference or perversity of humans, but it is neither merited nor unmerited by the animals themselves. However, it can have a positive effect on us, teaching the dignity of our fellow animals. "We would not see how strong was the desire for unity in lower animate creatures were it not for the pain suffered by beasts."[35]

Augustine's attempt to explain the suffering of children[36] seems particularly dissatisfying, but perhaps this is so because of the way in which the question is posed. In various places he suggests that there are two possible explanations for a particular case of suffering:

(1) It is a punishment for sin;[37]

(2) It is a natural result of the conflict between a created being's "drive to stay together" and its natural tendency to deteriorate.[38]

He uses the second reason primarily to explain the suffering in animals, but he could just as well have also used it as a partial explanation of the suffering of children. However he does not do so. Why? Perhaps because the objection raised by his adversary is posed in terms of sin, asking: "What evil have they (children) done that they should suffer so?"[39] Augustine, rather than answering the more fundamental question "Why do children suffer?"), responds to the question as posed, a question which assumes a connection between suffering and sin.

Augustine makes two different moves in his response. First, he turns the question around, noting that if one holds that there is no reason to punish someone who has not sinned, there is likewise no reason to reward someone for innocence when perversity is impossible. The context suggests that Augustine is not speaking about "eternal" reward but the "temporal" reward of protecting a naturally corruptible being from the unpleasant effects of that corruptibility (for example, death and disease). Such action would obviously be beyond the reasonable expectations of corruptible being. Created from nothing, every human can expect to die. We begin to die as soon as we begin to exist and we all move toward this end at the same speed.[40] For some it is closer than for others, but whether the years are many or few, life on earth is a short time for any of us.[41]

In a second approach, Augustine suggests that though the suffering and death of the young is indeed a sorrow-filled event, there is some good that can come from it. At least death brings the sufferer a relief from suffering. Moreover, we don't know what good things await such inno-cent sufferers on the other side of death. One thing we do know. In a universe where not even one leaf of the smallest tree is wasted, it is not possible that God would create a useless human being. There is a need for every human who exists, even those who die young. They are "wanted" by God and, despite their helplessness, even in their dying they can con-front others with the mystery of life and death and challenge them to make a decision for or against God.[42]

Though the comings and goings of individual things, their corrup-tion and disappearance, may be hard to understand in individual cases, there is an order in their passing. The two sources of good in being are existence and order,[43] and there is a certain majesty and message in the orderly "giving way" of the old to the new. Sometimes, of course, indi-viduals cannot perceive this majesty because they are too focused on their own condition. One cannot appreciate the mosaic in a cathedral floor if one's eyes remain riveted on one panel.[44] We do not see the beauty of the whole because "we are so entangled in our little corner of the universe that we cannot see the beauty of the total pattern of parts which, taken individually, seem so ugly to us."[45] If we could only raise the eye of our mind and expand its vision to see the whole, we could perhaps discover that there is nothing out of place.[46] But this takes hope and effort, and we may be just too tired. We cannot see the forest for being bushed.

Analogies for beauty coming from the passing of things are not lack-ing. The disorder of a poem's parts creates great beauty when brought together in a completed work.[47] A sentence makes no sense until each syllable is pronounced and then released to make room for the next.[48] Even one who complains about the natural passing of created things proves the need. As Augustine remarks: "Anyone who is so entranced by one phase of an argument that he refuses to move on to the next step is rightfully judged to be insane."[49]

It is foolish to say that temporal things should not pass away. The orderly process of old yielding to new is the essence of the beauty of creation.[50] It is likewise absurd to complain about the limits in their na-ture which make their deterioration inevitable. They come from nothing and their only two alternatives are to be corruptible or not-to-be at all.[51] Redwoods and butterflies must die because their roots are in nothingness. That one should live for centuries and the other for but a day is deter-

mined by the wisdom of a creator who arranges each one's timely existence so as to best contribute to the beauty of the whole.

Of course we are still talking about a beauty that is brought out of
corruption and it does not answer the question "Why have corruptible
being at all?" Why create anything if everything created is destined for
disintegration? It is claimed that God is good, but is it not a sign of malice
to give a gift of being that eventually must be taken back? Is it not better
"never to be," than "to be" temporarily? God seems no better than a cosmic blower of bubbles, creating flimsy fragile circles of nothingness for
the momentary pleasure of seeing the pretty colors reflected from its
quivering surface. There seems to be no love, no attachment, no valuing
of the creation. When it "pops" into nothing, it is quickly forgotten, its
place taken by another fragile creature already destined for dissolution.

The goodness or badness of the creative act depends on the purpose
it is meant to achieve. In Augustine's view, there is only one reason for
creation and that is love. God is infinite love and that love wanted to be
shared. The value of creation comes from the fact that for the brief moments of its existence it reflects an aspect of God, infinite immutable being. God sees this reflection and loves it. The reason for creation is to
reflect the infinite. The value of creation is given to it by the infinite love
that values it.

Is it better to be than not to be for this reason and with this value?
This is a question that each person must answer for himself. For Augustine the answer was a resounding "Yes." To be a sign pointing to an infinite lover is a great gift even though it is for only a time. Such a passing
existence is not absurd. It is glorious. What would be absurd would be for
humans to cling to such passing things, trying to make them be forever.

> Such transient things continue on the course toward dissolution that is
> set for them. If the soul loves them and wishes to find its rest in them,
> it will be torn by desires that can destroy it.[52]

Things pass; only humans are forever. The true tragedy, the true evil
in creation is the sometimes stupid and sometimes perverse human choice
of finite over infinite, of the temporal over the eternal. For Augustine this
is the real mystery: What causes moral evil in the world? It is to the solution of this mystery that he now turns his attention.

Moral Evil

In a review of his works completed toward the end of his life, Augustine distinguishes two issues in the problem of human evil. He writes:

> It is one thing to ask where evil comes from; it is quite another to ask how one can return to that primordial state of innocence or, perhaps, move forward to achieve even a better state.[53]

He goes on to say that his work *On Freedom of the Will* and, in general, all of his early works against the Manichaeans address the first question while his works against the Pelagians (for example, *On Nature and Grace*) deal with the second. He summarizes his position on both issues as follows:

> It is by free will that a person either sins or lives rightly. . . . However, unless the will is freed by the grace of God from the condition of servitude by which it is the slave of sin and is helped to overcome its vices, no human can live rightly and piously this side of death.[54]

Our present situation is such that we are good but wounded. We are born with ignorance about what we should do and an inability to choose easily the course that is good for us.[55] We are like those born addicted and we need help to overcome our addiction. We have been captured by the effects of past evil choice and now we need release from captivity before we can exercise the freedom to do good. How did we get this way? Nothing happens without a cause[56] and so we may reasonably ask: "What is the cause of moral evil and our present inability to overcome it without help?"

As we have seen, Augustine holds that the strict meaning of "evil" is "a blamable imperfection by which a being departs from the order demanded of it by its particular nature."[57] Evil, therefore, can be found formally only in free beings because only they can "choose" to depart from the order of nature. Since Augustine held that there were only three orders of free beings (God, angels, humans) the ultimate blamable source of moral evil must be one or more of these.

God could be "blamed" for human sin if humans by nature were incapable of avoiding sin. Angels could be blamed if they can and do "force" humans to sin by irresistible temptation. Humans are rightly blamed for their sin if, at least in their original state, they were not so dominated by nature or by environment that they were "forced" to choose evil. It is clear that Augustine believed that there was no true evil in the universe before angels and humans sinned and in both cases the choice of evil was not necessitated.[58] The human "falling away from God" was not like the falling of a stone, controlled by forces outside itself.[59] It was a self-controlled choice of oneself over God. That first sin was not a sin of weakness but a sin of pride. The free spirit became so satisfied with itself, so delighted with its own powers, that it tried to be God. It was ". . . like a prisoner who creates for himself the illusion of liberty by doing something wrong, when he has no fear of punishment, under a feeble hallucination of power."[60]

The effect was disastrous. The more the created being pretended to be great, the less it became. It desired to be more than it should be and became less than it could have been.[61] That first sin of Adam created in his progeny a condition of weakness which made them much more prone to sin than they would have been had they been preserved in Edenic innocence. Augustine stresses the point that when he speaks of the "freedom to do good" he is speaking of the way the will was when humans were first made.[62] Our situation is quite different now. We humans now are unable to do good without help either because we "do not see what we ought to be or because we do not have the power to be as we ought to be."[63] This ignorance of the good and this difficulty in doing good are not part of human nature. They are our inherited burden, part of the baggage of human existence after sin.[64]

Such burdens may be called unfortunate and even unfair but they cannot be said to be unreasonable. We are accustomed to such inherited disabilities on the physical level. The burden of drug addiction and genetic defects are passed from parent to child. Even more to the point, the scourge of AIDS can be passed to the newly conceived giving them from their very beginning an inability to fight off the poisons of the environment into which they are born. Even when an inherited physical disease is curable there is always need for outside assistance. Left on their own the diseased humans would perish. "Wishing" to be well and to act well, they find that such good is beyond their powers.

Augustine infers from his own experience and from his reading of scripture that such inherited weakness has infected the human spirit as well as the human body. Still rational and still free, humans can still choose evil freely. But they can no longer effectively choose good without outside help. Sin is still caused by human choice, but now it flows from a spirit wounded by the sin of those who have gone before. The healthy Adam sinned and the whole race became infected.

Is this not unfair? Augustine poses the question very forcefully:

If Adam and Eve sinned, what did we poor wretches do? Why should
we be born with the blindness of ignorance and the tortures of difficulty? Why should we first wander about, ignorant of what we should
do? And why, when we are finally moved to do the right thing, why
should we be unable to do it because of some sort of carnal desire?[65]

He answers by admitting that the objection would be valid if there
were not a way of overcoming our inherited dullness of mind and weakness of will. We will be condemned not because of these wounds but for
not trying to know, for not being open to the healing that can strengthen
our will.[66]

In any case Adam wounded himself by his sin and it was only natural
that this weakness should be passed along. "Nemo dat quod non ha-
bet . . ." No one can give what he does not possess. It would be contradictory for the wounded Adam to beget offspring better than himself.[67]
Humans are not like angels, each a separate species with no connection
with what has gone before. We are of one species and we share common
strengths and weaknesses.

Of course God could have intervened and protected the children of
Adam from the effects of his poor choice, but to what end? There is certain fittingness in his non-intervention. God respects thereby the natural
course whereby humanity reaps the harvest of its decisions for good or
evil. Furthermore, God even now gives at least some wounded humans
the means (grace) of overcoming their wounds and of doing good despite
their wounds. He thus proves how easy it must have been for that first
unwounded human to do good. Finally, just as we children of a fallen
father bear the weakness of his humanity, so he (now the human father of
children redeemed and made victorious by Christ) is honored and participates in our redemption.[68]

Even in our weakened condition we have many good things in our
favor. First, we are alive and, as Augustine says: "We should not despair
of any human as long as there is life."[69] Secondly, though happiness was
lost with Eden, it can be recovered. We are indeed born in ignorance and
with passions difficult to control, but we are not forced to stay in that
condition. We can admit our weakness and wait humbly for the healing
God to come. We have retained a natural wisdom which drives us to seek
peace and truth.[70] We have retained the zeal to dream of the highest goals
and we can receive the power to achieve these goals if only we use well
the gifts we have and pray to God for the additional gifts we need. Thus
(Augustine concludes) . . .

The author of the human soul should be praised because he created the
soul in such a fashion that with proper development and appropriate
effort it can achieve truth and right action.[71]

Still, if God can be praised for enabling humans to overcome ignorance and disordered will, can he not be blamed for making (or at least
allowing) such "overcoming" to be necessary? We have already seen that
Augustine traces human mortality and corruptibility to being created *ex
nihilo*. He also accepts the scripture story telling of those idyllic Eden
days when God "prevented" mortality and corruptibility from having
their natural effect. Sin ended that gift and certainly that sin was done by
humans, not by God. Why did God not "prevent" that destructive sin?
Why did he not, after sin, "prevent" death and corruption as he had done
before humans had sinned?

It was "possible" for God to have done both. He could have prevented sin by not creating free beings or by making them free but incapable of sin. There were at least two ways of doing the latter. As Augustine
says:

It cannot be denied that the possibility exists that God could so help the
human will that it would achieve not only that perfect righteousness
from faith spoken of in Romans 10:6 but even that perfection in righteousness which is the lot of the blessed in heaven who are face to face
with God for all eternity.[72]

However God did not choose to create free beings in such an invio-
lable state. Augustine gives the reason:

God had the power to make humans who could not sin. But he preferred to make them so that they had the power to sin or not sin as they
wished. As a result there would be humans who gained merit from not
sinning in this life and who received in the next the reward of not being
able to sin.[73]

Being able to sin did not mean that those first humans would sin, but
it did create the possibility and, considering the "draw" toward corruption
in a being coming from nothing, it was even likely that some free being
at some time would in fact sin.[74] God certainly knew about this likelihood. Indeed he foreknew who would sin. Knowing this, can he not be
"blamed" in some way? His knowledge of future events does not make
them happen,[75] but it does imply a conscious choice on his part for an
actual world where there would be freedom and sin rather than a world
without sin. God certainly does not "cause" sinners to sin in the actual

world. They are the cause of their sin. But he is responsible for the existence of this actual world in which sin exists rather than other possible
worlds where it does not.

Augustine on the "Best Possible World"

Of course God cannot be blamed if he did the best he could, if this
actual world is the best possible world. But is it? The answer to that question depends on the answer to a preliminary question: "Best for what?"
Before we can make a value judgment about this actual world, we must
determine its purpose. Why did God choose to create? What purpose did
he hope to achieve?

Augustine answers that God created by a free choice simply because
he wanted to.[76] God did not need to create. His action was not like that of
a human who needs to build a house for shelter or needs to make clothes
to cover nakedness. God created because he wanted to and the reason why
he wanted to was because creation was good.[77] The goodness of created
things is caused by the goodness of their creator.[78] Each one is modeled
on the perfections of God and each reflects an aspect of that perfection in
its own individual way.[79]

Each one also makes a unique contribution to the goodness of the
whole. Obviously losing some of the lesser parts of the universe would
have a negligible effect on its mass, but it would lessen its beauty. The
universe is something like the human form:

> Shave off one eyebrow and the loss to the mere mass of the body is
> insignificant. But what a blow to beauty! Beauty is not a matter of bulk
> but of the symmetry and proportion of the members.[80]

The purpose of this world is to reflect the beauty and goodness of its
creator. Is it the world best suited to achieve that end? Is this the best
possible world or is it, if not the lesser of two evils, the lesser of possible
goods?

Augustine states his view on the question very clearly in his *Confessions*. Speaking to God, he says: "Those who find fault with any part of
your creation are crazy."[81] Earlier he says of himself that once he started
to look at creation as a whole,

> I no longer wished for a better world. I had come to see that though
> higher things are better than the lower, the sum of all creation is better
> than the higher things alone.[82]

Augustine came to realize that it was wrong to wish that any created nature should not exist. Each gives praise to the God who made it for the time it exists. Things come and go but "All things that exist are fit and proper to the times and places of their existence and God is in all things and all things are in God."[83] There is nothing missing in the order of being.[84] If something is conceivable, it is possible but it is just impossible to conceive of anything better in creation which has escaped the maker of creation. With respect to the hierarchy of being in created nature, at least, it is clear that Augustine believed that this is the best possible world.[85]

But what about humanity's contribution to the mix? In fact this is a world in which sin occurs . . . a disruption of the order of the universe by perverse free choice. Moreover, it is a world in which this perverse choice results in some being condemned for all eternity . . . eternal failures in a hell of unhappiness. Would it not be better to have a world where sin, unhappiness, and hell were impossible?

Augustine answers "No!" for the following reason. The only way to make sin impossible would be either

1. not to create free beings;

2. or to create them free and then overpower them with grace or with the vision of infinite good.

But to do either would be to rob creation of the glory that comes to God from beings who praise God willingly when they could do otherwise. Human and angelic freedom reflects the perfection of God in an extraordinary way. God gave free beings the power to choose what they wanted. He also made them so that they could not be happy unless they chose rightly, that is, in accord with the order of the universe. He neither forced the angels and the first humans to sin nor prevented them from sinning.[86] He did however make them of such dignity that even in their sin they remained better than any other creature.[87] Augustine clearly believes that it is better for a free being to have lived and lost than never to have lived at all. God foreknew those angels and humans who would misuse their freedom and fail for all eternity, but he would not therefore refuse them the honor and dignity of existing second only to God in the order of the universe.

> Just as a stray horse is better than a stone which is not astray (because the stone does not have its own motion or perception), so the creature who sins with free will is more excellent than the creature who does not sin because it has no free will.[88]

Furthermore, though sin considered individually is an ugly blotch, it does not dim the glory of the universe any more than dark colors detract from the beauty of a portrait.[89]

Of course the unhappiness of those free-falling failures is sad, but it is simply contrary to true wisdom to say that beings who can and even will be unhappy should never be created. To say that there should be no free beings because we misuse our freedom and become unhappy is an example of our narcissistic tendency to judge "good" and "evil" on the measure of our own personal convenience.[90]

The fact of the matter is that the world would be imperfect if there were no created free beings. The hierarchy of being would be incomplete. And the world would also be imperfect if among such free beings the saints were unhappy and the sinners were happy. There would be no justice in that. As it is, "Since there are souls that gain happiness because they do right and souls that are unhappy because of sin, the universe is always full and perfect."[91] Punishment balances the disorder of sin and creates order in the universe.

The occasional distress of the virtuous in this life is indeed a riddle[92] but it does have a good result sometimes. We free beings are destined for eternal happiness. If we were too satisfied with our times, we would not want to move on.

> God wants us to love only eternal life and thus he mixes some unpleasantness with our innocent pleasures here. . . . We are taught to love the better by the bitterness of the less. Thus, as we move along on our way to our homeland we are not tempted to dawdle in a wayside inn rather than continuing our journey to our real home.[93]

Of course all of these arguments for this world being the best possible would be empty if it were in fact impossible for free beings to achieve their destiny. Now wounded by sin, humans must be able somehow to overcome their disability and to become successes for all eternity. But in order to do this they must effectively choose the good. How this is possible is a topic for later discussion.

Notes

1. *DUC*, 1.1.2, PL 42, 66.

2. *C*, 5.3.3, PL 32, 707.

3. *C*, 4.4.9, PL 32, 697.

4. *C*, 7.5.7, PL 32, 736.

5. *C*, 5.10.19, PL 32, 715.

6. *DUC*, 1.1.2, PL 42, 66.

7. *DO*, 1.1.1, PL 32, 977-79; See *C*, 7.5, PL 32, 736-37.

8. *C*, 7.12.18, PL 32, 743; See "Malum ex defectu non ex profectu." *CSM*, 15, PL 42, 590; See "Tendit ergo id quod est, facere ut non sit. . . . Idipsum ergo malum est . . . deficere ab essentia et ad id tendere ut non sit." *DMC*, 2,2,2, PL 32, 1346.

9. *ENC*, 11, PL 40, 236.

10. *DNB*, 4, PL 42, 553.

11. *DNB*, 3, PL 42, 553.

12. *DLA*, 3.17, PL 32, 1294-95.

13. *Ibid.*; See *DNG*, 1.3.3, PL 44, 249.

14. *DLA*, 3.5.17, PL 32, 1279.

15. G.R. Evans, *Augustine on Evil* (Cambridge: Cambridge Univ. Press, 1982), p. 97.

16. *DCD*, 11.22, PL 41, 335.

17. *DLA*, 3.8.22, PL 32, 1281-82.

18. "Videant ergo isti qui non dolent nec timent, ne forte non sint sani, sed mortui." *SER 348*, 2.3, PL 38, 1529.

19. "Amari mors non potest; tolerari potest." *SER 299*, 8, PL 38, 1373.

20. *SOL*, 1.9.16, PL 32, 877.

21. Possidius, *Vita Augustini*, 29 PL 32, 59.

22. See *DCD*, 22.24, PL 41, 788-92.

23. *DCD*, 22.22.1, PL 41, 784.

24. *DDQ,* 46.1-2, PL 40, 29-31.

25. *C*, 7.4.6, PL 32, 735.

26. See *DNB*, 10, PL 42, 554; *CEM*, 38, PL 42, 203; *CSM*, 15, P.L. 42, 590; *CJH*, 6.1.9, PL 44, 671.

27. *DLA*, 3.14.40, PL 32, 1291.

28. *DLA* 3.15.42, PL 32, 1292.

29. *DO*, 1.2.3, PL 32, 980.

30. *DLA*, 3.23.69, PL 32, 1305. Translated by Anna S. Benjamin and L.H. Hackstaff, *Saint Augustine: On Free Choice of the Will* (Ind.: Bobbs-Merrill, 1964), pp. 141-42.

31. *DNB*, 20, PL 42, 557.

32. *DCD*, 19.8, PL 41, 635.

33. *C*, 4.6.11, PL 32, 698.

34. *DNB*, 8, PL 42, 554.

35. *DLA*, 3.23.69, PL 32, 1305.

36. *DLA*, 3.23.66-68, PL 32, 1303-05.

37. *DLA*, 3.10.29, PL 32, 1285.

38. *DLA*, 3.15.42, PL 32, 1291-92.

39. *DLA*, 3.23.66, PL 32, 1303.

40. *DCD*, 13.10.29, PL 32, 383.

41. *SER 124*, 4.4, PL 38, 688.

42. *DLA*, 3.23.69, PL 32, 1305.

43. *C*, 7.13.19, PL 32, 743.

44. *DO*, 1.1.2, PL 32, 979.

45. *DCD*, 12.4, PL 41, 352.

46. *DO*, 2.4.11, PL 32, 1000.

47. *DO*, 2.4.13, PL 32, 1000-01.

48. *C*, 4.10.15, PL 32, 699.

49. *DLA*. 3.15.42, PL 32, 1292.

50. See *DCD*, 11.22, PL 41, 335; *DLA*, 3.15.42, PL 32, 1292.

51. *DCD*, 12.4, PL 41, 351.

52. *C*, 4.10.15, PL 32, 700.

53. *RET*, 1.9.2, PL 32, 595.

54. *RET*, 1.9.4, PL 32, 596-97.

55. *DLA*, 3.20.55, PL 32, 1297.

56. *DO*, 1.4.11, PL 32, 983.

57. *DLA*, 3.14.40, PL 32, 1291.

58. *DVR*, 21.41, PL 34, 139; *DLA*, 3.22.65, PL 32, 1303; *DNG*, 3.3, PL 44, 249.

59. *DLA*, 3.1.2, PL 32, 1271-72.

60. *C*, 2.6.14, PL 32, 681.

61. "... tanto fit minor, quanto se cupit esse majorem." *DLA*, 3.25.76, PL 32, 1308.

62. *DLA*, 3.18.52, PL 32, 1296.

63. *DLA*, 3.18.51, PL 32, 1296.

64. Augustine remarks (*DLA*, 3.18.51, PL 32, 1295) that this weakness is clearly implied in such scriptural texts as: "For I do not the good which I will to do, and I do the evil which I hate" (Rom 7:15, 19); "To will is present with me; to accomplish that which is good I find not." (Rom 7:18) It also explains why it took him so many years to "unscramble the twisted tangle of knots" that his early life had become and to find his way back to God from the barren waste that he had created for himself (*C*, 2.10.18, PL 32, 682). It is interesting to note his declaration that the final obstacle to his conversion was not lust but pride: "I was not humble enough to conceive of the humble Jesus as my God, nor had I learned what lesson his human weakness was meant to teach" (*C*, 7.18.24, PL 32, 745).

65. *DLA*, 3.19.53, PL 32, 1296.

66. *DLA*, 3.19.53, PL 32, 1297.

67. *DLA*, 3.20.55, PL 32, 1297.

68. *Ibid.*

69. "De nullo enim vivente desperandum est." *ENN 36/2*, 11, PL 36, 370.

70. *DLA*, 3.20.56, PL 32, 1298.

71. *DLA*, 3.22.65, PL 32, 1303.

72. *DSL*, 36.66, PL 44, 746. An example of the first alternative would be Mary, the mother of Jesus, who was prevented from sinning because of the superabundance of grace in her life. A more universal example can be found in all those angels and humans who have direct vision of God in heaven. In these cases freedom is present but in fact there is no sin.

73. *DC*, 6.16, PL 40, 359.

74. See John Rist, "Augustine on Free Will and Predestination," *Journal of Theological Studies*, vol. 20, pt. 2 (October, 1969), p. 433.

75. *DLA*, 3.3.8, Pl 32, 1275; See *DCD*, 5.9, PL 41, 148-52.

76. *DGM*, 1.2.4, PL 34, 175; *ENN 134*, 10, PL 37, 1745..

77. *DCD*, 11.21, PL 41, 334.

78. *DCD*, 11.22, PL 41, 335; *DVR*, 18, PL 34, 1137; *CSM*, 1.10, PL 42, 585.

79. *DDQ*, 46.1-2, PL 40, 29-31.

80. *DCD*, 11.22, PL 41, 335.

81. "Non est sanitas eis quibus displicet aliquid creaturae tuae." *C*, 7.14.20, PL 32, 744.

82. *C*, 7.13.19, PL 32, 744; See *DLA*, 3.6, PL 32, 1279-80.

83. *C*, 7.15.21, PL 32, 744.

84. *DLA*, 3.5.13, PL 32, 1277.

85. *Ibid.*

86. *DLA*, 3.5.14, PL 32, 1278.

87. *DLA*, 3.5.16, PL 32, 1279.

88. *DLA*, 3.5.15, PL 32, 1278. Augustine's position may be summarized as follows. The excellence of creation is manifested more by a universe containing free beings than by one without them. When a free being errs it is unfortunate but it is still better than not having the being at all. Similarly excellence is manifested more by a creation containing a being sensitive to environment and thus capable of pain than one that is not. When such a being suffers it is indeed unfortunate but it is still better than not having such a being at all. So too the creation of corruptible being is better than no creation at all. The erring of free being is justified by the glory of having a being which has a chance at choosing rightly. The pain of sensate being is justified by the glory of having a being able to perceive the environment in which it exists. The pain itself does not simply point to a weakness in a being falling apart. It also points to the strength of a soul which has a thirst for unity even when the body it informs is coming apart.

89. *DCD*, 11.23.1, PL 41, 336.

90. *DLA*, 3.5.17, PL 32, 1279.

91. *DLA*, 3.9.26, PL 32, 1284.

92. *ENN 91*, 8, PL 37, 1176.

93. *ENN 40*, 5, PL 36, 458.

1. knowledge involves a relationship between the knower and the thing known.

2. a claim of a knower to "know" the object known is a claim that in some fashion the "object known" is present to and indeed in the knower.

Simply put, knowledge implies a "union" between the knower and the object known and characteristic of this union is that it is in some sense firm. To know something means to have some degree of certitude about it. Putting all this together one may describe knowledge as follows: "Knowledge is certitude about a reality experienced (that is, the reality is as I experience it) and/or certitude about the truth of a judgment I make."

Various forms of knowledge seem to meet this description. First of all there is the accurate (true) and clear representation of a reality perceived. This may occur at the sense level through sense perception of a sense object (for example, color) or at the level of the intellect where a concept is formed (for example, redness). In later medieval philosophy this intellectual act went by the name of simple apprehension . . . "simple" in the sense that it involves only the formation of the idea and not anything beyond that. A second level of knowledge occurs when these ideas are united or divided through judgment. Knowledge is present when it is perceived with certainty that the unity/division asserted to exist between concepts (for example, "humanity" and "mortality" in the mental judgement "All humans are mortal") in fact is found in the described reality beyond the mind. Another kind of knowledge is the certitude we have about relationships between purely abstract entities. This certainty is present either because the relationship between the concepts is perceived to be self-evident (for example, If "p" is greater than "q" and "q" is greater than "w," then "p" is greater than "w"); or because we perceive that the judgment is consistent with other abstract truths previously accepted as true (for example, some theorems of plane geometry).

In all of these forms of knowledge it is crucial that there be certain possession of a truth. We cannot say we know something when we are ignorant of that something. We cannot say we know something when we are convinced with all certainty about something false. A something false (for example, a younger brother of the youngest in a family) is not something at all. It is a nothing and to know a nothing is the same as "not knowing" at all. Finally it is improper to say that we know something when we are doubtful about that something. In all these cases the union between the knower and the thing known is absent. In ignorance there is no connection at all. In error there is nothing that the "knower" can be united to. In doubt the bond is simply too weak and tentative to count as true union. Thus the conclusion: knowledge is certain possession of the truth.

But what is truth? The following points are consistent with Augustine's mind-set. First, in matters relating to my judgments describing the real world, truth is found in the correspondence between my judgment and the reality it claims to describe. Thus, the judgment "I am free" is true if in fact I am free. Second, in matters relating to purely abstract truths my judgment uniting or dividing concepts is true if it is consistent with other truths already accepted (for example, assuming a triangle has 180 degrees and 1 right angle, the other angles must be less than 90 degrees) or is demanded by the self-evident force of the assertion (for example, "x" is not "non-x").

We have said that knowledge involves a certain possession of a truth. Certitude may be defined as a quality of mind whereby the mind asserts the truth of a judgment without reasonable fear of error. Various degrees of certitude are possible. In metaphysical certitude the mind is certain of the judgment because the opposite judgment is simply impossible. Thus the judgment "Being is not non-being." In physical certitude the judgment is secured because the opposite judgment is improbable (though not impossible) taking into account the regularity of the laws of nature. Thus the judgment "Jumping from top of a tall building, I will fall to earth." Finally, in moral certitude the judgment is secured because the opposite judgment is improbable (though not impossible) taking into account the way human beings normally behave. Thus the judgment "This mother will act in the best interests of her child."

Although we speak about "false" perceptions, about the senses being "fooled" into committing some error, the fact of the matter is that with respect to knowledge "the true" and "the false" exist only in the judgment. We do not risk error in the "seeing" of a "red rose." We see what we see and that ends the matter. We are liable to error only when we make the judgment joining or separating concepts derived from that sense experience, saying "The rose is red" or "The rose is not red."

The truth of judgments about the real world can be arrived at in various ways. If the connection between subject and predicate is self-evident then it is just "unthinkable" that the opposite be true (for example, "X is either A or -A"). We become certain of the truth of a proposition by immediate evidence when we are in such direct contact with the reality that we cannot be mistaken about its existence (for example, when I know the truth of the proposition "I exist"). If immediate contact is lacking, then some sort of proof is required . . . a step by step process whereby we establish the connection between propositions known to be true and the conclusion that we wish to establish. Such lines of argumentation include proofs by induction, deduction, analogy, and authority. In each of these forms of argument the truth of the conclusion will depend on the truth of the premises and the logical connection with the proposition to be established. Since the truth of the conclusion depends on establishing several other truths, conclusions depending on proof are always more problematic than truths that are self-evident or immediately evident.

It is in the arena of "truths that need to be proven" that skepticism plays out its game most powerfully. Only the most radical skeptic will question whether we can be certain about any truth. The more moderate approach will be to question whether we can be certain about truths that need proof . . . especially any proof depending on an authoritative and credible witness. Such is the mystery of the human being that there is always an opening for the challenge: "Well, what do they know?" "What makes them so trustworthy?" Considering the immensity of the universe in time and space, such challenges are of momentous importance. Like it or not, most of what we know about past and present and most of what we hope for in the future depends on such testimony.

It is no wonder then that Augustine felt compelled to answer the challenge raised by skepticism. As we shall see, his interest was more than purely theoretical. He understood the position and for a period of time embraced it.

The Possibility of Knowledge: Skepticism

By the time he reached his thirtieth year, Augustine had long since become disenchanted with his long-standing devotion to Manichaeism. He had come to realize that their assertions about the nature of the real world were contradicted by the growing body of facts demonstrated by science. Being "burned once" he became "twice shy," and for a time embraced the skepticism proposed by the New Academy.[1]

It was a disastrous time in his life. Above all he wanted to be happy and he was convinced that to achieve happiness he had to know something about the real world . . . especially to know about himself and about God.[2] The skeptic Zeno's assertions made such knowledge impossible. Granting the premise that a proposition is true if and only if no possibility of error is contained therein,[3] it seemed at first to Augustine that no such proposition existed and that the only course for an intelligent person to take was to remain in the state of searching until some certain light should appear by which to direct one's destiny.[4]

What Zeno was demanding was metaphysical certitude before assent be given. What he was asserting was that such certitude is never achieved. Augustine came to realize that the assertion was false and that the original demand was unreasonably conservative. His argument proceeds as follows.

He notes first of all that the skeptic position was both odd (claiming that wisdom is in knowing nothing) and contradictory (protesting doubt while asserting the certainty that "I can know nothing with certainty"). He then goes on to show that in fact we do possess knowledge of some principles where the opposite propositions are just unthinkable and which therefore possess even the metaphysical certitude demanded by Zeno. We know the truth that "the world either is a unit or is not a unit."[5] We know that "3 x 3 = 9" is true even when all are asleep.[6] We are likewise certain of the laws of logic that control our reasoning.[7]

Such propositions not only have no "thinkable" contradictory in the actual world; they are necessarily true, that is, true in every conceivable possible world. They are therefore "eternal" and "unchanging" . . . mysterious and almost inexplicable characteristics considering that these truths are captured by a temporal changing being living in a temporal changing world. Wherever being exists, these truths exist. They are limited only by what is impossible . . . which is the same as saying that they partake of infinity.[8]

These absolutely certain and necessary truths may bring some satisfaction to a doubting mind, but they did little to help Augustine in his quest for happiness. The truths of metaphysics or mathematics or logic are so broad as to be almost devoid of content. They are indeed obviously a priori, completely independent (as to content at least) of previous experience of this actual world. They did not help Augustine find that "actually existing thing" (or things) in the real world which when possessed would bring happiness.

But is it possible to find truths about the actual world that have the same metaphysical certainty as truths of mathematics and logic? Augustine suggests that there are such truths. If people make a project of trying to be doubtful about all truths of the actual world, they will find that it is impossible. They may or may not be deceived about the truth of a particular assertion, but even if deceived about a particular assertion, the fact of their own existence is forced upon them with a clarity which is beyond doubt. "Si fallor, sum" . . . If I am deceived, I am![9]

The perception that "I exist" is the first indubitable truth I discover about this actual world. Although it is not an "eternal" truth nor an "unchanging" truth (there are possible worlds in which I do not exist) it is a truth that I grasp with metaphysical certainty. In raising the question, I force the answer. Knowing my "self" I do not depend on the vagaries of sense knowledge or the formation of ideas or images. In a way it is more intimate and more direct than even my knowledge of my ideas. It is a face to face contact.

In the same passage from the *City of God* (11.26) Augustine goes on to note that there are two other truths flowing from the first that are beyond doubt. Not only does he know that he exists; he also knows that he knows and knows that he delights in knowing and existing. The fact that he is an existing thing, a knowing thing, and a loving thing are the first responses to his prayer to know himself. They do not go very far, to be sure, but they are a beginning . . . a metaphysically certain foundation on which to build knowledge of the real world.

To go further demands "taking a chance." There are two kinds of knowable things: (a) those that are known directly by inward knowledge and (b) those that are known through the mediation of sense knowledge.[10] Only the former live in the land of metaphysical certitude. Once one gets outside oneself, it is possible to be mistaken. Knowing through the senses puts one at the mercy of the vagaries of sense organ and environment which make appearances literally deceiving. One can always doubt a testimony coming from outside whether that testimony comes from one's own experience or the assertions of an informed witness. It is always possible to doubt, but is it reasonable to doubt every experience, every witness? Is the way of prudence to live one's life in the narrow but safe land of metaphysical certitude? Augustine's answer is a resounding "No!" He insists that it is absurd to doubt everything that is reported by our bodily senses or to deny that we truly know that which is learned on the authority of others. To do so would be to doubt most of what we know about the world around us.[11]

Methods of Knowing: Faith and Reason

Through self-analysis Augustine discovered that his knowledge includes things that are passing or "temporal" and other things that seem fixed or "eternal." In both instances some of the things are known by direct experience while others are known only through others who act as credible witnesses. Thus in present time I know some things (the sun flooding this room) by direct experience while others (events even now taking place in Boston) by the testimony of others. Past events too may be captured by remembered direct experience or the testimony of historians. The future, if it is to be known at all, can only be known through reliable witnesses. Trapped here in my present, I cannot experience the world of the "not yet." Some "eternal" truths (for example, the principles of geometry) I know directly because I know and understand what they assert. Others (for example, unchanging truths about God as Trinity) I can only know by believing. I do not have direct experience of such realities. Indeed, I could not comprehend them even if I did have such experience.[12]

Augustine concluded that there were two broad ways of knowing: (1) knowing by seeing and (2) knowing by believing. The first Augustine calls "understanding" (the way of reason); the second he calls "belief" (the way of faith).[13] Both modes of knowing seek to bring about the union between knower and thing known which is the essence of knowledge. In the case of understanding there is an immediate contact between the two, a direct confrontation in which the knower perceives the object by a type of "vision." Since my experience of such truths is so immediate, they seem to "force" themselves upon me. I cannot deny the pain in my leg nor the noise of the street nor the remembered facts of my past. I may try to ignore them but I cannot deny them once they capture my attention. Moreover, once attended to, they have a tendency to move me by their presence. My contact is so intimate that once I see them as true, I easily move on to see them as "good" or "bad," desirable or abhorrent. I quickly move from being a "knower" to being a "lover," reaching out to embrace those realities which promise to bring satisfaction and happiness when possessed.

Knowledge by way of belief (faith) does not possess such power. The truth of the object known is not known directly but only through the testimony of others. Whatever is good and desirable about the object is known by hearsay, not vision. The immediate contact of the knower is with that witness who testifies to the truth perceived. It is not the truth of the object that forces itself upon the knower. It is the credibility of the witness, a credibility that rests on a conviction that this witness is (1) knowledgeable, that is, is in a position to know the facts, and (2) trustworthy, that is, is not likely to misrepresent the facts. Only rational beings can serve as such witnesses and since humans, angels, and God are wrapped in mystery, we are never overpowered by evidence of credibility unless we want to be. It is for this reason that Augustine will define faith or belief as an act of "thinking with assent."[14]

There are some important conclusions flowing from the definition. First of all, belief is a "thinking," an act of intellect rather than a pure act of will or an emotional ecstasy. To believe that "God is Trinity" one must first have some understanding of the meaning of the assertion. "No one can believe anything unless he first thinks that it is something to be believed."[15] What Augustine is saying is that it makes no sense to say that a person truly believes "Farasi buk flan" if he has absolutely no clue what the nonsensical phrase means. Moreover, the intellect must play a part in analyzing the credentials of the authority proposing the matter of belief. Without minimal use of reason, belief cannot be well-founded.

At the same time the will plays a more important role in belief than it does in understanding. In understanding we are forced to know the object by its very immediacy. The only escape is to shut down our knowing powers completely. As is the case with physical vision, we cannot avoid seeing the light once we open our eyes. This is not so in the case of belief. Here we are not present to the object known, but only to its witness. When we run into a wall or come face to face with our existence, we are forced to pay attention. But seldom if ever does this happen when we are confronted by a witness whom we must trust if we are to know the object. We can always find a reason for not believing. Thus, the final step in coming to believe is an act of will whereby we choose to believe. What Kierkegaard was to later describe as the "leap of faith" is nothing more than a choice.

Since it is so heavily dependent on choice, knowledge by belief is more fragile than knowledge by understanding. It is easily destroyed and even more easily ignored. Still, as we have seen above, Augustine holds that it can be just as certain as knowledge by direct experience if prudently exercised. In many ways it is more important. We know more things by belief than we ever could know by experience, and they are things that are much more important to our temporal and eternal happiness. As Augustine says:

> No institution of human society can remain stable once we have decided to believe in nothing which we cannot grasp with our senses.[16]

The trust that is at the root of faith is also at the root of the friendship, love, and respect that are the foundations of society.

Because belief is so dependent on choice, Augustine insists that personal purification is necessary for faith to be possible . . . at least that faith whereby we come to know about God and our own eternal destiny and duties.[17] Even in the best of conditions, belief would have been difficult for humans. Now after sin, it is even more difficult. Humans are in a weakened condition. Now there are obstacles in knowing, especially in knowing about God. Our minds are covered by cataracts of the spirit which make even the most brilliant truths seem cloudy and gray. Our wills are too weak to force our attention to any one thing for any appreciable length of time. We are easily distracted by new fancies. It is hard now for us to choose to believe any truth that demands a life-change. In our present condition, belief must be given and it is only given after a healing that prepares the person for the grand faith that is to come. Augustine writes:

> Will you be able to lift up your heart unto God? Must it not first be healed in order that you may see? Do you not show your pride when you demand "First let me see and then I will be healed"?[18]

It was impossible for Augustine to be either a pure rationalist or a pure fideist because he was convinced that understanding and belief were intertwined, each depending on the other.[19] If we were not beings of reason with a hunger to know, we could not come to belief.[20] Recognition of the need to believe rests on reason's awareness of its own limits. Recognition of the possibility of belief rests on reason's acceptance of the proposed truth as at least believable.[21] Finally, for belief to be truly well-founded there must be some rational analysis of the credentials of the authority on which the belief is based. In all of these ways reason seems to have priority over faith and justifies the truth of Augustine's assertion that: *"Intelligo ut credam"* ("I understand so that I might believe").[22]

On the other hand it is also true to say *"Credo ut intelligam"* ("I believe so that I might understand").[23] Even on the humble level of everyday living, belief opens the door to great vistas of knowledge that we only later come to understand. A baby left to its own direct experience and its purely personal interpretation of it would not progress far in accurate knowledge of reality. Probably none of us would have survived without the trust we developed in the friendly giants who were constantly telling us what was and was not good for us. And when it comes to beatifying knowledge, that knowledge that is crucial for our eternal happiness, the priority of faith is even more important. In our present condition we cannot know much about God except by believing. Once we believe in the fact of the Trinity, we can then go on to try to understand what the mystery means.[24]

Belief is a necessary means to beatification but it is not meant to be the ultimate stage in our knowing. We believe now so that someday we can come to a time and a place where we will finally and forever understand ourselves and our God. We seek now by faith; then we shall find by understanding.[25] Then we shall know the truth of Augustine's words: "Understanding is the reward of faith."[26] Then we shall finally see what now we can only believe.[27]

Notes

1. See *C*, 5.11 & 14, PL 32, 716-18; See John J. O'Meara, *op. cit.*, pp. 110-115.

2. *DO*, 2.18.48, PL 32, 1017; *CA*, 3.17.37, PL 32, 954.

3. *CA* 2.5, PL 32, 924-26.

4. *C*, 5.14, PL 32, 717-18.

5. *CA*, 3.10.23, PL 32, 946.

6. *CA*, 3.11.25, PL 32, 947.

7. *CA*, 3.13.29, PL 32, 949.

8. See *DLA*, 2.8.21, PL 32, 1252. The puzzling fact of these infinite, eternal, unchanging things existing in the human mind is the problem that leads to his theory of illumination to explain knowledge. It is also the reason why he believes that God can be found inside the individual soul.

9. *DCD*, 11.26, PL 41, 339-40.

10. *DT*, 15.12.21-22, PL 42, 1073-75.

11. *DT*, 15.12.21, PL 42, 1073-75.

12. *E 120,* 2.9-11, PL 33, 456-58; See *DT*, 12.14-15, PL 42, 1009-12.

13. *E 147*, 3.8, PL 33, 600.

14. "Quamquam et ipsum credere, nihil aliud est, quam cum assensione cogitare." *DPS*, 2.5, PL 44, 963. 15. *Ibid.*; See *E 147*, 3.8, PL 33, 600.

16. *DUC*, 12.26, PL 42, 84.

17. See *DCD*, 8.3, PL 41, 226-27; *DT*, 1.2.4, PL 42, 822. See Robert Cushman, "Faith and Reason," *A Companion to the Study of St. Augustine*, edited by Roy Battenhouse (Oxford: Oxford Univ. Press: 1955), p. 299.

18. *ENN 39*, 21, PL 36, 447; See Cushman, *op. cit.*, p. 299.

19. See *DVR*, 24.45, PL 34, 141-42.

20. See *E 120*, 1.3, PL 33, 453.

21. *DPS*, 5.10, PL 44, 968.

22. See *E 102,* 38, PL 33, 385-86; *SER 43*, chaps. 6 & 7, PL 38, 257-58; *ENN 118*, serm. 18, # 3, PL 37, 1552.

23. See *DLA* 2.2.6, PL 32, 1243; *E 120*, 1.3, PL 33, 453.

24. See *E 120*, PL 33, 452ff; *E 147*, PL 33, 596ff.

25. *DT* 15.22.42, PL 42, 1089-90.

26. *IJE*, 29.6, PL 35, 1630-31.

27. See *SER 43*, 1.1, PL 38, 254; *IJE*, 48.10, PL 35, 1741.

Chapter 4

The Nature of the Human Being: Soul and Body

General Introduction

As we have seen, Augustine was driven in his life and in his thinking by the desire for happiness. He believed that such happiness depended on the possession of actually existing goods, goods which were able to satisfy the special thirsts that he had as a human being. Once he had satisfied himself that some knowledge of the real world was possible and that there were two dependable ways of knowing (reason and faith), he set about trying to answer the two questions that he considered to be the most important for the pursuit of happiness: "What am I?" "What is God?"

He began with himself and some of the questions he asked were the following:

1. What am I? Is my human nature a composite of soul and body or is it just my soul?

2. What is the nature of the soul?

3. What is the nature of the body?

4. If my human nature is a composite of soul and body, how is the interaction to be explained?

"What Am I?"

The question "What am I?" seeks to identify those elements in me that are essential to my being a human. It asks: "What elements are so crucial to my being human that when they are absent it is no longer appropriate to speak of me as a human being?"

It is obvious that there are many things about human beings that are not constitutive of their humanity. A human is not made human by the clothes he wears. A naked human is still human. Even such deficiencies as the loss of limbs and the loss of memory do not diminish one's humanity. Amputees and the mentally retarded are still human beings. Infants are still part of the species even though their mental and physical powers are undeveloped.

A perfect body is clearly not necessary to claim humanity, but is it necessary to have a body at all? Am I essentially something "other" than my body, a "spirit" or "soul" or "mind" that for the time being is trapped in a confining "coat" of body that I could just as well do without? Or am I my body and nothing more?

The questions are obviously important for me, a human searching for happiness. My answers will determine whether happiness is possible and, if so, how I must go about acquiring it. If I am only body, my life should most reasonably center on taking care of that body. If I am only spirit [soul, mind] now trapped in a body, prudence dictates that I should do all I can to free myself from my fleshy prison. If I am a combination of both, then I must meet the needs of both. If I am a spirit-body combination, I may indeed recognize the priority of one over the other but I cannot neglect the legitimate demands of either. Even my lesser part has its own dignity and its legitimate claims on my attention. Though my lesser part has a somewhat humble condition, it is still an essential part of me. I cannot deny it without denying myself.

The procedure for discovering my "self" must begin with myself. My perception of humanity in others is always filtered through my sometimes defective senses or my problematic understanding of what others "tell" me about themselves. It is hard to get a clear vision of the human "self" through the cloudy lenses of sensation and belief. Better by far to begin with that human who is closest to me: namely, "me." I am in immediate contact with myself, and though I may make erroneous judgments about the information supplied and may even in some cases ignore it, I cannot mistake it. I cannot be mistaken about the fact that "I am being" or that "I am living," and both of these somewhat modest assertions have valuable content.

To be aware that I am "being" is to be aware that "I exist." I am part of the actual world. I am not "non-being," nor am I "purely possible" being [that is, being that "could exist but in fact does not"]. This perception "that" I am includes an awareness of "how" I am, an awareness that I exist contingently. I need not exist. I am not part of every possible world and my presence in this actual world is not demanded by my nature. I am here and remain here at the pleasure of forces beyond my ken and control.

However, knowledge of my existence still does not tell me anything about my nature. "That I am" says nothing about "What I am." It is the second assertion, "I am living," that begins the discovery of my nature. It also introduces a new set of questions. What specifically is "life"? Is there a substantive difference between life and non-life?[1]

Classical philosophers (for example, Aristotle and Aquinas) suggested that the essential meaning of "life" was that it was "the capability of performing immanent activity." By "immanent activity" they meant an activity which has its beginning and end in the agent who performs the action and which has the effect of perfecting that agent. Thus, the energy whereby the immanent activity of nutrition is carried on in a living being comes from within the living being itself. This is quite different from the transient activity of a blender compacting and dissolving food, driven by an electric energy that comes from outside. The end result of the vital process of eating/nutrition is the maintenance in life of the being who eats. Assuming that life is better than non-life, the activity thus perfects the being who eats. The effect of the electric blender is only on the food blended. It is only by a stretch of the imagination that one can say that the blender becomes "better" by its blending. In fact, this transient activity eventually wears it out.

I can perceive various sorts of immanent activity going on within me. I am aware of nutrition, growth, knowing and desiring. Indeed, the awareness of such activities within me leads to my awareness of "self." Aware of my "thinking," I come to recognize "myself" as thinking. At the same time I recognize that a person is still alive even though every level of immanent activity is not being actualized at this moment. Obviously when nutrition ceases the person dies, but it is absurd to expand this need to every other vital function. A person does not need to be always "growing" or "reproducing" or "thinking" or "sensing" or "desiring" to be classed among the living. We are still alive when we sleep. We are still alive in a coma. Indeed the very language "John is in a coma" expresses the conviction not only that this comatose body is still alive but also that it is still "John" despite its unconscious state.

The assertion "I am alive" makes no claim about there being a radical difference between being alive and not being alive. However if there is a difference, then there must be a cause of this difference; and, if the difference is substantial, then the cause must be of my very essence. If there is a difference and the "state of being alive" is perceived to be a higher form of existence than "not being alive," a reasonable explanation for the difference can only be that the living thing has a more noble "something" that the non-living thing does not have, that is, a principle which is the source of its immanent activity.

In classical thought the name given to this principle was "soul" and it was defined as "a principle of life." This simple statement makes no assertion about the nature of this soul. It does not claim that soul is matter or spirit, nor does it set limits on the extent of soul. It allows room for theories [for example, hylozoism] which bestow soul on every being in the universe . . . indeed, on the universe itself. It allows room for a gradual narrowing which begins by giving soul only to vegetable-animal-human, then proceeds to limit it to animal-human, then restricts it to "some" humans, ending up with the extraordinary elitism of one who might say: "Soul belongs only to me and thee and [to be honest] I am not quite sure about thee."

The view one takes on the extent of the soulful universe must be argued to be true, that is, in accord with the reality that sensible reflection reveals. It is a choice which has important practical implications. Historically, theories about the extent of life and the causes of life have been the basis for extending rights and value to the universe. The belief that the whole universe was alive limited scientific investigation for centuries. The belief that some members of the human species do not have as valuable a life as others has led to the most cruel persecution.

What causes life in a being is an important question and various answers have been suggested in the history of philosophy. Radical mechanism maintained that life is caused by purely material principles. At most, the difference between living and non-living is a difference in architecture. There is no qualitative difference between the two states. Both the living and the non-living have the same building blocks; living things just have these blocks arranged in a special way. The laws of physics and chemistry are sufficient to explain non-life and life in all of its variations.

Vitalism disagreed with this explanation. It held that there is present in living systems a substantial reality which gives to that system powers possessed by no non-living body. In living things (at least at the highest level of life) there is a qualitative difference between living and non-living things. Though not necessarily a non-material (that is, spiritual) principle at every level, the principle of life is different in kind from the principle that explains the unity and functioning of a non-living thing.

All vitalists agree on this much: there is "something" qualitatively different about living beings. They disagree on the explanation of how the soul exists in human beings. Extreme vitalism insists that the human soul is a non-material (spiritual) reality which dwells in the body but is not joined to it in any substantial way. The essence of the human being is the soul and not the composite of soul and body. Moderate vitalism maintains that the soul and the body are united to form one substance. The composite is the human being. Some [for example, Aristotle] emphasized the intimate union so strongly that it became impossible for them to claim that the soul [at least the whole soul] could survive death. Others [for example, Aquinas] emphasized the radically different substances in the union and hence had an easier time explaining how spirit could survive the corruption of the body. As we shall see, Augustine's view on the nature of the human "self" seems to be closest to this second opinion.

Augustine on the Nature of the Human Being

The Human Being as Composite

In a work written when he was thirty-four, Augustine posed the question "Is there anything better than the human being in the universe?" To answer this question about human nobility (he argues) one must first address the very difficult question about human nature: namely, "What is a human being?" He notes that almost everyone will admit that the human has a soul and has a body but are these essential to being human? For example, is the human being something like two horses tied together with a double harness, that is, a composite formed when soul and body come together as two different entities acting as one? Or is the human more like a centaur, a unity formed out of two very different kinds of things which lose their separate identity when they come together? Possibly the answer lies in how we use the word "human." Perhaps we use it as we use the word "lamp." A lamp is called "lamp" only because of the light that it produces and yet the name "lamp" refers to the object that contains the light rather than to the light which justifies calling this object "lamp." In the same way, perhaps we use the word "human" to refer to that body which contains the light of mind, that light which makes its containing vessel "human" rather than simply "animal." Or, finally, it may be that we call a person "human" in the same way we call one who rides a horse a "horseman." A horse is indeed necessary to speak of "horseman" but the term itself refers only to the one who rules, the rider. In the same way the word "human" [though it implies body as a necessary condition] may refer only to the rational soul, that part of the composite which rules. Put simply, the question comes down to this: "Is the human being the composite of soul and body or is the human the body alone or is the human the soul alone.?"[2]

Augustine states his answer to this question in the *City of God*. There he makes the following points:

> 1. There is a real difference between the human body and the human soul. The body is not a projection of the soul, nor is the soul only a more exotic power of the body.

> 2. The human person is the composite of these very different things. Neither is accidental to the human being. Without either the human as human ceases to exist. One may speak about the human soul separated from the body. One may even by extension talk about a "dead human body" [that is, the body separated from the human soul]. But it is only the union of the two that can be described as the human being.

> 3. The soul of the human being is specifically a rational soul, that is, a principle of life which can support such activities as thinking and deliberate choice. Any body with any other sort of soul can be described as a living body but it is not a human body.[3]

His conclusions follow from the human experience of "self." When I look inside myself, I perceive one and the same "self" thinking, feeling, and sensing. I experience pain and pleasure in both spirit and body. I both love other humans and feel satisfied after a good meal. I experience anxiety about the future and feel the pain of a present bodily wound. In all these cases, be they experiences spiritual or crassly material, I attribute them without reservation to myself. My pain/joy of soul or body is properly my pain/joy, because I am soul/body together forming the unity that is my person. This direct knowledge of myself as body and soul is an overpowering experience and it is good that it is so. Augustine remarks that it would be hard to accept a union of such radically different things on faith alone. Luckily we are not faced with that challenge because we are confronted with the reality of our composite nature every day of our lives.[4]

Admittedly, there are some texts in Augustine's earlier writings which suggest some ambivalence on the nature of the human "self." Thus, in one place he writes that the human being seems to be a rational soul using a body. In another place he describes the human soul as a rational substance which is fitted to a body as its ruler.[5] However, such texts from Augustine's early writings do not weaken the clear statements made thirty years later where he consistently affirms his conviction that to be a human being is to be the composite of rational soul and material body.

Characteristics of the Human Soul

The human soul is the most important part of the human being and is the most difficult to understand. When Augustine was sixty-one, he wrote a letter to St. Jerome in which he summarized both his convictions and lingering questions about the nature of the soul. He writes to Jerome that after a lifetime of reflection he is convinced of the following:

1. The soul is substantially different from the body and radically superior to it in the order of being.

2. The soul is the life-force of the body and is present totally in every part of the body . . . energizing each part and supporting each part in its particular function whether it be nutrition, growth, reproduction, sensation, desire, formation of ideas, making of judgments, or free choice.

3. The soul is not a part of God and indeed is radically different from God in the order of being.

4. The human soul is immortal.

Augustine then goes on to admit to Jerome that he remains mystified by other questions. For example, he still cannot explain how the soul comes to be in the descendants of the first humans.[6]

The pages that follow will examine Augustine's views on the soul's nature and its relationship with the body. The issues of its origin and destiny will be explored in later chapters.

The Spirituality of the Human Soul

Augustine's conviction that the human soul is radically different from the body and is superior to it can be seen as early as 387. In his work entitled *On the Magnitude of the Soul*, he describes the soul as a substance which has the power of reasoning and which is therefore well suited to direct the activities of the body.[7] Whatever one means by "body," it is clearly different from the soul. If the defining characteristic of the body is that it is "material," then the soul must be said to be a "non-material" substance, that is, a spirit.

The soul is clearly more in the order of a substance than an accident. It is not like "color," a modification of something else. Color as such does not exist; there are only colored things. Heat only exists in hot things. It does not have an existence in and of itself. Our awareness of our rational soul is far different from our awareness of our color or our temperature. The latter are "of us"; the soul is part of us, a part which in many ways seems independent of its material partner, the body.

The soul therefore is a "reality," but is it "spirit"? Augustine's argument for its spirituality proceeds along the following lines:

(1) It is generally accepted that a body is any reality that has the characteristic of "being extended" over the three dimensions of length, width, and depth.[8]

(2) But we do not perceive that these characteristics belong to the activities that are special to our rational soul. For example:

(a) we perceive ourselves as thinking beings, beings with a mind.[9]

(b) the content of our perceptions includes such things as memories, representations of extension, etc. which themselves have no extension.

(c) the principle "*Operatio sequitur esse*" establishes the expectation that "a being acts as it is." Reversing this principle, it seems equally reasonable to say that how one acts gives an indication of one's nature. "Non-material" activities can proceed only from a "non-material" source, that is, a person cannot perform a spiritual activity unless he is in some sense a spirit.[10]

(d) This conclusion is confirmed by our direct awareness that there is part of us [our thinking mind] that is beyond sense-perception, that type of knowledge which perceives material things.[11]

(3) It follows that there is a real part of us that is not a body and that this is precisely the energizing part of us, the principle of our life and activity . . . our soul. This soul is reasonably called spirit since spirit means nothing more than "an existing being which is not body."

Augustine's major concern in such argumentation is to show that if one accepts that "to be corporeal" means "to be extended" with parts outside parts where each part is less than the whole, then one cannot describe the rational soul as being corporeal. There is no special "place" in the body for the soul. Its vital activities manifest themselves equally in all parts. The fact of our experience is that the soul neither is extended in space nor is able to be perceived by the senses. Even if one wishes to call it "body," it still must be admitted that it is not like the crass bodies made of material elements such as earth, water, air, and light. The rational soul is a more excellent substance with more excellent activities than any of these.

Of course if one defines body in some other way, saying for example that it is "being that changes" and that spirit means "unchangeable" be-ing, then it would be logical to describe the human soul as being "body" since it is evidently subject to change. But Augustine rejects such useless "word-games" that are both devious and divorced from reality. The fact of the matter is that a body is much more than a being that changes. The specific characteristic that makes a body to be a body is extension, not mutability. All of creation changes, but only bodies are extended in space.[12]

The Soul's Superiority over the Body

Augustine bases his claim that the human soul is superior to the body on a number of facts known either by self-analysis or from scripture. Scripture teaches that the rational soul is the supreme created reflection of the infinite perfections of God. It and the pure angelic spirits are at the very highest level of created being. As Augustine says: "Only God is above it, only the angels are equal to it, and all the rest of creation is below it." Just as a mirror takes its value from the perfection of its reflection and the object that it reflects, so too the soul is the "best" of creation because it "best" images the "best" . . . the uncreated infinity that is God.[13]

Through self-analysis Augustine perceives that his rational soul is the active principle and that the body is the passive principle. His soul "works" on his body much as the artist works on undifferentiated clay to make beauty or as electric energy makes machines move and radios trans-mit sound and televisions project pictures.[14] The soul constantly "works" on the body and, since "A being is always inferior to that which causes an effect in it," it follows that the soul is never inferior to the body. The body can never be the "cause" of anything that may happen in or to the human soul.[15]

The soul is ever acting on the body in a number of different ways. For example, it gives the living body its form, that is, it is the principle of organization for the structure and perfections of the body. All created being exists only insofar as it is a reflection of the infinite perfections of God. The soul is the necessary intermediary bringing these divine perfections (ideas, forms) to the body so that it can exist in a structured way with its own specific quality and quantity.[16] This service of soul to body as the "transmitter" of perfection is important and necessary. It is important because without it the body cannot exist. It is necessary because the greater the ontological difference between two beings, the less they impact each other. God is the highest in the order of being and body is the lowest. An intermediary [an active agent with a "foot" in both camps] can make communication more orderly. Though the soul will always be a finite spirit it is at least a spirit and thereby is much closer to God the infinite spirit than the body can ever be.

The soul is the cause of the beauty of living bodies. It gives to body its order and is therefore the source of the "splendor of order" which constitutes its beauty. The soul is the channel through which divine beauty and harmony are reflected in every living animal, even the least worm.[17] Furthermore, soul brings to body the perfection of subsistence which enables it to exist as an individual, independent thing. It makes the body to be this body, and thereby sets it apart from all other bodies.[18]

Finally, the rational soul is the source of the body's life, that quality which makes it to be something much more than an organized grouping of pieces of matter [like some gigantic "tinker-toy" construction]. It makes the human body to be a living body capable of those immanent activities characteristic of living things. It is because of the soul that the body is able to participate in the vegetative, animal, and rational functions of the human being.[19]

There are good reasons for Augustine's description of the human soul as being "fitted" to rule the body. Not only is the soul, through its power of choice, the cause of the body's direction;[20] it is also the source of the very being of the body as an individualized, living, specifically "human" body.

The Soul's Presence in the Body

Augustine was convinced of the immateriality [spirituality] of the human soul by his experience of how the soul seemed to act in his body. This experience convinced him that the soul was not present in the body as blood was, diffused part by part throughout with different degrees of intensity and activity. Rather, the soul seemed to be totally present in each and every part of his body through a kind of awareness of what was going on, a sort of "vital attention" that was equally present in all parts of the body.[21]

No stranger to pain, Augustine remarked that it seemed that his entire soul felt the pain in a particular joint of the body without feeling it in the entire body. When there was an ache in the foot (he says) the eye can look at it and the mouth can speak of it and the hand can reach out for it. Somehow or other the existence of a pain in the foot is communicated to other parts of the body. This would be impossible if the soul present in the foot were not at the same time present in the entire structure. The whole soul feels the pain in the foot and that same soul in other parts of the body reacts appropriately.[22]

The rational soul expresses itself in different activities in different parts [the head does not nourish, nor does the stomach think] but at the same time it is totally conscious of every stimulus in any part of the body, suggesting that it is totally present in each part, not being limited by material space to have "parts outside parts."

The Soul Is Not God

The human soul is not a part of the body; neither is it part of God. In Augustine's day there was a special need to make this point clearly. Part of the Manichaean doctrine was that the human soul is much more than the "best reflection" of God in the universe. They maintained that it is actually part of the supreme principle of good, a "piece of God" that had been broken off and mixed with matter at the beginning of human history. Augustine rejected this view as being simply contradictory. God is unchangeable; the human soul is changeable. One cannot be the other. The essential characteristic of the divine nature is that it is unchangeable. It cannot suffer corruption or deterioration because it is infinite, containing all things. There is nothing it can change to. There is nothing that it can add because it already is everything; it cannot lose anything that it has. This is so because everything it has is "necessarily so." God exists necessarily not simply in terms of the extent of its existence [it can never "not-be"] but also in terms of "what" it is. All that it is is necessary and therefore cannot be lost or diminished. The human soul, on the other hand, is neither unchangeable nor incorruptible. The rational soul can perfect itself through virtues or lessen itself through vice. It can learn new things and have new feelings and forget or lose those of its past. Whether the soul moves itself or is moved by something else, it is still moved and thereby changed.[23]

In his debate with his former Manichaean friends, Augustine insisted that the human soul is not a "piece" of anything. It is neither part of God nor part of some common soul shared by all human beings. For good or ill, our destiny is in our individual hands and our ultimate happiness or unhappiness will be ours individually. Each person has his own particular rational soul.[24] Though made to be with God, this soul is radically different from God and is now separated from God by its own malicious choices. To achieve happiness it must now make its pilgrim way toward God by choice of the good. Dirtied by existence in a deteriorating world, the person has become somewhat corrupt, but still his soul remains the best reflection of the divine in all creation.

Radically different from the body, the human soul is yet the driving force behind all the wonderful living activity of the human person, that person who is constituted by the intimate union of body and soul. The human person can find happiness only when both body and soul are at peace, and it will be the rational soul [with the help of God] that ultimately will receive credit for being the energizing force if such peace is found in eternity. The soul is the superior part of the human person. But it is only a part. The body too is part and must be respected and understood as such. It is to this "lesser glory" of the human being that we must next turn our attention.

The Human Body

Introduction

In Augustine's various comments about the body, he tried to steer the middle course between the following extreme positions:

1. the contention of Manichaeism that the human body, indeed *all* matter, is essentially evil. Matter is part of the supreme principle of evil that is eternally in conflict with the supreme principle of good. Indeed the conflict which humans perceive within themselves is but a tiny skirmish of the war of celestial forces that goes on forever;

2. the contention of Pelagianism that every human is born in the same condition as Adam. Except for the bad environment created by eons of human malice, the human being born today has as much control over her/his body as did those first humans before their sin.

The task of understanding Augustine's views on the body is complicated by the fact that sometimes he seems to be saying one thing and at
times another. At times he will concentrate on the goodness and beauty
of the body. At other times he will morosely ponder the misery that it
causes the poor human slogging through this earthy world. In order to
understand any of his texts one must take into account the context of
where and why he is saying what he is saying. One must consider the
opponent of the day and the influences on his life at that particular moment. For example, when he wrote his dialogues at Cassaciacum (for example, *De beata vita*), he was only a few years away from being a
dedicated neo-Platonist. When he wrote his essay *De continentia*, he was
trying to disprove the assertion of the Manichaeans that the body was
evil. In his numerous later works against the Pelagians, his concern was
to disprove their contention that, apart from a few spiritual scratches and
bruises, the human condition was just fine.

The points that Augustine makes about the body will thus be deeply
affected by the objections raised by his opponents. In opposition to the
Manichaeans he argues: "The body is good and is worthy of our love."
Against the Pelagians he points out that the friendly partnership of body
and soul enjoyed by the first humans no longer exists. In fact, in our present condition: "The body is often a pain." The discussion that follows is
organized around these two contrary themes.

The Body Is Good and Worthy of Our Love

Throughout his writings, Augustine gives various arguments for the
goodness of the body. The primary reason for asserting this goodness is
the fact that the body was made by the good God. Thus, Augustine wonders how those who call themselves "Christian" can claim that the body
is evil when scripture clearly says that it, along with the rational soul, was
created by God.[25] God must have seen the body as a good, not something
evil in itself, otherwise the incarnation would not have occurred. Christ
was a true human being, a being of soul and body, and this proves that the
body is "not bound by the chains of evil."[26]

A second argument for the goodness of the body is that it fitted to
receive the rational soul and is necessary for that soul to exercise a whole
range of activities: for example, physical nutrition and growth, reproduction, sensation, the feeling and expression of emotions. If the rational soul
is recognized as being good, one must also grant such goodness to its

partner in human life, the body. Far from being at odds with the body, the soul has a natural inclination to be "in" the body.[27]

The goodness of the body is also shown by the fact that the human being cannot be perfectly happy without it. This is the reason why the prospect of death has such a wrenching effect on the human psyche. The song "I ain't got no body" when sung by the rational soul is not a song of triumph. It is a form of ontic "blues."[28] Death [the separation of soul from body] is the punishment for sin, not conception [the union of the two]. Augustine explicitly takes to task Porphyry and other philosophers who claim that humans must get rid of the body if they are ever to be happy. He dismisses their view as being just crazy.[29]

It is crazy because it contradicts our own experience and the fact that God, making humans to be body and soul and giving humans immortality, must have planned that soul and body be together forever.[30] Once the body gets beyond death its painful corruption will cease. It will run and leap lightly through heaven with a wonderful ease of movement, a wonderful lightness. It will experience a "lightness of being" that will tempt some to see it as a spirit. But it will not be so. It will be a body with parts outside of parts, with all its functions intact. It will be spiritual only in the sense that it will no longer be in conflict with the rational soul. There will no longer be any battles going on inside the human person. There will no longer be the insanity of one part fighting against another. There will be no more war, only perfect unending peace.[31]

Finally, the goodness of the material world in general and the human body in particular can be argued from the beauty that is found there. For Augustine "order" was always a good and he had a great appreciation for the "splendor of order" that was beauty. If order is a proper arrangement of similar and dissimilar parts, a body, with its extension of parts outside of parts in space, has a capacity for reflecting a special kind of beauty not realized in purely spiritual substances. Of course the rational soul has its own beauty when it exercises its special functions of understanding and choice in an appropriate way. When the rational soul grasps the truth and chooses the good, there is a splendor in the order found in comparing what it should do and what it actually does do. There is an ordered arrangement between what the rational soul is and what it does. Only the body can express beauty through what it is, that is, its existence in an ordered arrangement of parts outside of parts. Even though the body is now "falling apart" and is sometimes filled with pain and sometimes is a pain to the rational soul, it yet maintains a striking arrangement of parts. Even at the worst of times it remains true that there are many wonderful characteristics of this body of ours.[32] Indeed, considering all this, Augustine sees no paradox in the praise that God bestows on the human body through the Christian faith.[33]

It follows that if the body is good, there is nothing wrong in "loving" it. Indeed, the healthy human has no alternative. To perceive an object as "good" is to perceive it as "desirable" and "love" is nothing more than a "longing" for that which is desirable . . . a "longing" which seeks union with that which is loved. Of course it is possible for a person through some perversion or weakness in intellect to "make" something desirable. But this "desiring" does not make the object "good." For Augustine, the essential characteristic of a true good is that when possessed it makes the possessor "better." In an ideal world a reality would never be desired if it did not "make better." Unfortunately in the real world this does not always happen. Humans sometimes love things that are not "good for them" and sometimes they ignore or turn away from true goods. People can "make love" for anything real, but they cannot "make themselves to be happy" when false goods are possessed.

It is clear that Augustine believed that the body is good not because it is desired, but rather because it "makes better" the human being who possesses it. The rational soul is a noble creature, indeed more noble than its fleshy partner, but by itself it can only be part of a human being. Embodied, it is more fulfilled than when disembodied. It is not "forced" into the body. Rather, it was created as a life-principle that wishes to be embodied as much as it wants to live.[34]

It is therefore a mistake to describe the body as the prison of the soul. It is more like its spouse.[35] Certainly just now there are moments of conflict between spirit and matter, between soul and body, but such tensions are more like a lover's spat than an outright war between hostile forces.[36] Augustine finds support for this image of body and soul as disagreeing friends rather than revengeful enemies in his experience of himself and in the testimony of scripture, especially the letters of Paul. Admitting Paul's sometimes harsh words about the body, Augustine is yet impressed that Paul's favored analogies for body-soul relations are the gentle pictures of the affection between human lovers and, even more dramatically, the love that Christ has for his church.[37]

From this need to love the body comes the practical duty of protecting it. It should be cared for, not punished. Augustine [himself plagued with various illnesses] writes to a friend that bodily health is not to be despised. If people must live until they die, there is no good reason for not making the experience as painless as possible. Indeed, to do the maximum good in this life, to serve the purposes of God, there is a great advantage in having good health. Even the ascetic Paul rebuked Timothy for beating down his body too much, advising him to use a little wine for his stomach.[38] Augustine followed Paul's advice. He usually had wine on his table and, while he recommended fasting and abstinence at appropriate times, he made sure that his religious community had enough to eat to maintain good health.

Just as the body deserves reasonable care in life, it also deserves great respect at death. It had once been the faithful companion of the soul in all the good that the person had accomplished in life. In a poignant analogy Augustine asks if children value a treasured ring or a favored garment their dead parents used when alive, how much more should they treasure and respect that body which was of the very nature of the one they love.[39] The bodies of the deceased are worthy of respect; the living body is good. The body is not to be despised; it is worthy of our love. Such are the conclusions of Augustine's analysis of our embodied condition.

Body Problems

Having a body is a blessing but it is not an unmixed blessing. In our present situation the body is frequently the source of problems. Augustine recognizes this truth in numerous texts which speak about the body being a pain, at best a distraction for the spirit and at worst a maddened beast with bodily emotions and sexual drives far beyond the power of the rational soul to control. When he emphasizes these negative features of being embodied, Augustine stresses the occasional need to "beat down" the body by rigorous ascetic practices which will "chain the body-beast" in its lair and permit the spirit, now freed from earthy demands and feelings, to soar to the heavens. The distressing aspect of being with body can be fruitfully explored under the following headings:

   a. the body is a pain;

   b. we are passionate beings;

   c. we are sexual beings;

   d. the need for friendly asceticism.

The Body Is a Pain

Augustine was quite sensitive to the pains that can come from being a human being of body and soul. At times he had passions that seemed uncontrollable. His sexual drive expressed itself in his early years through intimate relationships (one long, one brief) with at least two women. Even in his later years when his sexuality was under some modicum of rational control, it still remained a force to be reckoned with.

The pain of having a body that was falling apart caused him to fear death and illness for most of his life. In his early years this fear was close to panic, pleading for baptism when as a boy he thought he was close to death. Even in his later years as a believing Christian sure of his immortality, he admits that though he was truly dying to get to the city of God he would much prefer to get there without dying.

Along with his fear of dying, he suffered the pains of living. Over his long life he endured the distress of recurrent asthma, bad digestion, a tendency toward malaria, and the assorted posterior problems not uncommon in old age. In his last years he looked back at all he had been through and remarked that, given the choice between dying and going back to infancy, he would rather die. Indeed, he considered it to be somewhat prophetic that babies enter this life crying rather than laughing. It is almost as though they knew what was in store for them.[40]

Human Passion

By emotions Augustine understands those movements in humans and other animals whereby they react to things presented as being good or bad, pleasurable or painful. What is characteristic of these "affections," these emotional responses, is that they involve some bodily reaction. People not only "fear" a coming evil; they break out into a cold sweat. Not only are they angry at a present evil; they are "hot" with anger. Not only do they desire their loved one; they "blush" with love.

Augustine agreed with the common scientific opinion of the day which identified four basic emotions: desire, joy, fear, and sadness.[41] He analyzed all of them as being aspects of love: a "thirsting" for a good which has its source in the rational soul. Emotions are not an action of the body on the soul [which Augustine regarded as impossible]; rather, they are the effects of the soul acting in and through the body. Emotions are the result of a person's will being attracted or repelled by things it desires or wishes to avoid.[42]

Just as it is wrong to describe the human body as being itself evil, so too is it wrong to describe these emotional responses to the desirable and abhorrent as being evil. Certainly in this "vale of tears" some of our emotional outbursts seem out of order but it is wrong to blame the body for this.[43] Emotions are neither good nor bad in themselves. They are described as good or bad because of the direction of the will's choice either toward the good or toward the perverse.[44]

No one with any sense would condemn a person for being angry with evil people in order to correct them, or for being sad for suffering persons so as to try to make them feel better, or for fearing lest a loved one die.[45] What is mercy but a feeling of compassion caused by the misery of another and compelling us to offer help? Such an emotion is not an enemy of reason but its servant when it gives aid without violating justice, for example in giving alms to the poor or in giving forgiveness to the wrong-doer who is repentant.[46] Emotions are evil only if person's love is evil; they are good if person's love is good.[47]

Augustine argues that even the best of humans (citizens of the city of God who are living even now according to the will of God) should make no apologies for fearing and desiring, grieving and rejoicing with the rest of the human race. Their love is well ordered; their emotional response is therefore appropriate.[48] They are moved by these feelings not only for themselves but also for those they care about . . . desiring their happiness and fearing their loss.[49] If emotions that flow from such love for true goods are to be called vices, then what indeed is worth the name of virtue? These emotions are directed to their proper objects and are governed by right reason. How can anyone dare to call them diseased or vicious?[50]

Even the incarnate God, Jesus Christ, expressed emotion during his human life. He was saddened and angered by his enemies. He felt joy when someone seemed to believe in him. He wept at the grave of Lazarus. He desired to eat his last paschal meal with his friends. When faced with his own final suffering and death, he broke into a bloody sweat.[51] How can emotions be evil when the good God deigned to express them?

The debate about what to do about the emotions is a useless exercise. We can't live without them and a person who tries to do so is attempting a non-human life.[52] It is true that some of the emotions will not last beyond death but some will endure. There will be no sorrow in heaven but there will be infinite joy. Joy will be absent in hell, but the depths of grief will be unending.[53]

As for now, there will be times when each of the emotions will be useful. Fear and sorrow may be out of place in heaven but here on earth even those disturbing feelings can be therapeutic. A person who in this life feels no fear or sorrow for anything is in deep trouble. It is a sign that he does not know what is going on. Even that quiet apathy [so cherished by the Stoics] where the person has emotions but is not disturbed by them is impossible. The wildness of desire that is concupiscence gone mad will be a threat as long as we live. We may control it but we cannot do away with it. It will disappear only when our bodies return to us glorified in resurrection. Then we shall still "feel good" in a physical way but the desire for such good feelings will not tempt us to turn aside from the infinite good standing before us.[54] Such controlled emotion is truly a good devoutly to be wished for, but it is not one that can be attained in this life.[55] And, as far as that extreme state of apathy which is devoid of all feeling is concerned, this is a stupor worse than any vice.[56]

Augustine believed that emotional reaction to the pleasant and un-pleasant is an aspect of being human. Feelings are not bad. They are part of human nature. Apathy is not the Christian ideal; controlled fervor is. Indeed, he suggests that without some fervor in one's life, one can never hope to understand the divine passion for humans and the human passion to seek the infinite. It was probably because of this conviction that one day, when Augustine was trying to describe to an apparently apathetic audience the joy of infinite love, he cried out (no doubt emotionally):

> Give me people who are in love! They will know what I mean. . . . But if I speak to cold persons, they will just not know what I am talking about.[57]

Sexuality

Augustine felt the force of his sexuality as long as he lived. He knew its power and was somewhat afraid of it. Still, his own felt weakness did not lead him to condemn the human sexual drive as evil in itself. He was convinced that to be sexual is as much a part of being human as to have emotions. Human sexuality is therefore a good and to say otherwise comes close to blasphemy, accusing God of creating humans with a fatal flaw.

It is true that when Augustine warns about the dangers of concupis-cence ["desire gone mad"], he often uses the sexual drive as the primary example. It is also true that the occasional harshness of his rhetoric seems to support the view that the sexual drive is the most dangerous aspect of the body's domination of the soul. But it must be remembered that when he rails against concupiscence with his thunderous prose, the concupiscence he speaks about is not an evil in the body but a wound in the soul and that even in the soul it not so much the desire [*concupiscentia*] that is evil as the will's lack of control of the desire.

In Augustine's usage, "concupiscence" is a neutral word. It neither means something always good [like the word "God"] nor something always evil [like the word "sin"]. Augustine notes that it is only by custom that words like *cupiditas* and *concupiscentia* have come to be used with a negative connotation. In itself the word "concupiscence" means nothing but "desire" and it may be used to stand for good desires as well as bad. Thus, Paul speaks about the "desire to be with Christ" [Phil 1:23] and the author of the Book of Wisdom praises the "desire for justification."[58] When the word "concupiscence" is used in a pejorative sense, it refers more to a perverse will than a wild bodily urge. Evil in its primary meaning is bad choice in the fulfillment of a desire, and what makes the choice "bad" is that it is disordered. It is the choice to fulfill a desire for a lower good rather than a higher good, choosing, for example, matter over spirit, creation over the creator.

These "bad" choices in fulfillment of desire and the desires themselves are activities which come from the rational soul, that one and only source of all human activity. The desires are vital actions which move the person toward perceived goods . . . goods which may be either material or spiritual. At any one time a human may have a whole range of competing "hungers" . . . for food, for faith, for comfort, for love. Evil enters in when the will chooses a lower good over a higher, or when it chooses to let a desire for a created good go unregulated. Only God can be desired without limitation. All other human desires must be limited for them to be in their "proper place."

Thus, the source of the true evil in a disorderly expression of a bodily desire is not the body; it is the soul. The body is of course a necessary condition for this particular brand of evil. A person could not perceive bodily satisfaction as a good if he did not have a body. Devils may be damned for many vices but they cannot be accused of having bodily lust.[59] Any human desire, including sexual desire, can get out of control in our present condition. But Augustine is at pains to emphasize that this does not point to some tragic flaw in the way humans have been made. It is a wound or weakness that humans have made for themselves. It was not so in the beginning of the human race. Concupiscence in the sense of desire comes from being human. Disordered concupiscence comes from being wounded. The frenzy that sometimes drives humans comes only as a result of sin.[60]

The urge for sexual pleasure may be a powerful expression of this disorderly frenzy, but it is not the worst.[61] Augustine always maintained that the ultimate perverted desire is not the wish to live like an animal; rather, it is the desire to be God. Sexual sins are mostly sins of weakness. Pride is the truly satanic sin of pure, cold malice.

Augustine's primary argument that human sexuality is natural is the same as his defense of emotions: namely, this is the way God made humans to be. It is clear in sacred scripture that when God created the first human beings, he did not make them merely beings of body and soul; he made them man and woman. Humans were made male/female from the beginning and God must have willed that they exercise their sexuality. He commanded "Increase and multiply" and there is no hint that he intended that this "multiplication of the race" should occur in any other way than by sexual intercourse. God intended that those first humans propagate and he planned that they should be driven toward that end both by their growing love for each other and by the sexual drive that made them want to express their love through the intimate act of coitus. From the very beginning the sexual drive was as natural to the human race as the drive which moved them to eat when they were hungry and drink when they were thirsty. Human sexuality was not the result of sin; it was part of the divine plan for human beings.

A further sign of the goodness of human sexuality is that it will last forever. Augustine is firmly convinced that in heaven there will not only be a difference between man and woman; there will also be a continuation of their love. Thus, he consoles a widow with the following words:

> You must not grieve as the unbelievers do who have no reason to hope. We have hope based on the firm promise that we do not lose our loves who have left us in death. We have sent them on ahead of us so that when our time comes to die, we shall come to that life where they will be more than ever dear to us. Best of all, we then shall love them without any fear of ever losing them again.[62]

Of course in heaven there will be no sexual intercourse. Its purpose will have ceased to exist. But just as we shall have the means of eating and drinking with no longer any need to do so, so too we shall have the different sexual characteristics that defined us a man or woman in this life. The original reason for human sexuality comes from the determination to make humans as "animals" designed to propagate their young by an intimate union in which two people not only express their love for each other but also join together with God in the noble task of creating a new human being. Augustine saw this ability to "have children" as one of the greatest blessings left to the human race after sin. It was a continuing sign of God's love and respect for a fallen humanity.[63] In heaven there will no longer be a need to propagate. Citizens of the city of God will be produced by virtue, not by coitus.

Our sexuality is important to our being human, but it would be wrong to overdo its importance. Augustine was firmly convinced that being man or woman was natural but that it was not part of the essence of "being human." A human being is a rational animal and nothing more. Being female or male is neither of the essence nor even a property of being human. My "maleness" is as accidental to me as my color or weight or height. Of course I cannot exist as human without having some form of sexuality, some combination of male and female. But what my dominant sexual characteristics may happen to be neither enhances or detracts from my status as a human being.[64]

It is of our essence to be social. The drive to form a community of friends with other humans is so much a part of being human that one cannot envision a human being without it. However, one's particular sex has nothing to do with this sociability. Being a "friend" with someone does not demand that that person be of a particular sex. This seems to be the point that Augustine wants to make in those places where he provocatively suggests that if Adam needed only a friend, someone to rescue him from loneliness, God could just as well have made the second human a man also. The first two humans did not need to be "man" and "woman" to be companions. The need of humans for social interaction with others of their kind could just as well have been satisfied by a single sex society. I suspect that if Eve had been the first human created, Augustine would have just as innocently suggested that it was not necessary to give her a man for a friend. The only reason for humans to be made "man" and "woman" was so that the human race could cooperate with God in its continuation.[65]

Not only is one's sex not of the human essence, its roots are in the less important part of one's nature. It is more of one's body than one's soul. Augustine will say that when Adam and Eve were created, the only radical difference between them was in their bodies. As far as their rational souls were concerned [the seat of the mind "where God's image is best revealed"], there was absolutely no difference between them.[66] It is perhaps for this reason that, though he recognized and often preached about the practical problems for virtuous living that come from a person's sexual drive, he was little interested in sexuality as an object of speculation. There were too many more important things to think about: one's nature, one's soul, one's friends, one's God . . . to name but a few.

Sexuality would not have even been a practical problem if Adam and Eve had not sinned. If they had remained in their original state of innocence, the expressions of their sexual drive would have remained firmly in control of their reason. Loving God above all, they would have been able to love each other passionately but in a way which neither subordinated God nor denigrated their humanity.[67] There would have been no tension between spirit and body. Their friendship with God, the union of mind and heart at the root of their conjugal friendship, would have dominated even in their coital union.[68] In the midst of their innocent human passion, they would have remained first and foremost good friends and that friendship would have continued to be the root of their loving conjugal relationship.[69]

Augustine recognizes that such peace is not part of our present condition. But the source of our present "dis-ease" is not the body; it is the soul. The evil in us comes not from our sexuality; it comes from the wounded will which so often chooses to satisfy any of our desires in inappropriate ways. The task facing humans now is not to "deny" or try to "do away" with their sexuality but to find balanced ways to place rational control on its exercise. In Augustine's view there were only two possible paths to follow. Either one must choose a life of total abstinence from sexual activity (continence) or choose a life of controlled exercise within the framework of the family. Both alternatives are good. The way of continence may be described as being better only because this is the way humans will live eternally in heaven. In this life neither way provides a safe haven from temptation. As long as we live and wherever we live there will be troubling temptations, but these troubles do not make our sexuality evil any more than the troubles in living make our lives evil.[70] On the positive side, our sexuality can add "warmth" to the friendship that should unite all human beings. It can contribute to that "oneness of heart" that friendship demands.

This is especially important in the family. To the very end of his life Augustine defended marriage and conjugal desire against those who argued that both were somewhat disreputable . . . effects of sin if not sin itself.[71] Thus when he spoke to his people about married life, he assured them that he had no intention of forbidding them the pleasures of conjugal love. Indeed, he said that it is not only un-Christian, it is even inhuman to deny love to one's spouse. The only requirement in such love is that husband and wife must love Christ more than each other. But they must love each other too, loving in their love the Christ living in their goodness and hating in them only those things which are obstacles to Christ's presence.[72]

His conclusion is that there is a proper place in this life for the pleasures of food and drink and sexual union. When we are told not to love these things, this cannot mean that we are forbidden to eat or drink or have children. What it does mean is that these pleasures should be indulged in moderation so that we are not encumbered by them.[73] The only problem with the human sexual drive after Eden is that it sometimes tends to demand an inordinate amount of attention from the spirit and it sometimes sways the will to choose sexual fulfillment over other higher goods. It certainly will be necessary and useful for all humans making their pilgrim way to heaven to embrace a healthy asceticism, but the purpose of such self-denial is not to "beat down the body." Rather it is to train the spirit to indulge its earthy pleasures in a rational and orderly way.

Friendly Asceticism

The relationship between body and soul just now is that of friendly enemies. They are like lovers who do not always get along. They are "meant" to be together and yet they often seem to be acting at cross-purposes. The problem is not that the body is evil but that it is just "heavy." Augustine's famous phrase "My love is my weight drawing me wheresoever I go"[74] has special application here. The body is of the earth and can draw the human being [who is both part of heaven and part of earth] toward earth and away from heaven. Our fear of death is a sign that our spirit has a deep love for the body and fears separation from it,[75] but united to it in this life it is not quite sure how to love it. We must be taught how to love our body so that we do not give in to its every impulse. At the same time we must not ignore its legitimate needs.[76] Loving our body too much can turn us away from the pursuit of higher things, those spiritual goods we need for happiness. If we ignore these goods of the spirit, we become restless and disturbed.[77] Even if our spirit is successful in governing the untoward passions of its earthy partner, the very effort pulls us apart, tires us out, and can make our lives somewhat miserable.[78]

Because of the combative nature of our appetites, we must train them for useful service as one might train young colts, using reins that are neither too slack nor too firm in order to channel their natural vigor toward the good.[79] As has been suggested, this training is not so much a training of the body as a training of the spirit to respond to the feelings and hungers and pains of the body in a reasonable way. To expand on the equine analogy, when trying to achieve a perfect union between horse and rider it is not so much the horse that needs correction as it is the rider who either tends to let his steed drag him wherever it wishes or destroys his faithful friend by unreasonable beatings and denial of true needs.

In heaven after the resurrection, we shall be at peace with our bodies[80] but just now there will always be need of cautious care for our sometimes rambunctious friend.

Body and Soul: Mysterious Partners

Augustine believed that one of the great mysteries of human nature was how such radically different entities as body and soul can so "stick" together and "work" together that we experience not two agents acting in us but only one.[81] Indeed in his argument for the "believability" of God becoming a human being, he goes so far as to say that it is easier to accept a union of the changeable human spirit with the unchangeable spirit of God than it is to believe in the union of a changeable spirit with the changeable body of the human person. He goes on to say that if such union were not the common experience of every human being, it would be hard to get anyone to believe in it.[82] And yet this is our experience. When we analyze ourselves, we do not perceive two entities working in tandem. In some strange way body and spirit come together to form one human being while at the same time maintaining their very different identities. The soul is neither absorbed by the body nor is the body consumed by the soul.

Augustine uses various analogies to try to understand this mysterious union. For example, he says that it is something like the Trinity where three distinct divine persons are yet "one God."[83] Or again, it is like a marriage between ill-matched lovers where the spouses have little or nothing in common except for their love of each other.[84] Such love explains why these lovers fear to be separated in death even though it gives no insight into how such different beings can live together in peace day after day. Augustine ruefully noted that, because of a lack of common language, it is easier for people to be friends with their dogs than with a foreigner.[85] The problem of communication between body and spirit is even more difficult. In body-soul relationships, one is confronted with two realities separated not simply by language but by the very order of their being. They are radically different in that one is radically inferior. Augustine admits that the soul has a natural desire to "manage" the body, but how this is effected in practice remained a mystery for him.[86] Even in the last decade of his life we find him saying that no one knows how the soul is able to act on and through the body.[87] And, as far as the body being ever able to act on the soul, that is simply impossible.

The puzzle of body-soul interaction has mystified philosophers ever since Augustine's day. The fact that there seems to be some cause-effect relationship is supported by immediate experience. When my body touches a hot stove, my mind (my perceptive power) is aware of pain. When my mind (my power of choice) "decides" to run to the store, my body does the running.

How to explain these experiences? A system that may be called dual interactionism takes a straightforward approach saying that indeed mental events can sometimes cause bodily events and bodily events sometimes cause mental events. The theory of occasionalism, stressing the radical difference between body and spirit, will argue that all apparent cause-effect relationships are but fantasy. The apparent interaction is better explained by having recourse to God. When I put my hand on a hot stove, God uses that "occasion" to cause the feeling of pain in my perceptive powers. When I decide to move my leg, God uses that occasion to move my leg. Parallelism also assumes that the body and spirit are so different that one cannot cause an effect in the other. It explains their apparent interaction by asserting that, like two perfectly correlated clocks, they have been set in parallel activity from the beginning of their existence. Just as two clocks set in tandem motion will strike the hour twelve together without one causing the other's striking, so in the human being the events that occur in the body are timed perfectly with concordant events in the soul, and vice versa. Finally, epiphenomenalism solves the problem by denying any real difference between mind and body. In fact mind and body are two aspects of one and the same material thing. Mental events are like the froth generated by an angry sea. Though its translucent bubbly state makes it appear different from the dark heavy mass below, in fact froth (mental events) and sea (body events) are of the same nature. Mental events are only "epiphenomena" (by-products) of body events.[88]

All of these theories were developed formally long after Augustine had died, but had he been asked to make a choice among them, he would have leaned toward an explanation that could be appropriately termed: "one-way interactionism." Our various bodily events [for example, running into a wall] are but the conditions for the various acts that the soul performs in response to what it perceives is happening in the body. The soul can "cause" effects in the body, but the body cannot "cause" effects in the soul.

Augustine's conclusion on body-soul interaction rests on two assumptions:

1. Whatever causes an effect [that is, "works"] on another is superior to that on which it "works."[89]

2. The body is never superior to its soul.[90]

These assumptions forced him to deny that the body can ever have an effect on the soul and this conviction created great difficulties for him when he came to explain how we come to know things. The "content" of our knowledge comes through experience of the real world, but how can the mostly material world of our experience become "known" without causing that knowledge? How can the material objects of our experience become "dematerialized" so as to be understood by our mind? Augustine's answers to such questions will be examined in the chapters that follow on the process of knowledge.

Notes

1. See "Life & Death," *The Great Books of the Western World*, vol. 1 "The Syntopicon," Mortimer Adler ed., (Chicago: Encyclopedia Britannica, Inc., 1990); "Life, Meaning and Value of," *Encyclopedia of Philosophy*, vol. 4, Paul Edwards ed. (New York: Macmillan, 1967).

2. *DMC*, 1.4.6, PL 32, 1313.

3. *DCD*, 15.7.11, PL 41, 1065; *DCD*, 13.24.2, PL 41, 399; *DT*, 7.4.7, PL 42, 940; *DA*, 4.5.6, PL 44, 527-28. Other texts suggesting that the human being is the composite include the following: *IJE*, 19.15, PL 35, 1553; *DDQ*, 7, PL 40, 13; *SER 150*, 4.5, PL 38, 810. See G. R. Evans, "Augustine on the Soul: The Legacy of the Unanswered Questions," *Augustinianum*, xxv, 1 (1985), p. 287.

4. *DCD*, 10.29.2, PL 41, 308.

5. *DMC* 1.27.52, PL 32, 1332; *DQA* 13.22, PL 32, 1048.

6. *E 166*, 2,3-4, PL 33, 721-22.

7. "It seems to me that the soul is a substance which through a certain participation in reason is fitted to rule the body." *DQA*, 13.22, PL 32, 1048. The following points should be noted:

[a]. The definition is precisely that of the *human* soul (*animus*). As Hölscher notes, Augustine uses four terms in speaking about that principle [soul] which gives life to the human being:

1. *anima* . . . is used to designate the principle of life in any living being. In the human being it will include seven levels of activity (*DQA*, 33.70-76, PL 32, 1073-77)

2. *animus* . . . is used specifically to refer to the *rational* soul, that is, the soul of the human being which supports not only vegetative and animal functions [nutrition and sensation] but also the specifically human functions of intellectual knowledge and free choice.

3. *mens* . . . is used to designate specifically the intellectual faculty of the human soul whereby the person is able to understand and know wisdom and truth.

4. *spiritus* . . . though used by analogy of many things, its primary meaning is "a non-corporeal being" and as such is used to refer to God, the angels, and the human souls.

See Ludwig Hölscher, *The Reality of Mind: Augustine's Philosophical Arguments for the Human Soul as a Spiritual Substance* (London: Routledge & Kegan Paul, 1986), fn. 52, p. 228. See also Gerard O'Daly, *Augustine's Philosophy of Mind* (Los Angeles: University of California Press, 1987), pp. 7-8. See Etienne Gilson, *The Christian Philosophy of St. Augustine*, trans. L. Lynch (New York: Random House, 1960), p. 269, fn 1.

[b] The definition emphasizes that the rational soul is a substance, that is, a being able to exist in itself and not in another as an object of inherence. (for example, color can exist only in a colored thing; tall can exist only in a tall thing). Such accidents have no independence. They must inhere in another for their very existence. There is no difficulty in understanding how a substance and its accidents (color, shape, taste, etc.) can be united to form "one." There is severe difficulty in understanding how two different substances (body and soul) can come together to become one. Augustine constantly refers to this in the human being as being a mystery.

[c] The definition also clearly states the rational soul's superiority to the body and points to the root of the superiority in the fact that it is a *rational* soul.

8. *DQA*, 3.4, PL 32, 1037-38; *DGL*, 7.21.27, PL 34, 365. Hölscher [*op. cit.*, pp. 20-21] summarizes in fourteen points Augustine's view on the nature of "body." However the central characteristic of any material being would seem to be that it occupies a specific extension in place (*DT*, 10.7.10, PL 42, 979) with all that *that* entails, for example, having parts outside of parts, the whole is greater than any part, an inability to be in two places at the same time, etc. Hölscher in fn. 18, p. 232 lists numerous references in Augustine where he makes this point.

9. *DT*, 10.10.13, PL 42, 980.

10. *DQA*, 5,9, PL 32, 1040-41; *Ibid.*, 14.23-24, PL 32, 1048-49.

11. *DT*, 10.10.15-16, PL 42, 981-82. See Gilson, *op. cit.*, pp. 48ff. In various other places Augustine pursues his argument for the spirituality of the soul. Thus, in his work *On the Soul and Its Origin* he argues first that it is possible to have a substance which is not corporeal [4.18.12] and then goes on to point out that some of the non-corporeal activities of the human being [for example, dreaming] point to such a substance being part of the human nature. [4.25.16].

12. *E 166*, 2.4, PL 33, 721-22; *IJE*, 20.10, PL 35, 1561.

13. *DQA*, 34.77-78, PL 32, 1077-78.

14. *DCD*, 22.24.2, PL 41, 789.

15. *DM*, 6.5.8, PL 32, 1167-68.

16. *DIA*, 15.24, PL 32, 1033.

17. *DVR*, 41.77, PL 34, 156-57.

18. *DIA*, 15.16, PL 32, 1033-34.

19. *DCD*, 13.2, PL 33, 377-78; *DDQ*, 7, PL 40, 13. In his discussion of the human being, Augustine will sometimes speak of human nature being composed of *three* entities: spirit, soul, and body. By "spirit" he means the highest powers (*mens*) of the rational soul (*animus*) whereby it reasons and understands. He will use the word "soul" (*anima*) to stand for the more general function of *any* soul (rational or irrational) in giving life to the body it perfects. Thus irrational animals may truly be said to have "soul," but not "spirit." See *DA*, 4.32 & 33, PL 44, 544-46.

20. *DIA*, 13.20-21, PL 32, 1031-32.

21. *E 166*, 2.4, PL 33, 722; See Gilson, *op. cit.*, pp. 48ff.

22. *DIA*, 16.25, PL 32, 1034.

23. *E 166*, 2.3, PL 33, 721; See *DGL*, 7.2.3, PL 34, 357.

24. *DLA*, 2.7.15-19, PL 32 1249-50.

25. *DC*, 8.20, PL 40, 362. See Margaret R. Miles, *Augustine on the Body*, American Academy Of Religion Dissertation Series # 31 (Scholars Press: 1979), p. 62. See *DVR*, 11.21, PL 34, 131-32.

26. *DC*, 12.26, PL 40, 367.

27. *DGL*, 7.27.38, PL 34, 369; *ibid*, 7.25.36, PL 34, 368-69; *ibid*, 12.35.68; PL 34, 483. Augustine suggests not only that is the soul made to rule the body but also that it cannot be perfectly happy after death until it is reunited with the body. See *E 166*, 2.4, PL 33, 722.

28. *DA*, 4.2.3, PL 44, 535.

29. *SER 241*, 7.7, PL 38, 1137.

30. *DCD*, 22.24, PL 41, 788-792; *E 118*, 3.13, PL 33, 438.

31. *SER 241*, 7.7, PL 38, 1137-38; *SER 242*, 8.11, PL 38, 1142-43; *SER 155*, 13.14 & 14.15, PL 38, 848-49; *DCD*, 22.30.1, PL 41, 801-02.

32. *SER 241*, 7.7, PL 38, 1137; *DCD*, 22.19, PL 41, 780-82; *ibid.*, 22.24, PL 41, 788-92.

33. *SER 30*, 7.7, PL 38, 1137.

34. *DGL*, 7.27.38, PL 34, 369; *ibid.*, 1.35.68, PL 34, 483. See *DCD* 14.16, PL 41, 424-25; *DNC*, 1.24.27, PL 44, 429; *DUJ*, 4, PL 40, 709-11. For an extended

discussion of how natural it is to love one's body, See *DDC* 1.23-26, PL 34, 27-29.

35. *ENN 140*, 16, PL 37, 1825-1826.
36. *SER 155*, 14.15, PL 38, 349.
37. *DC*, 9.22, PL 40, 363.
38. *E 130*, 3.7, PL 33, 497.
39. *DCM*, 3.5, PL 40, 595.
40. *DCD,* 21.14, PL 41, 728; *ibid.*, 22.22.3, PL 41, 785-86; *SER 277*, 7.8, PL 38, 1261-62; *ENN 102*, 5-6. PL 37, 1319-21.
41. *DCD*, 14.7, PL 41, 410-11.
42. *Ibid.*, 14.6, PL 41, 409.
43. *Ibid.*, 14.5, PL 41, 408-09.
44. *Ibid.*, 14.8.3, PL 41, 413.
45. *Ibid.,* 9.5, PL 41, 260.
46. *Ibid.*, 9.5, PL 41, 261.
47. *Ibid.*, 14.6, PL 41, 409.
48. *Ibid.*, 14.9.1, PL 41, 413.
49. *Ibid.*, 14.9.2, PL 41, 414.
50. *Ibid.*, 14.9.3, PL 41, 415.
51. *Ibid.*
52. *Ibid.*, 14.9.4, PL 41, 415.
53. *Ibid.* 14.9.5, PL 41, 416.
54. *SER 128*, 9.11, PL 38, 718.
55. *DCD*, 14.9.5, PL 41, 415.
56. *Ibid.*
57. *IJE*, 26.4, PL 35, 1608.
58. *DCD*, 14.7.2, PL 41, 410-11.
59. *DGL*, 10.12.20, PL 34, 417; *DCD*, 14.3, PL 41, 406-07. See Miles, *op. cit.*, p. 71; Peter Brown, *op. cit.*, pp. 405-18. In Augustine's later work, especially his writings against Julian, he seems in many places to describe concupiscence as being in itself evil. However, even here two things should be noted. First he is always speaking about conconcupiscence [specifically the drive to sexual union] as it exists now after sin. Secondly, in calling it evil now he seems to be speaking more about the disruptive effect it has on the person's seeking "higher things." See *CJH*, 4.2.11, PL 44, 741-42.
60. *CJH,* 3.9.18, PL 44, 711.
61. Chadwick offers the following comment: "In the Pelagian controversy he came to say with a mounting crescendo that in human nature as it is now, the sexual impulse is the supreme symptom or expression of the irrational, the uncon-

trollable, the obsessive condition of the human psyche in its fallen condition."
Henry Chadwick, "The Ascetic Ideal," *Studies in Church History*, 22 (1985), p.
19; See Peter Brown, *The Body in Society*, pp. 406-07.

62. *E 92*, 1, PL 33, 319; *DCD,* 22.17, PL 41, 778-79.

63. *DCD*, 22.24.1, PL 41, 788. Along the same lines, Augustine makes clear
to Julian that the *only* persuasive reason for having two sexes is because of procreation through intercourse. Thus he writes: "You say: 'The reason for the existence of the sexes is the union of bodies,' and you want me to concede this to you.
I do concede it." *CJH*, 3.7.16, PL 44, 710.

64. *DGL*, 3.22.34, PL 34, 293-94.

65. *Ibid.*, 9.5.9, PL 34, 396. Augustine goes on to make the interesting point
that whatever the combination of sexes in that first community, some arrangement would be necessary to make sure that "opposing wills would not disrupt the
peace of the household." And the basis for determining which one should "command" and which one should "obey" could still be found in that one was created
before the other and even more so if one was made from the other. This suggests
that the subordination of woman to man in the family that he recognized was
based not so much on her being a woman as that in the order of creation she was
created second and made from Adam. Augustine concludes his discussion by
saying that if woman was not necessary to help man in work, and if woman was
not necessary for man to have a friend, the only way in which specifically a
woman was necessary to be a helper to that first human being (who happened to
be male) was for the sake of "bearing children." See *DGC*, 2.35.40, PL 44, 405.
See also *CJH*, 3.7.15, PL 44, 709.

66. The fact that Augustine relegates sexual differences primarily to the body
perhaps explains why he did not make too much of the culturally accepted subordination of woman to man in his society. For him, in the part of human nature that
was the most important, the spirit, there was absolute equality. See *DGL*, 3.22.34,
PL 34, 293-94. See Richard J. McGowan, "Augustine's Spiritual Equality: The
Allegory of Man and Woman with Regard to *Imago Dei,*" *Revue des Études
Augustiniennes*, 33 (1987), p. 260.

67. *DCD*, 14.24, PL 41, 432-33; See *ibid*, 14.10, PL 41, 417; *DGL*, 11.42.59,
PL 34, 454.

68. *DGC*, 2.35.40 & 2.36.41, PL 44, 405-06. See Brown, *op. cit.*, pp. 402-03.

69. *DBC*, 1.1, PL 40, 373.

70. *CJH*, 3.11.22, PL 44, 712-13; *ibid.*, 3.10.22, PL 44, 713. See Brown, *op.
cit.*, p. 419.

71. *E* 6*, 3.2-3, CSEL 88, 33.

72. *SER 349* 1-2 & 7, PL 38, 1529-33.

73. *IEJ*, 2.12, PL 35, 1996; See *CJH*, 5.16.61, PL 44, 817-18.

74. *C*, 13.9.10, PL 32, 849.

75. *DGL*, 12.35.68, PL 34, 483-84.

76. *DDC*, 1.26.27, PL 34, 29.

77. *DMU*, 6.13.39, PL 32, 1184.

78. *DGM*, 1.20.31, PL 34, 187-88.

79. *C*, 10.31.47, PL 32, 799; *DUJ*, 3.3, PL 40, 709.

80. *SER 155*, 14.15, PL 38, 849.

81. *DCD*, 21.10.1, PL 41, 725.

82. *Ibid.*, 10.29.2, PL 41, 308.

83. *E 238*, 2.12, PL 33, 1042; *DGL*, 8.21.42, PL 34, 389.

84. *E 140*, 6.16, PL 33, 545.

85. *DCD*, 19.7, PL 41, 634.

86. *DGL*, 12.35.68, PL 34, 483-84.

87. *DA*, 4.5.6, PL 44, 528.

88. For these theories See "Mind- Body Problem," *Encyclopedia of Philosophy*, *op. cit.*, vol. 5.

89. *DMU*, 6.5.8, PL 32, 1167-68.

90. *Ibid.* Miles has suggested that Augustine's emphasis on abstinence points to a tendency toward a two-way interactionism. She writes: "Augustine would be totally without any rationale for abstinence if a two-way interactionism were not implicit." [Miles, *op. cit.*, p. 65] However this would not seem to follow if, as we have suggested, abstinence is more a training for the will denying the body some of its desires than of the body itself. Moreover, if the soul pains itself because of some disruption in the body [for example, an upset stomach], it would seem logical to say that it feels peace when, through a process of reasonable abstinence, such disturbance ceases.

Chapter 5

The Process of Knowledge I:
Sensation & Memory

General Introduction

For most human beings the problem of knowledge is not a problem. Although we "know" things, we usually do not "know" that we are "knowing," not because we cannot but simply because we do not. In ordinary life we are just not that reflective about what is going on inside us. In a vague way we are aware that we do know, that we do love, that we do feel; but seldom if ever do we think about the process: how we know, how we love, how we feel.

Augustine realized this as well as anyone else. On a day by day basis he did not worry about how he knew things. He was more concerned about the truth of what he knew (especially about himself and God) and how to convince others of that truth. He did not preach about the process of knowledge in his daily sermons. His goal was to get his people to believe in God and to choose to lead a moral life. He knew that "doing good" was more important than being able to define "good." As he remarked in his *Confessions*, it is preferable by far to be a simple farmer who has a tree and blesses the creator for such a wonderful gift than to be an eminent scientist who is able to list accurately the exact specifications of a tree but who neither knows nor loves its creator.[1] At the same time, as one who proclaimed that he wished to "know himself" and "know God," the question of "how" one knows anything was an issue of great interest to him. As in so many other topics, he "wondered" at the mystery he found there and quickly moved from self-analysis to praise of the God who created humans so complex and wonderful.

The first question about knowledge that he had to address was, "What indeed do I know? What seems to be the content of my knowledge?" If we asked the same question of ourselves, we would discover the following:

1. I know myself as a being who exists, who is alive, who thinks, who has perceptions of individual material things that seem to be external to myself . . . that is, things that are not part of me.

2. I perceive "objects" of my sensations, the "hardness" of this desk, the "color" of the walls of this room, etc.

3. I have memories of past experiences of the material world . . . past events that go to make up my history. I can also remember purely abstract events . . . for example, the solution to a geometry problem, a "definition" of a term in logic.

4. I have imaginings created by combining past experiences of the material world. Thus I can imagine what a "centaur" looks like by combining images of horse and human. I also have creative imaginings which allow me to discover new ideas and new proofs from previously known ideas and lines of argument.

5. I have an awareness of purely "abstract" things, for example, ideas of justice, beauty, goodness which I use as absolute norms, ideals against which I measure just actions, beautiful sunsets, and people whom I call "good."

6. I have an awareness that I make judgments whereby I mentally connect my ideas about the actual world: for example, "Sarah is the sister of Mary"; "A human being is a rational animal." I also makes judgments about purely abstract matters: for example, "Two things equal to the same third thing are equal to each other." Some of these judgments are not only certainly true; they are necessarily true, that is, they must be true not only in this actual world but also in every possible world.

Performing a similar analysis, Augustine created a simpler list by separating the objects of knowledge into three categories. First of all (he says), we know material things, corporeal things of "body" like the "heavens and the earth and everything in them that can be perceived by our senses." Secondly, we know the images of material things that we remember from past experience or create for ourselves by combining remembered images into new "imaginations." Finally we know immaterial things, ideas such as justice and wisdom and charity which can be understood but are far beyond imagining.[2]

In order to know these three classes of objects, the human employs three distinct kinds of vision:

1. corporeal vision: the vision exercised through the external senses;

2. spiritual vision: the vision exercised by memory and imagination;

3. intellectual vision: the vision exercised by the mind.

Augustine uses the following example to explain his meaning. When I hear and understand the commandment "You must love your neighbor as yourself," I experience three sorts of knowledge. First of all, I see the words by my power of sight, a corporeal vision whereby the material marks made by the words on the paper impact my eyes with their reflected light. Corporeal vision is thus the physical contact between the object and the sense organ. It is not yet the act of sensation. This occurs only at the next level of vision, a spiritual vision where the rational soul creates an image of the words and retains them in memory. It is also through this spiritual vision that we can recall a memory of the sentence and of an actual neighbor even when they are not before us. Though this vision is "spiritual" (in that it forms non-material images of things) it is far less than the "intellectual vision" whereby we come to understand the meaning of the word "love," a reality that can be thought but not imagined.[3]

All of these "visions" have only one source: the rational soul of the person knowing. It is the person who sees the sun, remembers the moon, understands the science of astronomy, and even sees from time to time the glimmering light of "perfect beauty" and "necessary truth." Even though the cognitive power of the human is "one," Augustine finds it convenient to use different names for the rational soul as it moves from one level of vision to another. He makes the following distinctions:

a. Mind (*mens*) is the highest exercise of our cognitive power by which we are able to know purely intelligible things: that is, realities that cannot be known by the senses directly. It is through mind that one can even come to knowledge of God.[4] When the mind is directed toward God as its object it is called "intellect" and the truth discovered is called wisdom. Directed toward anything less than God, it is called "reason" and the truth discovered is called science.[5]

b. Spirit (*spiritus*) is that aspect of the human cognitive power whereby it is able to produce the "images" of material things and present them as objects of thought. It is thus a bridge between sense and mind.[6]

Spirit plays an important part in the process of sensation in all animals able to perceive and react to the world around them.[7] It is the source of the internal sense, memory, and imagination that are so crucial for the internalization, organization, retention, and evaluation of the stream of stimuli impacting the external senses. Though "spirit" is constantly under the barrage of bodies, it yet cannot be called body because it reacts by producing incorporeal images of those corporeal things.[8]

There are many mysteries in this complex process reaching from object sensed to thought conceived. Augustine was puzzled by questions like the following:

1. How can I perceive material things far distant from me? I seem to know such things, things like the sun and moon and stars. Even seeing something or hearing something on the other side of this room is mysterious. Knowledge is a vital power limited to those places where I live. I cannot see or hear or smell or taste or touch places where I am not. I am not among the stars; how can I know them?[9] Knowledge demands contact with the thing known.[10] How can I explain my contact with distant things? Do I in some way "reach out to them," extend my vital cognitive powers out into the infinite heavens; or do they come to me, the distant galaxies indeed spinning through space far away and yet being at the same time here, impinging on me, touching me and thereby awakening my awareness?

2. How can such different things as matter and spirit have any impact on each other? It seems reasonable to expect that the "thing known" should be close to the "knower" not only physically but even ontologically. At least on the level of created being there should be some parity between the knower and the thing known. A two-dimensional being necessarily would always be ignorant of a three dimensional world. A being of planar mind would probably find it difficult even to think with any depth. How much harder, then, must it be for any connection to be made between spirit and matter! Their difference is much more than a matter of a single dimension. One is the antithesis of the other; indeed, its very contradiction. How can there be understanding? It is like the doomed marriage of the elephant with the mouse. Their lack of communication was sad but really it was no one's fault. It's just that they did not have very much in common.

3. How can a being of a lower order cause an effect on a being of a higher order?[11] If matter in general and the human body in particular are radically inferior to the human soul, how can the soul be "moved" to acquire knowledge of the material world through its corporeal partner, the body? It would seem that for the mind to acquire knowledge

of the material world, it must subject itself to the experience of that world and to that extent be subordinate to it.

4. How can one grasp any reality (so as to know it) in this ever-changing world? The event that impacts us at one second is never quite the same as the next. In some way this "moving picture of the world" must be frozen so that an individual frame can be "captured" by our cognitive powers. How can this be done?

5. How can we have knowledge of the perfect, the necessary, the eternal? Our whole experience is of the imperfect, the contingent, the temporal. Everything we come in contact with seems to be "more or less" . . . more or less beautiful, good, just, etc. Moreover none of these things of our experience are necessarily so. It is certainly true that "I exist" but it could be otherwise. Everything experienced (even myself) is in constant flux. How is it that we seem to know unchanging perfect expressions of these changing imperfect objects . . . things like perfect beauty and perfect goodness and perfect justice . . . ideal norms on which we base our judgments about the ever-changing degrees of beauty and goodness and justice that we find around us? How is it that some of our judgments about the real world seem to be not only certainly true (such as "I exist") but also necessarily true (such as "two things equal to the same third thing are equal to each other"). To use an analogy, if contingency and the imperfect are colored red, and necessity and perfection are colored blue, how is it that some of my knowledge is blue when the universe of my experience is all red?

These are some of the questions Augustine sought to answer as he pursued his analysis of the three levels of human vision: the corporeal, the spiritual, the intellectual.

An Overview of the Cognitive Process

Before examining the three levels of vision in detail, it will be helpful to make some points about the process as a whole.

The first thing to note is that Augustine believed that to truly know something we must grasp it by reason. Pure sense knowledge (for example, in animals) is knowledge only by analogy. The perfection of knowledge is in the ability to distinguish, differentiate, evaluate, and organize the content of our experience into a rational structure.[12] Any stage of perception less than this is on the way to true knowledge, but it has not yet arrived.

The second general point about Augustine's theory of knowledge is that he recognizes only two sources for our knowledge. There is knowledge that comes through our sense perceptions of the material world. There is also that inner knowledge which comes from our direct awareness of ourselves, for example, the recognition that "I exist," "I think," "I desire." Though such self-knowledge is most evident (indeed, is beyond doubt), it is very restricted in its extent. Although it can be multiplied infinitely (for example by carrying out the string of "I know that I know that I know, etc."), it does little to expand what may be called "important" knowledge, that is, knowledge that is important for achieving happiness.[13]

Augustine distinguishes three elements in every act of knowledge:

1. the object perceived;

2. the cognitive power to be "informed" by the object perceived;

3. the will which brings together the object and the cognitive power to produce the vision.

For example, in sensation the object is the external body itself: the sun that is seen, the rock that is felt, the sounding bell that is heard. Joined to the sense power by the will's intention and choice to pay attention, the characteristic (ontological form/species) of the external object is changed into an incorporeal image in the sense power . . . a species/form which reflects the content of the form as it exists in the object but which is different in its nature. This image of the present object is then joined by will to the memory where it is stored. Now the object can be seen even when absent through its remembered image. This stored image becomes a potential object of thought. It becomes actual when the will joins it to mind by recollecting it, by paying attention to it, by holding it before the gaze of the mind so that the mind can ruminate, evaluate, and place this bit of experience into an organized context. If this knowledge is about matters of this world, it is called science. If it deals with God and eternal truth, it is called wisdom.

Augustine perceived in this process of knowledge a unified trinity of visions, each one itself a trinity of object, power, and will. It was thus a faint reflection of the triune God who created it. God was thus not simply a distant creator; the presence of God was carried in a very intimate way in every human being.

Sense Knowledge

Augustine had no doubt that he had perceptions of a material world external to himself. It was part of his direct awareness of himself as an existing, thinking, desiring being. Furthermore, he trusted (rather than proved) that these perceptions gave reliable information about a world of material beings beyond himself.[14] To have such secure information about this external world was of immense practical importance for him. He knew that he wanted to be happy. He was also convinced that his happiness depended upon finding that good, that being, that really existing thing which when possessed would slake all his thirsts. He knew that this "good" was something other than himself. It was thus crucial that he be able to break out of himself and touch that "other" world, to know something about it and, perhaps, find there some good that could make him happy.[15] He trusted that his sense knowledge could be a valid bridge to that external world, but to support that trust it was important for him to understand something about the process.

In his search to understand sensation, the first problem he faced was the problem of "contact." In order for us to "know" a material thing, that "thing" must somehow or other be "in us." But material objects are corporeal and external; the power by which we "know" is both internal and non-corporeal (that is, spiritual). In some way or other those perfections, those characteristics, that "form" (to use the technical term) which makes that "thing" to be that particular thing must be present to us and in us. The green of the tree, the aroma of its leaves, the roughness of its bark . . . these must in some way or other become "part of us" to be known by us. But the process cannot be such that we take on these characteristics. To "see" a green tree is not like brushing against a fence recently painted green. Our perception of "green" is not a surface event, and though we are "changed" by every new knowledge we gain (the "I" seeing green is slightly different from the "I" without that perception), we are not changed into the thing perceived.

There is a special difficulty in explaining such contact for someone like Augustine who believes in the radical difference between matter and spirit. The problem is twofold:

1. How can the characteristics of the "form" of a crass material body be absorbed by a spiritual power?

2. Indeed, can anything as gross as a body have any impact on a rational soul so far above it?

Augustine answered the first question by suggesting that the movement from matter to mind was through a series of stages in which that specific material form that gave being to the body was gradually dematerialized until it could be expressed as a thought by the mind. The second question was answered by positing what has come to be called his "active" theory of sensation.

Augustine's theory is called "active" because it asserts that the cause of sensation is not the material object sensed; it is the spiritual soul of the one who senses. Augustine readily admits the obvious fact that the act of sensation is a reaction to a sensory stimulus. We are in a real way "moved" by what we "see."[16] We can "imagine" anything we want by combining previously received sense impressions but we cannot "sense" what we want. We cannot "hear" what does not sound, nor can we be indifferent to the external sounds if we allow ourselves to be impacted by them and pay attention to them.[17] We cannot "look out of a window" and see an oncoming tornado when there is no tornado there. A real tornado is at least a condition for us to see a tornado. Simply put, we cannot see what is not there.

Having granted this, Augustine is yet unwilling to say that the tornado "causes" knowledge in the rational soul. To have a material object, whether it be an oncoming tornado or even our own body, act on our spirit is to make the spirit subordinate to matter. Just as the stone shaped by a sculptor is proved inferior by the fact that it is worked and shaped and molded by the artist's hands, so too would spirit be inferior to matter if matter could truly "effect" something in the spirit.[18]

How then does Augustine explain the act of sensation? He first emphasizes the mystery of the process. Even such an ordinary event as hearing a sound may be beyond our understanding. This being said, however, some things are clear. It is clear, for example, that the sounds and sights, the tastes and smells, the touches and brushes with things do have an impact on us. They cause a reaction in the body, a change which is either favorable or unfavorable, a change which is either pleasurable or painful. Whatever the nature of the change, it causes the soul to pay attention and note the change. It is this act of the soul that is sensation. It happens something like this. The soul is in all parts of the body like a calm pool of spirit filling all crevices of its bodily container. In a state devoid of all sensation, the spirit is undisturbed with no special focus. When this restful state is upset by sensory stimuli impacting the body, the soul's attention is drawn. It becomes focused on the event. The body is affected by the stimuli; the soul's attention is drawn and effects the sensation. To paraphrase Augustine:

> It seems to me that when the soul senses something occurring in the
> body, the body does not cause anything to happen in the soul. Rather,

because the soul's attention is drawn to the pleasurable/painful event, it becomes aware of what is happening in the body.[19] Thus when I look out of my window and see an oncoming tornado, I run out of my room. The tornado did not cause my running. Its winds did not "blow" me through the door. Rather "I" was the one who initiated the running once I became aware of the approaching storm. I caused my running; the tornado was but a necessary condition for my action. This explanation of my "running" is analogous to the explanation of my "seeing" or "hearing" and indeed every act whereby I sense the world around me.

Augustine accepted the conclusions of the science of his day that humans had five external senses: sight, hearing, smell, taste, and touch.[20] He also accepted the existence of a sixth power, an internal sense which allows the higher animals to pull together the reports of the external senses and attach them to one and the same object. Thus, the same flower is perceived as being red and soft and sweet-smelling. Through this sense the animal becomes aware of its own act of sensation, for example knowing that its eye is seeing. This internal sense also reports objects perceived as being dangerous or attractive, something to be avoided or embraced.[21]

Augustine recognized that sensation has both a physical and psychological aspect. The soul acts through the body and when this is defective, sensation cannot take place. The external organs of sense are the gates through which the person must pass to know the material external world; when they are shut, access to this world is impossible.[22] Many things can go wrong because the physical organs are complex, including not only the external organ [for example, the eye] but also the brain and the connecting nerves.[23]

Augustine's explanation of how these internal connections occur reflects his conviction that realities must be somewhat similar to work together. Thus when he tries to show how the soul can move in the brain and nerves and eye to bring about sight, he supposes that all parts are filled with some sort of refined material element like air or fire or light. Such materials are still not spirit, but at least they are closer to spirit than bulky earth or water. Whereas science today speaks about "electrical" impulses as the connectors in the nervous system, Augustine suggests that "fine air" is the instrument for exchange, an instrument able to be moved by the stimulus of external bodies and also by the soul becoming aware of that stimulus.[24]

The connection between the sense power and the object perceived is a more serious problem for Augustine, especially when trying to explain hearing and sight. There is less of a problem with touch and taste and smell. These seem to imply an immediate contact with the object perceived. But when we see things and hear things there is often an intervening distance. We see the sun and hear distant thunder. How are we present to such distant sights and sounds? For a time Augustine seemed to lean toward a ray theory to explain sight. When we "see" the sun, rays stream out from our eyes carrying our presence with wonderful swiftness far out into space to "touch" the distant star.[25] However, when he comes to explain hearing distant sounds, he seems to favor the now familiar explanation that the sounding objects causes movement (waves?) in the intervening air which come across space to impact on our ear, there to be noticed by the soul.[26] Augustine was not terribly convinced by any of the various explanations of the contact between the object sensed and the person sensing. All of them seemed to involve some absurdity.[27] However, he was certain that, just as there must be some contact between perceiver and perceived in sensation, so too there must be some distance between them. The sense of sight cannot see itself. Only another sense (for example, the internal sense) can perceive that we are seeing.[28]

Augustine spent little time pondering the physics and physiology of sensation. He was more interested in the inner workings of the soul in producing the sense act. As we have noted in our introductory summary, he believed that the will played a crucial part in every level of knowledge. Thus, when he comes to discuss the act of sensation, he concentrates on what he calls the "intention of the soul." This "leaning toward" of the soul may be manifested in several ways.

First, in some cases there will be a preliminary desire or choice to seek or to avoid a particular sensation.[29] We desire a particular food for its pleasant taste. We choose to avoid going to the dentist because we wish to avoid the imagined pain. Secondly, in all cases, whether we seek out a sensation or have the sensation thrust upon us, there must be a choice to pay attention or at very least "not to ignore" the sensation which has already begun.[30] Using sight as an example, Augustine remarks that it is only by the "attention of the soul" that we can keep the sense of sight focused on the object.[31] Turning our attention away from it, we lose the sensation even though our eyes remain open and the object remains in our field of vision. We must be conscious of the world in order to know it. It is not enough simply to have an experience. It is possible to have an experience which makes an impact on our body and which may even lodge in the "vat" of our unconscious mind without our being aware of it. We look at something but never see it.[32] As we walk down the street, we are constantly bombarded by visual stimuli. But we only see what we pay attention to. Preoccupied with other matters, we lose awareness of where we are and how we came there. We are always surrounded by a world of sensate objects, but sometimes we remain living in a world of our own because we do not choose to pay attention.[33]

Once we decide to pay attention to the external world, then we move to the second step in our perception of it: the gradual dematerialization of the "ontological form" in the object perceived . . . an activity that is absolutely necessary if our spiritual soul is ever to absorb and retain it as a cognitive form. Augustine outlines the gradual steps in the process as follows:

> When we consider the logical arrangement of the various species beginning with the species in the body to be perceived and ending with the thought in the mind of the one thinking, it is possible to identify four species, each one "born" as it were from the one that preceded it: the second from the first, the third from the second, the fourth from the third. Thus, from the species of the body perceived arises the species which is made in the sense organ of the one perceiving. From that species in the sense organ flows that which is made in the memory. And from that "memory-species" is made that species (idea) occurring in the mind of the thinker.[34]

The word "species" used by Augustine is a technical term that is not easily explained in one sentence. When it is applied to an actually existing thing, for example a human person, it stands for those special characcteristics which separate that person from all other existing things. My species is that formal element (or "form") which makes me to be the particular thing that I am. Since this form constitutes a reality in its order of being, since it makes it to exist in this fashion and no other, it may rightly be called ontological: that is, constitutive of the being of the thing. Some of the characteristics it brings to an individual are essential; others are accidental. Thus, for example, to have body and soul is essential to my being a human person. However, as I actually exist here and now I also possess other characteristics which, though accidental, also identify me as the particular person that I am. I have a particular color, size, sound, health, history, etc. For me to be sensed by another, my special characcteristics (my species) must begin to exist in the one who senses me. But they must exist in them in a different way. The need for this difference is crucial in a theory like Augustine's which claims that the "knowing power" does not have the characteristics of matter. It has neither a lens limited by spatial dimensions nor a capacity confined by narrow limits. I can see sunsets much larger than myself. I can contain within my limited person unlimited memories of past and present experiences.

The color of the sunsets seen and remembered are obviously corporeal. Spirit has no shades. The very light by which color is revealed is itself material. An incorporeal power (the rational soul) absorbs and records a corporeal thing. How can this happen? Only through dematerialization of the material. Those characteristics which give the corporeal object the quality of being this color, this shape, this mass, etc. must begin to exist in an immaterial way for it to be perceived. It is for this reason that Augustine will insist that in sensation the perception is of the "images" of things, not of things themselves. The images must be incorporeal, for how else to explain our ability to embrace a universe much larger than ourselves? How else to explain the almost infinite clutter of remembered and half-remembered experiences? We reflect on the heavens not as a mirror reflects an image. Even the largest mirror shines back only a bit of the heavenly immensity around it. But we, when we look at the heavens, can embrace all of it in a succession of remembered images. Indeed, these images of huge distant stars seem to take up no space in us at all.[35] In a poetic expression of this movement of the forms or species of things from the material world into our senses, memory, and mind, Augustine writes:

> Bodies freely reveal to us their particular forms, each making its contribution to the pattern of this beautiful world we see around us. It's almost as though, realizing that they will never be able to know us, they wish at the very least to become known by us.[36]

How these bodily forms become dematerialized forms in the sense power is a mystery. Seeking understanding, Augustine resorts to analogies. He says that the transfer of forms is something like pressing a signet ring into soft wax. The wax replicates the design on the ring exactly and yet the "image" in the wax is different in substance from the metallic "form" in the ring. Furthermore, when the ring is pressing into the wax we cannot distinguish the form in the ring from the image it creates. We only realize that the image is present when we remove the ring and see that its image is retained by the wax. We can "see" the characteristics of the ring even when it is absent. In a sense the wax "remembers" the image.[37]

Of course any physical analogy for the process of sense perception must limp at best. The wax is completely passive as the ring presses into it. When I see the ring's configuration (for "configuration" read "ontological form"), the creation of the "image" in my sense power is not an effect caused by a ring acting on a passive receptor. Rather the image is created by the action of the one sensing, reacting to the stimulus of the ring's "touching." This description is suggested by Augustine's careful use of language where he writes that "the sensation proceeds (*procedat*) from the living body of the one who senses but it arises from (*gignitur*) the body that is sensed."[38] The active agent is the one from whom the sensation proceeds, that is, the knower, not the thing known.

An analogy used by Bubacz is helpful here.[39] He says that Augustine's process of sensation is something like a painter painting a beautiful landscape. The painter passively receives the vision of the actual landscape impacting the sense organs; but then the painter actively produces an image of the scene . . . an image that is not created by the landscape (as it might be by a huge mirror) but is rather the effect of the vital action of the one painting. The resulting picture is an image which is different in kind from the reality that it depicts; but, assuming the skill of the artist, it is still an accurate representation of the perceived landscape.

We may summarize Augustine's theory of sensation as follows. A material thing impacts the external sense organ of the body. This is corporeal vision, the first level of the cognitive process. The soul becomes aware of the change in the body and reacts to it by producing and retaining an immaterial image of the object perceived. This is now a spiritual vision. This act of seeing the object through its image created by the soul is the act of sensation.[40]

Imagination and Memory

The ability of the mind to create and retain images of things is a crucial step in coming to knowledge of the external world. This ability is present in other animals also, but in a much humbler fashion.[41] Beasts and birds certainly remember how to find their lairs and build their nests but they know nothing of geography or architecture. Humans can go beyond the memory of simple events and build science, an ordering of memory images into an organized body of knowledge of temporal affairs. It is this ability of memory and imagination which allows the human alone of all animals to take a truly rational approach to living this complex life.[42]

Memory and imagination are the foundation for coming to knowledge of the rules of science. They are also necessary for discovering the rules of wisdom, those rules based on eternal truths which allow the individual to lead a life of virtue.[43] Some experience of this universe, retained and recalled, is a prerequisite for discovering such truths. We must spend some time mulling over short-term goals before we can know and desire an eternal destiny. We cannot choose temperance without experience of our various desires. Wisdom begins in contemplation of everyday experiences and without memory our mind can be nothing more than a conduit through which such experiences rush, leaving nothing behind but a certain clinging dampness on the walls. Memory and imagination are the only bridge between this passing world and the mind. They are also rungs on the mind's ladder to eternity, that kingdom where unchanging truth and infinite being dwell.

This climb to the heavens begins on earth with the pedestrian act of sensation. As we have seen, the core of sensation is that moment when the mind forms an incorporeal image [a "phantasm"] of the corporeal object impacting the sense organ.[44] The retention of this image in mind is called memory. When the mind combines this image with others to form images of beings never experienced, it is called creative imagination. To use Augustine's example, I see Carthage here before me by forming an image of it. I remember Carthage when that image is placed in memory, able now to be recalled at will. I imagine Alexandria [which I have never seen] by combining and manipulating images of the many cities I have seen.[45]

In this "interior I" that is my rational soul there is no room for neat distinctions. Memory is the whole rational soul conscious of the contents of its past knowledge, just as sensation is the whole rational soul perceiving the material world, and intellect is the whole rational soul thinking. Augustine discusses memory and imagination in various places in his works but perhaps his most lyrical description is found in chapters 8 through 27 of book 10 of his *Confessions*.[46] There his desire for knowledge about himself and knowledge about God come together. After a fruitless search through the external world for a clear vision of God, he finally turns into himself deep beyond that "exterior I" that must deal with the external world. He plunges into the dark mystery of the "interior I" that can be seen only by the self and God. There in his own mind, remembering, thinking, imagining, he finds the clearest trace of God. He finds a trinity in memory-will-spiritual vision, but even more in the trinity which is revealed in intellect-will-intellectual vision, that highest of all human visions which produces the thought-word sounding silently deep in the rational soul.

In seeking to touch the heavens, Augustine dives deep into himself. He lingers for a moment seeking God-prints in his sense experience but then moves on to memory, that grand mind-palace where rest all the trea-sures of images created by sensation's contact with the material world. There he finds the storehouse for every human thought. Whatever we think or dream about the external world, indeed whatever we think or dream about that personal world that is ourselves must come from this depository. Though memory can exist without images [for example, we remember ourselves by direct contact with "self," not through an image of "self"] we cannot have images independent of memory. Even our most fantastic imaginings can be nothing more than creative manipulation of remembered experiences of self or others. New ideas flow from old ideas reconsidered. New "art" is but a different combination of remembered colors.[47]

Memory serves that which comes after; it also supports that which came before. It is the foundation for thought and the glue that makes sense perception possible. The fullness of sense knowledge depends not only on the creation of the image of the object in the act of sensation; it also depends on the retention of that image in memory. Without memory an adequate knowledge of the ex-ternal world is impossible. The corporeal vision of sensation must be filled out and organized by the spiritual vision of memory and imagination. This is so because every perception of a material thing is in reality a series of successive perceptions. In order to know what this room looks like, I must move my eyes to "look at" its various parts. If when I turn my head I lose the image of the wall in front of me, I will never get a full picture of my place. To appreciate a sunset, I must be able to freeze in memory and then integrate through imagination the quickly passing moments of time which capture the colors of my evening.

This need for memory is clear from even such simple experiences as understanding speech or listening to song. Augustine suggests that we judge a song to be pleasant or unpleasant on the basis of whether or not its harmony is in accord with the "sense of harmony" or order that is present in our minds. But to hear a word with many syllables or to listen to a song of more than one note, we must let go of each part, retain it in memory, and join it with the syllables or notes that follow. Without this ability to retain, recall, and join together a succession of sounds, a song or a word would have no more impact on us than the disparate "bytes" of rolling thunder bouncing off a concrete wall. Only beings with memory can have the experience of a raucous storm or a rolling golden field of grain because it is only through memory that we can capture the "whole picture" of events extended over time and space.[48]

The images of the material world experienced are kept safe and ordered in the recesses of memory. Each imaged sound and sight and smell
and taste and touch enters through its own sensory gateway. Augustine
admits that he has no idea how the soul forms these images but he also
has no doubts that such imaging is taking place. How else (he argues) to
explain the colors that I can still "imagine" even in the darkest cavern?
How else to explain the sounds I can still hear even in the most silent
room? These various sights and sounds remain with me even when the
reality captured by the image is long gone. And they are not mixed together. They do not interfere with each other. It is almost as though each
has its own proper space deep inside me. There is no conflict or confusion. I can still recall the colors of last winter even as I sing yesterday's
song. Even in the most stygian dark and most silent space I can remember
the colors of my days and "with quiet tongue and silent voice I can sing
inside myself as much as I wish."[49]

The will plays an important part in all memory and imagination.
Even in the first act of sensation there must at least be a decision to let
"nature take its course" as sense stimuli continuously line up to be imprinted on memory.[50] To recall such memories takes even more energy of
will, especially if the events are now only half-remembered. Augustine
describes memory as the stomach of the mind[51] and like our more humble
"innards" it contains dark crevices and hidden spaces into which food for
thought can easily disappear. Every memory begins to fade as soon as it
is made. It may be true as Augustine suggests that every past experience
of the material world, every past internal experience (an insight into self,
a problem solved, a new idea generated) leaves footprints in the mind, but
some of these prints are quite shallow, quickly filled in and covered over
by the shifting sands of passing times.[52]

Of course some of our memories return quite easily. Things once
arduously memorized now flood back swiftly in proper sequence . . . word following word, sound following sound as I recite remembered poems and old songs. But other memories are retrieved only
with great effort. Sometimes I must dig deep into the hidden recesses of
my mind, following faint clues to that dusty place where the memory
sought rests passively waiting for a call to act. As I search for my long-
lost remembrance, I am sometimes hampered by undesired memories that
rush forward to distract me, crying out: "Are we the ones you wish? Pay
attention to us!" Remembering (falsely) that a forgotten friend's name
begins with "B," I am temporarily blocked from remembering her true

name is "Helen." In order to make progress, I must first brush aside the unwanted memories "from the face of remembrance with the hand of my heart until that which I wish for is reborn and seen again, called back finally from its hidden place."[53]

The content of memory is immense. In it I enclose heavens and earth, the sea and the land, all perceptions received and all perceptions formed by creative imagination adding to and subtracting from, multiplying and dividing actual experiences. In the mysterious depths of memory I even meet myself, seeing myself not through image but face to face. I have not only the remembered images of doing things (for example, holding a loved one) and going places (for example, a Roman holiday), I remember also how I felt: the past joys and sorrows, ecstasies and depressions, all those streaming emotions that are experienced directly rather than through images. Working and reworking these accumulated past experiences and recalling the "self" present to me now, I can even begin to think about the future, plan for its happenings, give a foundation to my hopes. Thus, I pray "Keep my loved one safe!" as I remember her face and recall the dangers that can threaten any human life.[54]

This memory of mine seems like a vast unexplored cave and yet it is part of me; it is my mind. Why is it, then, that the mind cannot understand this thing which is its memory, which is itself? Is my mind too narrow to contain even itself? Thinking about such things, Augustine is amazed that humans spend so much time entranced by the mountain's peaks and the waves of the sea, the mighty rushing rivers and the ocean's limitless horizon, and yet they ignore the greatest marvel of all: that tiny capsule called "rational mind" which contains all of these grand spectacles. Augustine always had a great appreciation for the beauty of nature, but when he began to consider what was happening inside his own mind he was struck dumb, overcome (as he says) with a "mighty amazement."[55]

Even more amazing than the memory's store of images of external things are memories generated by the mind itself. Humans can remember the rules of logic and the nature of literature and the skills of rhetoric. These realities are present, not through images, but as they are in themselves. We do not see them through anything; we just see them. We may remember examples of a good speech through images; but the rules for good speech are seen directly, learned once by the mind and thereafter retained in memory to be recalled as needed.[56] So too, when I hear someone saying "Two things equal to the same third thing are equal to each other," I of course "see" the words through images. But the truth expressed by the words seems to have been already in my mind. Once I understand the meaning, I see the truth. Augustine argues that this truth is not "transferred" by these word-images. Proof of this is shown by the fact that the same truth can be expressed in different languages, different words, different signs and therefore different images. Humans who cannot understand each other will yet understand this "truth" once its meaning is brought to their attention. Somehow or other such truths are brought out of the mind, brought from passivity to actuality by the words of the "teacher" who by explanation uncovers the "truth" that was always there at least potentially in the mind of the student. Once brought to the fore and actualized, the truth can be returned to memory to be recalled at some future time. For example, I cannot say that I ever thought of the truth "If A= B and C= B then A= C" before I took geometry. After it was first explained to me, I "saw" it in my mind, knew that it was true, and then deposited it in memory for future reference. It seems that such truths are in me even before I learned them. But how can this be? How did they get there? Augustine answers simply: "I have no idea. But this I do know: they are there, buried deep in the mind's recesses."[57]

To learn such fundamental laws, to come to an awareness of such "eternal truths," we must think and we do this by collecting the disparate and dispersed contents of our memory and setting them down together as one remembered unit. We pay attention to them as an organized body of fact and in them we discover truths that go beyond the individual items that they explain. Once such truths become familiar to us, they can be allowed to slip back into passive memory, to be easily recalled when wanted. But if they go too far back into the distant caverns of memory, we can only rediscover them by going through the arduous task of re-thinking them again, ". . . drawing them together again so that they can be known" and expressing them again through that "thought-word" which is the product of a mind thinking.[58]

The memory contains more than images of things and the laws of science regulating these things. It contains also more abstract matters, things like "numbers" and elements of geometry. The things we count are all around us but the numbers by which we count exist only in our minds. I can see two elephants and three monkeys, but I cannot see "2" or "3." Such pure numbers are present to me because I understand them, I remember them. I see them as they are, not in their images. I can imagine many things of a triangular shape but I "see" triangle only in my mind. Though my days for pondering geometry are long past, I carry its figures still in memory.[59] There is a mystery here too, because I do not exactly remember all of my geometry. I have forgotten much of it. And yet I have not forgotten completely. At least I remember I have forgotten something and know that there was a time when I remembered.[60] Such is the power of memory that even such a tenuous hold on the past can be the beginning of recollection. It is a memory trace that can be the beginning of search. But I must have something to begin with. As Augustine says: "We cannot look for something lost if we have [completely] forgotten it."[61]

An examination of the content of my memory reveals many paradoxes. For example, I remember past feelings without now feeling their passion. Indeed, remembering joy forever past I may now be sad. Past feelings once swallowed in memory can be tasted no longer. Remembering passion is not the same as being passionate. And yet my passion and its memory cannot be completely different. Otherwise I would not be remembering it but would be remembering something entirely different. Perhaps the explanation is that feelings are like the objects that impact our senses. They must be experienced to be remembered and they are remembered only in their images. When I recall a pain, I do not feel pain because I recall only pain's image. But I must at least have this representation. Without such accurate imagining I could never remember how it was when I felt bad or how I felt when I was truly healthy.[62]

Perhaps the deepest mystery in memory is how it can remember forgetfulness. Does this mean that forgetfulness or oblivion is somehow in memory? How can it be in memory without destroying it? Is it there through its image? But to say this does not help much. For an image of something to be impressed on memory, it must first be present to memory. I have an image of the sun because one day I was in contact with it. But how could "forgetfulness" have been present to my mind without destroying all memory? Perhaps we must say here the same thing we said about remembering joy: to remember it is not to experience it. The only conclusion that Augustine seems to come up with is that he just does not know the answer. To use his own memorable words: "The place where I work is called 'myself' and this 'self' has become for me a land of toil filled with too much sweat." He is frankly amazed that he should have so much trouble understanding. After all [he says], it is not as though he was trying to lift the earth or measure the stars. All he is trying to do is to take the measure of that being closest to him in all the world: namely, himself.[63]

Again and again he comes back to the point that memory is a dark abyss, boundless in depth and extent. This is an obstacle to self-understanding because my mysterious memory is nothing more than my mind remembering. Indeed, I am my memory. Losing memory, I lose myself. Those parts of my life that I no longer remember have ceased to be me. I look in albums recording my infancy and see a stranger. Others testify to the continuity between today and that distant yesterday and I good-naturedly accept the fact on hearsay about my infant "self." But they remain stories about a stranger, one that I either have never known or have at least recently forgotten. Like an Alzheimer patient, I smile and say "Yes, as you say, that is me," hiding the deeper fear that I will never ever know who this strange "me" is. We search for ourselves and sink in that black hole of memory from which escapes little light. We cry with Augustine: "God, what am I? What sort of being am I?" and hear the fearsome and yet challenging answer in our hearts: "You are a terribly complex being with many facets, a life of infinite possibility."[64]

Memory is the source of those possibilities because it is the reservoir from which my thoughts can drink. I cannot think of anything not in memory. But where do my memories come from? Do they indeed give my mind a bridge to the real world? The origins of our memories of the material world seem clear. They come either through the external senses or through the creative imagination working over the images received from sensation. My memory of self and the things of self also come through direct experience of an actually existing thing. But what of those necessary truths that I remember? What about my notions of "perfect" beings such as perfect beauty and perfect justice and perfect goodness? How did they get into my memory?

For example, all human beings seek "perfect happiness." Augustine asks:

> How do we humans know this thing that we so fervently desire? Where and when did we come in contact with this "perfect happiness" that we love so much? There is no question that we do know it, that we see it, but how this happens I just do not know.[65]

Knowledge of perfect happiness must be part of the content of our memory. Though we do not consider it all the time, we can at will "recall" it, place it before our attention, ruminate over it, worry about it, love it. How does it come into our remembering mind? It is certainly not there as our memory of material things or the memory of ourselves and our past passions. In all of these cases we have experienced the reality that we now remember. But who has experienced the "perfectly happy life"? No one has had such a wonderful experience, and yet everyone desires it. They therefore must "know" it in some way. Where does this knowledge come from? It is a mystery, to be sure.[66]

Augustine's knowledge of perfect happiness and his desire for it was the force that drove him to seek God. This revealed another mystery. He wanted to find God so that he could possess happiness but where did this "memory" of God come from. He had learned about God long before, but only when he looked into memory did he find God. He says:

> I found my God [truth itself] in that place where I found truth. Once I learned about you, my God, you lived on in my memory. Now it is there that I find you, remembering and delighting in you. Seeing my need, in your mercy you have given me such holy pleasures.[67]

It seems clear that when Augustine speaks about his mind "containing God" he is speaking about an experience far more intimate than learning about God. He is saying that somehow or other the very reality of God is present in him. Of course he is not claiming a full vision of God. His earthly perception of God is not like the heavenly beatific vision that will be the source of human eternal happiness. But it is a real presence in his mind. Augustine says to God: "You have given the great dignity (of your presence) to my memory by remaining in it." He then asks God how and where this happened. He does not seem to have gotten much of an answer. He knows that it is useless to seek to find God in the remembered images of things or in the mind's remembered passions or even in the mind's memory of itself. All of these are limited and changeable and this God that is known is infinite and unchangeable.[68]

One thing is certain. God is not in memory until one learns of God. Knowledge of God remains in potency until the person comes to recognize something in the content of knowledge which is greater than the rational soul itself. Augustine discovers God through finding in himself truths that are both eternal and necessary. He finds God in those notions or ideas that are beyond imagination: notions of the "perfect." How these ideas and truths came to be in the mind and retained in memory now becomes the central question. The answer to that question will be the foundation for explaining both the desire for perfect happiness and the presence of God in individual minds.[69] This question and Augustine's answer to it will be considered in the chapter that follows.

Notes

1. *C*, 5.4.7, PL 32, 708.

2. *E 120*, 2.11, PL 33, 457. See Bruce Babacz, *St. Augustine's Theory of Knowledge: A Contemporary Analysis* (New York & Toronto: Edwin Mellen Press, 1981), p. 98.

3. *DGL*, 12.6.15, PL 34, 458-59. See *DGL*, 12.7-12.16-26, PL 34, 459-464. As O'Daly notes, Augustine calls the second level "spiritual vision" only because the image of material things which is its object is obviously not a body, though it does have some likeness to bodily things. Gerard O'Daly, *Augustine's Philosophy of Mind* (Berkeley: University of California Press, 1967), p. 96. See *DA*, 4.17.25, PL 44, 539.

Bubacz, *op. cit.*, p. 98 argues that the Latin term used by Augustine, *visio spiritualis*, refers to images of both things not present and also material things which are here and now being sensed by us. In this latter sense it is crucial for the perception of present objects and thus must be found in the lower animals who seem to have this power. Thus, Bubacz suggests four levels of vision in the human being:

Visio intellectus ...... "intellectual vision"

     ┌───────────────────
     | "spiritual vision"
Visio spiritualis ....|
     |
     | "animal sight"
     └───────────────────

Visio corporis .... "bodily sight"

4. *DT*, 9.2.2, PL 42, 962; *ENN 3*, 3, PL 36, 73-74.

5. See *DCD*, 11.2, PL 41, 318. Here Augustine speaks about " ... the mind, in which the intellect and reason are naturally present."

6. *DGL*, 12.9.20, PL 34, 461.

7. *DLA*, 2.3-4.7-10, PL 32, 1243-46; *DGL*, 12.11.22, PL 34, 462.

8. See *DGL*, 12.11-12.22-26, PL 34, 462-64; See *ibid.*, 12.24.51, PL 34, 474-75. See John H. Taylor, "The Meaning of *Spiritus* in St. Augustine's *De Genesi* XII," *Modern Schoolman* 26 (1948-49) 211-18. See also Gilson, *The Christian Philosophy of St. Augustine* (New York: Random House, 1960), n. 1, pp. 269-70. See Margaret Miles, *Augustine on the Body* (Missoula, Montana: Scholars Press, 1979), pp. 24-25.

9. *DQA*, 32.68, PL 32, 1073; *DT*, 11.1.1, PL 42, 984-95.

10. *DT*, 11.2.2, PL 42, 985-86.

11. *DMU* 6.5.8, PL 32, 1167-68.

12. *DLA* 2.9-10.25-29, PL 32, 1254-57.

13. *DT*, 15.12.21, PL 42, 1073-75.

14. *CA*, 3.11.24, PL 32, 946; See *ibid.*, 3,9.18, PL 32, 943. O'Daly (*op. cit.*, p. 95) remarks that Augustine assumes rather than demonstrates the validity of sense impressions. This is not surprising. The question "Do my senses give an accurate picture of a world beyond me?" is an example of a "limiting question," a question about something so fundamental that there is nothing prior to it that can be used as a basis for a direct argument. How can we know that the world of our experience is nothing but a great dream? The answer is that we cannot know for sure, but to act as though it were a dream would be absurd. This seems to be the approach that Augustine took on the issue.

15. Of course Augustine was not the first or last thinker to raise questions about the trans-subjectivity of sense impressions. The problem centers on the reality of and relationship among three elements: the one knowing, the percept, the thing known. For a discussion of the various opinions See Beloff, *The Existence of Mind*, pt. III, "Perception"; Pap & Edwards, *A Modern Introduction to Philosophy*, pp. 566-67.

16. *DGL*, 9.14.25, PL 34, 402-03.

17. *DMU*, 6.8.21, PL 32, 1174.

18. *DMU*, 6.5.8, PL 32, 1167-68. Nash notes that in subscribing to an active theory of sensation, Augustine separates himself from Aristotle, the Epicureans and the Stoics who explained sensation as a passive experience, See Ronald H. Nash, *The Light of the Mind: St. Augustine's Theory of Knowledge* (Lexington, Kentucky: University Press of Kentucky, 1969), pp. 43-44.

19. *DMU*, 6.5.10, PL 32, 1169. In speaking about the phenomenon of hearing, Augustine says that the soul constantly exercises its "vitalizing" function in the ear whether the ear is stimulated by an external sound or not. When the stimulation occurs, the soul notices the "difference" in the two states. As Augustine

puts it, the difference "does not escape the soul's notice when it senses" (*DMU*, 6.5.11, PL 32, 1169). In another place he will say that sense perception is the soul's awareness of the experiences of the body (*DQA*, 23.41, PL 32, 1058; cf *ibid.*, 25.48, PL 32, 1063). In sum, "Sensation belongs not to the body, but to the soul acting through the body" (*DGL*, 3.5.7, PL 34, 282).

20. *DLA*, 2.3.8 PL 32, 1244; See *SER 43*, 2.3, PL 38, 255.

21. *DLA*, 2.3.8, PL 32, 1244; See *ibid.*, 2.4.10, PL 32, 1246; *ibid.*, 2.5.12, PL 32, 1247.

22. *DGL* 12.20.42, PL 34, 471; See *ENN 41*, 7, PL 36, 468; *SER 126*, 2.3, PL 38, 699.

23. *DGL*, 7.13.20, PL 34, 362.

24. *DGL* 3.5.7, PL 34, 282; See *ibid.*, 7.19.25, PL 34, 364-65.

25. *SER 277*, 10.10, PL 38, 1262-63.

26. *DMU*, 6.5.11, PL 32, 1169.

27. *E 137*, 2.6, PL 33, 518.

28. *DT*, 9.3.3, PL 42, 963. On this question of the "ray" theory and the general problem of *actio in distans* See O'Daly, *op. cit.*, pp. 81-82 and Nash, *op. cit.*, pp. 44ff.

29. *DT*, 10.7.10, PL 42, 979; *ibid.*, 11.8.15, PL 42, 996.

30. *DT* 11.2.5, PL 42, 988.

31. *DT*, 11.2.2, PL 42, 986.

32. *DQA* 27.53, PL 32, 1065-66.

33. *DGL*, 7.20.26, PL 34, 365.

34. *DT* 11.9.16, PL 42, 996. The Latin text reads as follows:

In hac igitur distributione cum incipimus a specie corporis, et pervenimus usque ad speciem quae fit in contuitu cogitantis, quatuor species reperiuntur quasi gradatim natae altera ex altera: secunda, de prima; tertia, de secunda; quarta, de tertia. A specie quippe corporis quod cernitur, exoritur ea quae fit in sensu cernentis; et ab hac, ea quae fit in memoria et ab hac, ea qua fit in acie cogitantis.

35. *DQA*, 5.8-9, PL 32, 1040-41.

36. *DCD*, 11.27.2, PL 41, 341.

37. *DT*, 11.2.3, PL 42, 986-87. In sense perception, if the image is retained, memory is playing a part. If one were to speak about "pure" sensation where objects impact our power but the image is not retained once the experience ceases, a better analogy would be pressing a ring into a calm pool of water. We know the image of the ring is contained in the displacement of the water surface but we cannot see it either during or after the experiment. When the ring is present, the image is hidden. When the ring is removed from the water, the displacement (image) ceases.

38. *DT*, 11.2.3, PL 43, 986.

39. Bubacz, *op. cit.*, p. 120.

40. See *DGL*, 12.24.51, PL 34, 474-75, where Augustine clearly states that at the first level of vision the soul perceives through the body corporeal objects such as the heaven and earth and through the spirit it perceives the likenessess of bodies. The body may or may not be passive in the first vision, but clearly the second level of vision is the act of the soul creating an image. Since sense knowledge is the perception of images of things, it is at the level of "spiritual vision" that sensation occurs.

41. *C*, 10.17.26, PL 32, 790; *DQA*, 33.71, PL 32, 1074; *ibid.*, 28.54, PL 32, 1066; *DGL* 7.21.29, PL 34, 366; *CEM*, 17.20, PL 42, 185-86.

42. *DT*, 12.13-14.21, PL 42, 1009.

43. For a discussion of these rules See *DLA*, 2.10.29. PL 32, 1256-57.

44. *DMU*, 6.11.32, PL 32, 1180-81. For the various ways in which the mind creates, retains, manipulates images See *DGL* 12.23.49, PL 34, 473-74.

45. *DMU*, 6.11.32, PL 32, 1180-81; See *DT*, 8.6.9, PL 42, 954-55; *ibid.*, 9.6.10, PL 42, 966.

46. Other discussions of memory and imagination can be found in the following works: *E 7*; *DT* 11.11-18; 14:13-16; 15.39-43; *DM* 6.4-6.

47. *C*, 10.8.12, PL 32, 784; See *E 7*, 3, PL 33, 69; *DT*, 11.8.14, PL 42, 998; *DMU*, 6.11.32, PL 32, 1180-81.

48. *DMU*, 6.8.21, PL 32, 1174-75.

49. *C* 10.8.13, PL 32, 785; See *E 162*, 4, PL 33, 706.

50. *DT*, 11.8.15, PL 42, 996.

51. *C*, 10.14.21, PL 32, 788; *DT*, 12.14.23, PL 42, 1010-11.

52. *DT* 10.8.11, PL 42, 979; *DMU*, 6.4.6, PL 32, 1166.

53. *C*, 10.8.12, PL 32, 784; See *DT*, 11.5.8, PL 42, 990-91; *E 7*, 6, PL 33, 70.

54. *C*, 10.8.14, PL 32, 785; See *DIA*, 3.3, PL 32, 1023.

55. *C*, 10.8.15, PL 32, 785.

56. *C*, 10.9.16, PL 32, 786.

57. *C*, 10.10.17, PL 32, 786.

58. *C*, 10.11.18, PL 32, 787.

59. *C*, 10.12.19, PL 32, 787.

60. *C*, 10.13.20, PL 32, 787-88.

61. *C*, 10.19.28, PL 32, 791; See *ibid.*, 10.18.27, PL 32, 791; See *DT* 11.7.12, PL 42, 993; *DMU*, 6.8.22, PL 32, 1175.

62. *C*, 10.14.21-22, PL 32, 788-89; See *ibid.* 10.15.23, PL 32, 789.

63. *C*, 10.16.24-25, PL 32, 788.

64. *C*, 10.17.26, PL 32, 790; See *ibid.*, 1.7.12, PL 32, 666.

65. *C*, 10.20.29, PL 32, 792.
66. *C*, 10.21-23.30-34, PL 32, 792-94.
67. *C*, 10.24.35, PL 32, 794.
68. *C*, 10.25.36, PL 32, 794-95.
69. *C*, 10.26.37, PL 32, 795.

Chapter 6
The Process of Knowledge II: Mind

Introduction

The world of the mind is the world of what Augustine calls intellectual vision.[1] It includes the acts whereby the mind forms ideas, makes judgments, and performs the process of reasoning. A brief explanation of each of these may be helpful before going further.

Idea formation (or, to use a technical term, simple apprehension) is a process whereby the mind creates purely abstract "cognitive forms" that represent and reflect the concrete (for example, Villanova University) or purely abstract (for example, "justice") focus of its attention. Just as "material things" are the proper objects of sensation and "images" are the proper object of memory, so "ideas" are the proper object of the human intellect. These ideas differ from the percepts of sensation and the images of memory in that they are "completely" dematerialized. I can have ideas about things for which I have no image because they themselves are immaterial (for example, spirit) or because though they reflect a material event they are not part of my experience (for example, the end of the universe).

Judgment is the activity of the mind whereby I unite or divide ideas. Thus, I say:

"A human fetus is a human being."

"A person who is clinically brain-dead is not a human being."

In the first case I unite two ideas; in the second case I separate two ideas. Here in the land of judgment I confront truth and falsity for the first time. Sensations, memory, ideas merely report what they see. Only when I begin to make judgments do I face the possibility of error. Augustine took the common sense view that a judgment will be true or false insofar as the union or separation of ideas in my mind reflects the reality it purports to describe.

Some judgments are made easily and immediately. Others demand a further activity of mind, the activity of reasoning whereby the mind moves somewhat laboriously from judgments previously known [premises] to a new judgment [a conclusion] which by the laws of logic must be true if the premises are true.

There is no special mystery in the ideas I have of the changing, contingent, somewhat imperfect world of my experience. The process of forming the idea may be somewhat complex, but at least I know its source. My idea comes either from my direct experience of self or from the external world impacting my external sense organs and reflects the contingency, imperfection, and ever changing nature of its object.

Other sorts of ideas that do not seem to come from the world of my experience are more perplexing. For example, I have a direct awareness of the fact that not only am I having perceptions of what is presently happening in the material world (for example, the person passing my window); I also have ideas of such things as perfect justice, beauty, goodness whereby I am led to make judgments such as the following:

"Measuring beauty on a scale of 10, the person passing my window is a definite '4.'"

Now, I could not make such judgments if I did not know in some way or other what perfect beauty is. And yet I have never experienced such perfection in this world. Moreover I can "see" that these paradigmatic ideas are so unchanging and absolute that they would have to be part of any possible world. Beauty as the "splendor of order" would be the same in whatever fantastic world I can imagine. Justice is "giving what is due" even in the world where it is never observed.

The mystery in such judgments has to do with their content, but a second sort of mystery is found in the quality of connection found in some other judgments. I am constantly uniting, separating ideas in the act of judgment. Some of these judgments seem within my control, that is to say, it is as easy to think of uniting the two ideas as separating them. For example, in the judgment "Today it is raining," there is no necessary connection between the ideas "today" and "raining." Sometimes they are joined; at other times they are separated. Their truth today (when it is actually raining) is a contingent truth. But other judgments have a quite different character. In these the connection between the ideas is not contingent. The judgment proclaims a necessary truth. For example, consider the following statement:

> "I cannot be alive and not be alive in the same respect at the same time."

This judgment obviously says something about this actual world since "I" am actually existing and "my life and death" are more than mental constructs. However it is also clear that this judgment will be true at any time imaginable. It will have a place in any possible world.

The problem with such judgments about the "perfect" and those that assert a "necessary" truth has to do with their origin. How can we make judgments based on ideas of the perfect when all of our experience is of the imperfect? How can I see a "necessary" connection between two ideas in a world that is "not-necessary." What is the source of such "eternal" truths? And indeed, how in the world can I see these ideas of the perfect, how can I see these necessary, immutable, eternal truths when I and all my faculties (mind included) are imperfect and ever-changing. To use a color analogy, if the world in which I live and the powers by which I perceive that world are totally "red," how is it that some of my ideas and some of my judgments are so dramatically "blue"?

These are some of the questions to be considered at the end of this chapter. But first we must examine Augustine's answer to a more fundamental set of questions, namely:

How is any idea formed?
What is the nature of intellectual vision?
How does the mind work?

Augustine on the Mind

The Formation of Ideas:

Augustine believed that the mind is the most precious gift possessed by human beings. No sensible person would trade mind for treasure; better by far to be poor than to be insane.[2] The mind is the human's greatest glory because it is there that one can find the most perfect image of God in this sad and weary world.[3]

Augustine recognized two quite different powers of mind. First of all, it is able to deal practically with temporal affairs, organizing the concepts and principles which help us live rationally in this world. It is thus the basis for science, especially the science of virtue which guides humans in living noble lives now so as to enjoy happiness hereafter.[4] Secondly, the mind has the capability of understanding truths that go far beyond this world of change and time, truths that are eternally and unchangeably true. Here it moves beyond science to wisdom, the contemplation of those things that are not subject to the vagaries of passing time. It is in the midst of this wise contemplation of eternal truth that the human mind best reflects the image of its Creator-God.[5]

Augustine believed that all of our knowledge comes from one of three sources:

1. direct experience of an external body captured through the act of sensation;

2. the testimony of others telling us of some reality or event that they [not we] have experienced;

3. the knowledge acquired by intellect reflecting on itself and its contents.

In each of these cases the thing known is retained as a mental image in memory and it is from this "memory-image" that the "mental-word" ("idea") is formed.[6]

In his work *On the Trinity* (15.12.22) Augustine outlines the process for the formation of ideas about the external material world. It involves four steps:

1. The "species" (ontological form, actual characteristics) of the body perceived impacts the body of the person perceiving.

2. The rational soul of the person chooses not to obstruct the experience and then to pay attention to it. The soul thereby "becomes" aware of the stimulus and forms a non-material "species" (cognitive form, "image") of the body's actual characteristics).

3. The rational soul chooses to commit this cognitive form, this image to memory. Now the object can be "remembered" even when it is absent. This is a necessary step because the image created in the act of sensation is by nature passing. It is something like pressing a signet ring into a pan of quiet water. The image on the surface of the ring is present in the water only so long as the ring is held there. Once removed the water regains its unmarked surface. The analogy for memory is pressing the same ring into soft wax. Even though the ring is removed, the image is "remembered" by the wax. A permanent "impression" has been made.

4. Finally, the rational soul presents this memory-image to itself for rumination and contemplation and from it forms a "mental-word" or idea which expresses its understanding of the object reflected in the image.[7]

The following points seem implied in this text:

1. Although the primary thrust is to explain our ideas about the material world, it is clear that Augustine believed that some sort of movement from memory to mind was necessary for the formation of "word-thoughts" about anything the rational soul knows, whether it be known:

a. through itself [*per se*],

b. through the senses of the body [*per sensus sui corporis*], or

c. through the testimony of others [*quae testimoniis aliorum percepta*].

As we shall see, even "eternal" truths are not thought eternally. Sometimes they need to be recalled. Furthermore, even in their first discovery they must be "held still" at least for a while so that the mind can turn them over and over in its quiet rumination.

2. The "word-thought" is always "true" in the sense of being an exact replica of the "image" held before its view by memory. As Augustine puts it, the mind "adds nothing of itself to the content of the thought." If there is absolute perfection reflected in the idea, if the judgment has about it the air of necessity, these characteristics can only come from the reality perceived. They are not imposed on the reality by the mind. Of course even though the word-thought is true, the mind can still make a mistake in judging it. It can, for example, [in the midst of a nightmare or day's delusion] become convinced that ideas coming from images supplied by creative imagination are images of some actual object. It can also fall into error by making assumptions that go beyond the facts communicated by the image, for example that the apparently bent stick in water is in fact actually bent. But such errors come in judgment, not in the formation of the idea. The idea must correspond exactly to the image presented to it by memory, an image which itself must be reasonably assumed to be an exact replica of the object perceived. There is nothing in the mental-word [idea] except that which comes from the remembered perception from which it is born.[8] It is through these ideas that we speak to ourselves the speeches of our heart.[9]

The four-step process for the formation of ideas outlined above applies to all intellectual knowledge of the external world, whether the source of the knowledge is direct experience of an object or the testimony of someone else about an object. In the latter case the words spoken by the other person may refer to incorporeal realities [for example, the words of theologian speaking about God] but the words themselves must be perceived by the senses, committed to memory, etc. before the mind can form a "word-thought" of their content. When the source of the knowledge is the mind itself reflecting on itself and its contents, there is no need to dematerialize the object since the object itself is spirit. The mind's act of seeing itself is direct and immediate even though some means of "retaining" the experience would seem to be necessary in order to get a complete picture of the "self."

There is an important connection between memory and the formation of ideas. As we have seen in the previous chapter, Augustine recognized a crucial role for memory/imagination in sense perception. It is only through the "image" of the object that the object is able to be seen in the first place; and, in order to have continuity and completeness in our sensations, each moment's image must be retained so that the "whole picture" of the sight or sound or feel of the object can be captured. There is a similar need for memory in the formation of ideas. Just as the object itself must in some way "touch" our external senses for our rational soul to sense it, so the image of the object in memory must first "brush the mind" before our rational soul can react by creating the idea of the object, the intelligible species or word-thought which in a purely non-material fashion expresses the content conveyed by the memory image of the material object revealed by sensation.[10]

Moreover, there is a need for a "retentive" function of mind even when it is reflecting on itself and its contents. Obviously there is no need to "dematerialize" the object into a spiritual image for it to be known. The objects themselves are spiritual entities. When the rational soul looks at itself, it is spirit looking at spirit. However, my perception of self and the eternal truths that I find there are perceptions that must last to be fully understood. Understanding an abstruse principle [and certainly a complex argument to that principle] is an activity that must be spread over time. Any experience, whether it be of ourselves thinking or someone singing a song into our ear, is constituted by a series of passing points of time. In order to see the continuity of these experiences we must be able to comprehend them as whole. A melody is a succession of sounds, each striking its note and then disappearing never again to reappear. To create a new tune in my mind, I must soundlessly hear each note individually and then hear them together in the melody they create. The same is true when I am trying to understand a proof in mathematics. My understanding of the conclusion comes only after I have considered the premises and the logical pressure that irresistibly forces me to move beyond them to the conclusion. Once one focuses on the truth of the conclusion, the premises are past. They are no longer the center of my attention. And yet, at the same time they are still somehow present. They have been frozen in their passing so that the whole proof may be understood as a whole.

Indeed, it seems that some sort of "retentive ability" [whether one calls it memory or mind or intellect is irrelevant] is necessary to grasp even the first "byte" of an idea.[11] Understanding implies a pondering, a revolving of concepts in the mind, "a thinking them over" so as to see all sides of the issue. But such pondering implies stillness in the object. The mind may be hyperactive as it looks at a particular object, switching suddenly from a microscope to a wide angle lens, searching for its essence and then swiftly seeing it in its whole intellectual environment . . . its relationship to other truths, its assumptions, its alternatives, its application. This frantic activity must be stilled somehow. The object must be fixed in our attention to be known. You cannot truly see something passing by at the speed of light. You cannot measure mercury until it is confined. And you cannot get an idea of something until it is held quietly before the mind's gaze. Whether our "word-thought" is of the ever-changing material world or of those "immutable," "eternal" truths the mind discovers by contemplating itself, the process of formation is the same. We must put our mind into a "scan" mode whereby (to paraphrase Augustine):

> . . . we cast (our mind) this way and that by a kind of revolving motion, now pondering this aspect of the matter, then moving on to the next . . . until the mind arrives at the truth to be known and is formed by it, taking its exact likeness into itself and thereby coming to the "thought" of it.[12]

A more pedestrian need for memory comes into play once we have grasped the truth, once the idea has come. What Augustine said about memory in general applies here too: we begin to forget as soon as we know. There is no guarantee that any idea will be forever before our mind. To say that some truths are eternal does not imply that we will always think about them. Even the most intimate and ever-present experience of "self" can fall to the back of our minds as we begin to think other things or do other things.[13] In some way or other the "representation" of half-forgotten truths must be stored somewhere. Otherwise we could never recall them and would be forced to learn them all over again as though for the first time.

For example, I was not born with an understanding of the meaning of justice or truth. I did not know of the principle of sufficient reason nor of the principle of excluded middle nor of that bane to adolescent existence: the theorems of plane geometry. Once my attention was directed toward them, I came to see them (that is, understand them) and they became part of my memory. Thereafter I did not need to discover them anew. I only needed to remember them. They come now to my attention not as newly experienced strangers but as old friends. Such remembrance of familiar ideas would be impossible unless in some fashion or other they remained with me even when I was not thinking about them.[14]

Putting all of this together, we can see that there were at least four good reasons why Augustine was convinced that memory was the foundation for the formation of ideas:

> 1. it is necessary so that material objects can be seen and retained in a non-material form in the soul of the knower;
>
> 2. it is necessary to bring continuity to our thinking by holding together the successive moments of activity that are part of the contemplation of an idea;
>
> 3. it is necessary to bring a "stillness" to even that first instant of an idea so that it can be pondered completely and leisurely;
>
> 4. it is necessary as a reservoir from which we can recall and recollect ideas formed before but now partially forgotten.

It is no wonder that Augustine calls memory the stomach or treasure-house of the mind.[15] Like our physical stomach, it is not as dignified as the master it serves, but its quiet operation is necessary for its noble partner's health. It is this humble "stomach" that freezes the passing frames of experience of world and self, revealing on demand both the beauty of the universe and the mystery of being human. It gives humans a great gift. It makes them beings of past, present, and future and thereby permits them to know something about these their times.

The Principal Ideas

In the history of philosophy the word "idea" has been used to stand for two things:[16]

1. a mental image or representation which is the proper object of the mind. The idea is created and pondered and arranged by the mind in the same fashion as the image of material things is created, stored, and rearranged by the powers of sensation, imagination, and memory. Thus, after seeing you I form an image of you which I may remember even when you are absent. At the same time I have an "idea" of "human being" which I can apply to you and to many others.

2. a perfect exemplar that is the pattern on which all things of our experience are modeled. Thus, people are deemed human because they conform to the "Idea" of humanity that exists as the eternal, perfect, standard of what a human being should be. A somewhat limping analogy for such paradigmatic ideas is the standard meter bar that in past years was kept in Paris as the one final norm for all meter bars created throughout the world.

It is "idea" in this second meaning, the principal ideas, that is the topic examined in the pages that follow.

In question 46 of his work entitled *83 Various Questions*, Augustine gives a concise statement of his views on the principal ideas. He makes the following points:

1. They are the primary forms of creation; all created things are modeled after them.

2. They are unchangeable; they can neither come into being nor ever pass away.

3. They are not dependent on anything else for their formation.

4. The place where they exist eternally is in the mind of God.[17]

In saying that these principal ideas are the primary forms of creation, Augustine is speaking about what we have called the ontological form, that which is the source of all the perfections (characteristics) which go together to make a created being to be the particular thing that it is. The principal ideas are called primary in that there is nothing beyond them on which they are modeled. All things of our experience came (ultimately) from a creative act of God and these principal ideas are where creation had to begin. For anything to exist, it must exist differentiated from all other existing things. It must be built on a specific model which is distinct and different from all other models. In sum, it must have its own plan. God as creator does not act irrationally. He does not confuse his creations. Each species, and, indeed, each individual must be "thought" before they are "made."[18]

Augustine had no doubts about the primary place of these principal ideas. It was the mind of God. Before creation there was simply nothing else in existence. Indeed, it would be something of a sacrilege to suppose that when God planned to create the universe, he had to look outside himself for a perfect model. The principal ideas, therefore, had to be in God and as such had to be eternal, immutable, and perfect in their own order. Furthermore they had to be true in the sense of ontological truth. In a superior way they possessed that transcendental property whereby a being is what it is and nothing other. Not only are they "ideas," the foundation for things, they are in themselves true because they are eternal and remain forever the same.[19]

The place of the principal ideas is the mind of God. But Augustine goes further. Since God is absolute unity the "mind of God" is simply another name for God's "nature," that is, what God is. Since all created being participates in these principal ideas, it follows that creation is much more than a replica of an "idea" or "plan" in the mind of God. Each created being is a reflection [dim and cracked as it may be] of God's very nature. In whatever humble fashion it exists, even the least creature is a reflection of something holy. God created by inserting something divine into nothingness, making something that became good because it carried an image of the divinity.[20]

Combining the Platonic principal ideas with the Christian triune God, Augustine becomes even more specific. He defines the eternal place of these principal ideas as being God's nature personified in the "Word", the second person of the Trinity . . . that eternal person who at a specific moment of time became human in the person of Jesus Christ. All of creation was present in this one and only Word from all eternity. All creation lived in God even before it came to be.[21] Creation moved from possibility to actuality through the choice of God the Father working in accordance with "the eternal, unchangeable, and fixed exemplars present in the co-eternal Word" and through a kind of brooding action of the equal and co-eternal Holy Spirit.[22]

Thus, the eternal "principal ideas" or "forms" or "paradigms" are present in all created reality since every part of nature participates in, is modeled after, is formed in accordance with, these eternal prototypes. But they are also present in the mind in a special way. The mind not only participates in the principal ideas which are the exemplary cause of its existing as a human mind; it also knows them. It has a cognitive aware-

ness of such things as "absoluteness," "necessity," "perfection," those
characteristics which can be predicated only of God.

That we perceive these characteristics within ourselves is a fact of
consciousness. That most pay little attention to this phenomenon is a fact
of life. Augustine was one of those who paid attention. He was mystified
by the experience for most of his life. The principal ideas as found in our
minds are not like bodies which come and go. They are ever present,
ready to be seen by the glance of the mind just as the material objects
around us are ready to be perceived by the glance of our eyes.[23] He speaks
about this mystery in a number of places in his writings. For example, in
the *City of God* he argues that it would be impossible for us to appreciate
and pass judgment on the beauty of the material world around us if there
did not already exist in our minds the "idea" or "cognitive form" of perfect beauty which we could use to measure the beauties of creation. This
idea exists in us timelessly, ever present with no bulk or shape or sound.
By it we appreciate nature and create in our art the precious shapes and
sights and melodies that lighten our lives. Despite our occasional ugli-
ness, we yet know what beauty is and rejoice in its presence.[24]

It is only because we have ideas of absolute values, perfect exemplars, that we are able to make our everyday "more or less" judgments
that "A" is more beautiful than "B," that "Z" is wiser than "X." To make
normative judgments implies that we have knowledge of, we understand,
we "see" in some way the norm. We cannot approve some things as good
and other things as bad unless we had some knowledge of what "pure"
good is.[25] But if the traces of such absolute values are so common in the
human mind, why is it that so few seem to see them? The answer for
Augustine was plain. "Like knows like" and many humans are far divorced from perfection, stability, and eternity in their daily lives. They
are cracked pots immersed in a world of change where the only perspective taken is that of short-term advantage. To put it simply, only the pure
and holy can "see" the traces of the absolute and eternal present in their
minds and few of us have such purity and holiness on a continuing basis.[26]

Augustine describes the process as follows:

> The human soul is the best of all created being. When it is pure and
> unblemished it is the closest thing to God. As long as it remains
> "glued" to God, it is filled with light. Through this light it is able intel-
> lectually to see the reasons for things [those principal ideas or perfect

forms or eternal species or whatever else you wish to call them] which
bring happiness when they are seen perfectly.[27]

The clear implication of the passage is this. Since the "principal
ideas" are in God, in order to know them one must become like them.
That is to say, one must become like God by drawing closer and closer to
him, imitating divine purity, and finally "grasping him" with an act of
perfect love. Knowledge of this eternal, immutable, perfect realm of being can never be a passive event. Some activity on the part of the knower
is required and it is an activity more of will than of intellect. A potential
knower (which every human being is) must become an actual lover before
he can become an actual knower of the principal ideas. And to do this
there must be some effort at purification of self.

Once people have purified themselves through love, then the activity
shifts to God who through "illumination" helps the mind to recognize the
"the unchangeable, the perfect, the eternal" paradigms by which it is able
to measure the changing, temporary, imperfect world of experience.
Through this "enlightenment" it is able to understand those laws which
regulate the way reality is, the way we think, and how we should act. It is
able to understand that in this world of passing truths, there are some
truths that are necessarily true.

The effect of such knowledge is two-fold. From a practical point of
view it gives us the measures and the laws and insights by which we are
able to organize our daily lives in a rational fashion. The principal ideas
reveal the standards by which we make our judgments about the material
world. They thus provide the principles of organization which are the
foundation of *scientia*, the organized understanding of creation.[28] Such
knowledge also brings pure pleasure to those dedicated and gifted enough
to enjoy it. The principal ideas become purely and simply objects of the
mind's delighted gaze. The effect of successful contemplation of the
ideas is "full blessedness." The meaning of this last assertion seems to be
that the mind of the person comes to "full blessedness," that is, perfect
achievement of its function and the subsequent peace of accomplishment.
The beatitude or blessedness of the person comes not through contemplation of the principal ideas in God but by the possession of God through
love, a love that comes from seeing not through a cognitive image but
"face to face." There is no indication that Augustine believed that anyone
(except perhaps those gifted with an instant of mystical vision) "saw" the
"Principal Ideas" as they are in God. We see them only as they are present
in us. But for anyone in this life even this is a great gift.

To sum up Augustine's view on the presence of the principal ideas, it is clear that he believed them to be present in the universe in three very different ways:

1. primarily they exist in God as that "eternal truth" from which all temporal things are made;

2. they also exist in each part of creation through participation, that is, by "informing them." In this function they are that "from which all temporal things have been made." They are the "form according to which we (and all other created things) are;"

3. they are also present as objects of cognition in the mind where their "eternal truth is perceived" and whereby we are able to "effect something either in ourselves or in bodies with a true and right reason."[29]

The question remains: "How do the principal ideas come to be in the human mind?" This question can be broken down as follows:

1. Where does the "material element" [the content] of these principal ideas come from? Granted that they all are "unchanging," "perfect," and "eternal." Granted that some of them do not have qualitative content (for example, "one" or relationships such as "equality" or "similarity"), others do have a very specific content, a content which distinguishes them from all others. Thus, "charity" is not "justice." "The beautiful" is different in meaning from "the good." Where does that content come from which make "charity" to be charity, "justice" to be justice, "beauty" to be beauty, "good" to be good, "happiness" to be happiness, etc.?

2. Where does the "formal element" of these principal ideas come from, that is, those special characteristics of being "perfect" or "eternal" or "unchangeable" which all of them share? Where does the formal element of "necessity" come from that attaches itself to at least one of our ideas [God] and is characteristic of the truth of at least some of the judgments we form by uniting/dividing ideas?

3. Are these principal ideas in our minds prior to any experience of this world? Or are these ideas dependent in some way on having experience of this world. Do they come into our mind only after such experience? Are they a posteriori both in content and form, somehow present in and absorbed by the mind from the real world of our experience?

As might be expected, various answers to such questions have been suggested in the history of philosophy. For example:

1. the theory of direct vision: This view [sometimes called ontologism] maintains that we see the principal ideas as they exist in the mind/nature of God. God both "lifts up" the mind and illumines it so that it is able to stand face to face with God and see there the principal ideas in all their perfection, immutability, and eternity. The mind is also able to perceive there those relationships between ideas that are "necessarily" true.

2. the theory of knowledge by infusion: According to this opinion, the knowledge of the principal ideas is poured into our mind by God either at our creation or throughout the course of our lives. God "installs" both the form and content of the principal ideas in our mind much as a computer buff "installs" software into the memory of a newly acquired computer.[30]

3. the theory of reminiscence: This is the classic Platonic position which maintains that our knowledge of the principal ideas comes from an experience that occurred in a previous life and different world. In that world our souls were "face to face" with the principal ideas and saw them clearly. Having literally "fallen" into this life and become shackled in the body, our soul's knowledge of these perfect paradigms now comes from a "remembering" of what we saw then.

4. the principal ideas are materially a posteriori but formally a priori: This view holds that the material content of our knowledge of the principal ideas or of judgments "necessarily" true may indeed come from experience but the formal element of these ideas/judgments [their "perfection," their "immutability," their "eternity," their "universality," their "necessity"] comes from the mind itself. As Kant might say: "they are categories imposed by the mind on the content of our experience rather than being characteristic of or even having a foundation in any real world beyond our mind."[31]

5. the principal ideas are materially and formally a posteriori: This theory maintains that the mind through its own natural powers and without special outside help discovers the special characteristics of the principal ideas in the world of experience. These characteristics are not apparent to the senses. But the mind, working on the raw material of experience supplied by the senses, can uncover these characteristics by a process of abstraction. The only a priori element in this process is the way the mind itself was constructed with a natural tendency, under the right conditions but without any special illumination from God, to perceive the eternity, perfection, immutability, and universal applicability of these principal ideas.[32]

6. the theory of modified ontologism: This is a term is used by Nash to name what he believes to be the position that Augustine actually held. It is like classical ontologism in that it says that we do indeed "see" the principal ideas in seeing God. However, it separates itself from the classical position by insisting that we do not "see God as he is," only as he exists in the mind. We see an "image" of God rather than God himself. The principal ideas and unchanging truths exist perfectly only in God [who alone is perfect and unchangeable] but they are impressed on the heart of humans and are seen there by the individual once grace overcomes the obstacles coming from the wounds caused by sin.[33]

In trying to determine Augustine's explanation of how the principal ideas come to be in the mind, it is helpful to begin by identifying the answers that he clearly rejects. First of all, Augustine certainly does not believe that the principal ideas, these perfect "Forms," are merely aspects of the human mind. This they cannot be for the simple reason that they are radically different from and superior to the created vessel that contains them. They are unchangeable while the mind never stops changing. They are the same in every mind, but no two minds are ever the same. Two people will arrive at very different conclusions about fact, using the same norm as the basis for their judgment. For example, it would be extraordinary for any random group of people to agree on the degree of beauty contained in any painting. Even one and the same individual will change his view about the degree of beauty present. The minds passing judgment are subject to change but the principal idea of perfect beauty used to pass judgement on creation is ever the same.[34]

Secondly, Augustine rejects the view that we see the principal ideas through some sort of direct vision of the nature of God. He agrees with Paul that in this life we see God "only through a glass darkly" (1 Cor 13:12). We may become like God to the extent that we come to see his likeness all around us and especially in us and act accordingly; but we can never achieve any sort of direct vision of God on this earth because as long as we are here our mind remains clouded and our will is weak and distracted. We cannot hold onto God perfectly just now and hence we cannot "see" God directly.[35]

Thirdly, Augustine argues against those who maintain that the content of all of our principal ideas is revealed through sense experience. Ideas such as "equality" and "similarity" have no sound. The number "1" has no color. The world that our senses reveal is a world of multiplicity, not unity. We cannot see "the one," only "the many." We cannot sense the

unchangeable in a material world of change and contingency.[36] The laws
which govern the abstract sciences of logic and mathematics cannot be
seen by the senses. In a pithy statement that perhaps reflects his unhappy
boyhood experience of being beaten in school for his ignorance, Augustine observes that it is easier to sail a ship over the sand than to navigate
mathematics using sense knowledge. It is just as impossible to "navigate"
the sea of morality on the ship of sensation. There is no smell to moral
depravity and moral goodness has no sweet taste. Moreover, sense perception is different in every individual. How could it reveal truths like
"Good is to be done; evil is to be avoided" or "Justice is giving to each"?
Sensation is simply not up to the job of conveying such unchanging moral
absolutes.[37]

Finally, it is certain that the older Augustine did not accept the Platonic view that we know the principal ideas because we remember our
immediate vision of them from some previous existence. In his *Retractions* [written in his seventies] he is at pains to make clear that the statement from his work *On the Magnitude of the Soul* [written when he was
thirty-three] that "learning is remembering" should not be understood to
mean that the soul existed in some previous life.[38]

Augustine states his own view in a text from his work *On the Trinity*.
There he says that instead of maintaining that truths like the laws of geometry are recollected from a previous experience,

> . . . it should instead be maintained that the mind of the human being
> was so planned and formed by God that, when it is in the presence of
> intelligible objects which are illuminated by a "spiritual" light, it is
> able to see them in much the same way as the body's eye is able to see
> surrounding objects when they are illuminated by a material light
> which is in accord with the limits set by the eye's physical capacity.[39]

He argues that even those with little or no experience of intellectual
matters have the ability to "dig out the knowledge of the liberal disci-
plines which is buried deep within them." Assuming that they have some
mental capability, if they are skillfully questioned and encouraged to
think about such matters [no easy task], then "the light of eternal reason
by which they perceive unchangeable truths" becomes present to them
and they are able to reply to the questioner with true answers. He emphasizes that this is not because these "intellectual innocents" suddenly remember something from a previous experience.[40] Rather it is because
here and now in every rational soul there is present: [1] the potentiality

for intellectual activity and [2] the intelligible immutable objects of that activity, that is, the principal ideas.

How these intelligible objects became present in the mind becomes clear once one studies Augustine's explanation of how this world came about: namely, his theory of creation. Augustine believed that God is not only the efficient cause of the world of our experience. He is also its exemplary cause. This means that the principal ideas not only exist primarily and perfectly in God; they also exist in every created thing by participation. All creation is modeled on these eternal forms of things. In seeing nature we are seeing an image of God, an incomplete image of varying perfection, but an image nonetheless. With some effort the rational soul can see these traces of the principal ideas even in the most humble part of nature. These ideas can be seen even more clearly when the soul turns its attention inward, because it is the mind itself that contains the most perfect image of God on earth. The face of God is written on the very fabric of the soul. There is thus no need for a special infusion or face to face "seeing" of the principal ideas in God. They are already present in the fact that the rational soul has been "formed" in God's likeness.[41] When the mind pays attention to these objects ("moves toward them") or even more generally simply reflects on itself, then the mind is able to "see" these intelligible objects and appreciate their truth.[42]

In this process, the mind is not remembering ideas experienced in the past; it is reflecting on ideas that have been impressed on it. As was mentioned before, the process is something like the seal of a ring being impressed on soft wax. However this analogy cannot be taken too far because, whereas the wax is purely passive toward the seal's "impressing," the mind must choose to cooperate with the process and is able to see and understand the result.[43] Coming to knowledge of the principal ideas is nothing more than a movement from the "latent" to the "actual." The ideas do not "actually" exist (either in mind or memory) until the person forms them for the first time. Until thought they do not exist, except potentially. And we need some experience of our world before the cognitive powers begin to operate. Our mind needs to be "drawn" to pay attention to eternal things and this does not happen without some previous encouragement from temporal things. We do not come to think about "beauty" until we have experienced beauty. We begin to understand and consciously desire "perfect happiness" only after we have had some experience with passing joy.[44] Augustine outlines the process as follows:

The human mind first comes to know created things through sense perception. Then, if it has the intellectual ability to do so, it forms ideas of these created things. Next it begins to ask itself how these things came about, hoping that it will eventually come to discover those causes which exist eternally and immutably in God. Through these unchanging forms and causes of things, it seeks to come at last to knowledge of the hidden attributes of God. This is no easy task. Even though the soul is aflame with desire to rush after and grasp forever such heavenly things, it is held back by the weakness of the body.[45]

It is obvious that any the ideas or truths about the material world, the world of time, depend on some such sense experience. We come to recognize the immutable laws of science only after we have experienced the objects that they regulate. It is hard to see how we could come to know laws such as efficient causality or sufficient reason without some experience of "things being caused," "events happening." Our ideas of the material world are limited by the images stored in memory and all of these images (even our creative imagination) are traced ultimately back to our sense experience.[46] We must experience the world of change before we can come to know the unchanging laws of change. Once experiencing the multiple, we can go further and contemplate the "infinite."[47] If we are among the select few who strive and are capable of making such leaps, then at least for a few moments we come to "touch" the immutable through our experience of the mutable.[48]

Even those principal ideas that do not depend on experience for their content [for example, the idea of "unity"], are still a posteriori in the sense that they move from potentiality to actuality in the mind only after the person has had some experience with the world of creation . . . moving from knowledge of "the other" [the external material world] to a knowledge of "self" [as distinct from that world of other], coming finally to knowledge of the content and powers of self. It is there, finally, that knowledge of the principal ideas and necessary truths becomes actual.

We may sum up Augustine's position on human knowledge of the intelligible [what he calls "intellectual vision] as follows:

1. Human knowledge of the immutable principal ideas [the "perfect" forms of beauty, etc.] and of judgments that are necessarily, eternally true depends on some action of God.

2. Since one cannot see an object if one does not have the capacity to see (no eye) or if the object to be seen is not present to sight or if there is no light to illumine a present object, and since the human knower

has no control over such capacity, presence, or illumination, it follows that the divine action supporting knowledge of the purely intelligible must include at least the following:

a. the creative action of God making the rational soul in such a fashion that it has the capability (and desire) to know "the perfect," "the unchangeable," the "necessary";

b. the creative action of God whereby the rational soul is made in the divine image and thereby has the principal ideas/eternal truths "impressed" upon it;

c. the cooperating action of God whereby these ideas and truths are "illumined" so that the eye of the mind can see them.

3. Given this divine assistance and assuming the capability of the individual's mind for intellectual activity, if the person now chooses to pay attention to the principal ideas and necessary truths "imprinted" in the fabric of the soul, then they can come to achieve that "intellectual vision" whereby the ideas/truths are "seen."

It must be admitted that Augustine's view on how we come to have the principal ideas and necessary truths present to us remains a matter of dispute. What is clear, however, is his firm conviction that no human could ever have knowledge of these things so superior to the human mind without the act of God illumining them in some way. It is to this mysterious process of illumination that we must now turn our attention.

The Process of Illumination

Till the end of his days Augustine continued to be amazed at the mind's ability to perceive entities which were unchanging, eternal, and perfect exemplars of their class. By comparison, our knowledge of material things is easy to understand. When we see a color or hear a sound, at least the spiritual power by which we know it is of a higher order than the crass matter that it reports. But when we come to know ideas of the perfect and truth that is eternal and never-changing, the objects known far surpass our imperfect, ever-changing mind. To explain the presence of such objects in the mind is not enough. When we are present to beings so far better than ourselves, they may be so different that we are unable to see them. These extraordinary intelligible objects are something like those ordinary material things which are around us all the time but which cannot be seen until they are illumined by a special ultra-violet light.

Augustine explained the presence of the principal ideas by noting
that [a] all creation [the human mind especially] is made in their image
and [b] God has so "formed" the mind that it is capable of perceiving
them under the right conditions. The mind, then, has an "eye" capable of
seeing these perfect, unchanging, eternal things just as the human face has
an "eye" for the multicolored ever-changing material world. The rational
soul has the potentiality for seeing these preeminent realities by turning
its "inner face" and looking at them with the mind's eye. Of course many
never rise to this level of vision because they are not fit for it. They do not
have the holiness and purity necessary to make the mind's eye sound
enough, clean enough, serene enough to comprehend the perfection and
purity they are trying to see.[49]

However, for either the external eye or the mind's eye to see there
must be light. For intellectual vision to occur the light must match the
perfection of the object. "White" light is not sufficient to see objects that
are revealed only by ultra-violet, and the changing contingent light of
created suns cannot reveal the eternal and unchangeable. To see that
which is "better" than itself, the soul must be enlightened by a light that
is similarly "better." Brute animals may have a keener eye for seeing material things, but only we humans [driven by a remarkable urge to know]
have been given the gift of "an incorporeal light" by which our minds are
so illumined that we can judge rightly about the world: seeing what is just
and what is unjust, recognizing the absolute certainty present in such
judgments as "I exist" and "I know that I exist."[50] This incorporeal light
is fitted both to the intelligible objects known and to the mind's eye that
sees them just as the sun's rays are such that they are able to be reflected
by the colors of our days and perceived by the eyes of our body.[51]

The exact way this illumination occurs remained an enigma for
Augustine, but he was absolutely certain of the fact. As far as he was
concerned, it was the only rational explanation for the mind's knowledge
of the eternal and unchangeable. As he wrote to his friend Consentius:

> The light by which we perform and differentiate all of our mental acts
> does not shine only on a particular spot [like the sun or other physical
> sources of light] and it does not enlighten our mind with any sort of
> physical brightness. Its shining is invisible and beyond description and
> yet it is as certain as the realities which we perceive as being certain
> because of it.[52]

Though he did not understand the exact nature of this intellectual
illumination, Augustine was certain about some of its characteristics. He

was absolutely certain that the source of this illumination could only be God. He insisted that only God can show a person what truth is.[53] Just as we see the world through the light of the sun, we come to understand the laws of science that regulate it by the light of God illumining the mind. Very simply, it is God who makes things to be known.[54]

He was also sure that this "intelligible light" was not to be identified with God. God is the source of the light; it is not God. Writing to Faustus the Manichaean in the year 400, he argued that the light illumining the mind cannot be God because the light is a creation while God is the creator. The light is "made" and can come and go. God is its "maker" and is forever immutable.[55] Sometime later (413) in a letter to Paulina he says that if we spend any time at all thinking about matters of the mind we must come to realize that God is something greater than our intellect and that the light which is God is immeasurably more than the illumining light by which the mind is enlightened. We may wonder at the invisible light of the mind, but the Light that is God is incomparably superior.[56]

But if this illumining light is not to be identified with God, neither is it simply another power of the mind. It is not like the Aristotelian "active intellect" implanted as a power of the soul from the very beginning. This light operates *in* the mind but is distinct from and superior to it. Just as it is different from the object revealed, so too is it different from the rational soul illumined.[57] Though the primary focus of this illumination is to allow humans to see the realm of God, it permeates every level of human knowledge. It is one and same light by which we are able to categorize and evaluate all levels of our knowledge: purely intelligible objects (such as number), objects which are believed but not known (for example, God as Trinity), the material shapes we recall (Carthage), those we imagine (Atlantis), and those now perceived by the senses (the colors of nature I see through my window). Each of these various objects are judged and differentiated through the one and the same invisible and immaterial light that enlightens the mind.[58]

Augustine was convinced that the search for knowledge of the principal ideas and eternal truths is as much a moral as an intellectual quest. Only the morally healthy can come to this knowledge because knowledge of these intelligible objects is in a way knowledge of God. The farther away a person is from God, the harder it is to see. It is only the pure rational soul that can come close to God. Such a soul glues itself to God by love, and the tighter this connection, the more it is able to see. Stuck to God by its love, it becomes bathed by light, illumined by its divine friend. Then it is able to see with the mind's eye those truths which, when understood, make it most happy.[59]

Knowing where the light of the mind comes from, what it is not, and what we must do to benefit from it does not answer the question: "What is it?" Here, as in so many other issues, Augustine's view remains a matter of dispute. For example, Bubacz suggests that this "light" is nothing but the "truth perceived" illumining itself. He argues that Augustine's own analogy of "light" standing both for the flame and the lamp points in this direction.[60] Although I am attracted by the simplicity of the explanation, it does not seem to hit the mark. Clearly the "light" which illumines the mind is distinct from the object illuminated (be it a principal idea or necessary truth), the mind enlightened, and the God who is the source of the light.

It is of course possible that the light "flows through" and thus "illumines from within" these principal ideas and necessary judgments. The point that I would emphasize is that these ideas and judgments have not been given the power to initiate the light. Whether light shines through them or shines on them, the source of the light is still God himself, operating not like a deistic God who builds a self-contained one hundred year lamp in each individual human being and then goes about other business. Rather, God is a continuing active presence in the individual person, helping each not only to do the good but also to see the true.

This illumination is available to all humans, not because they are made in such a way as to generate it, but because all are capable of receiving it. God in his goodness would not withhold the light from those who sincerely want it and purify themselves (by withdrawal from matter) in preparation to receive it. Thus, humans have a very active role to play in the process. They must recognize what they do not know and desire to know it. They must purify themselves of distractions. They must take time to think. They must pay attention. It is true that, given the present wounded mind and will in human beings, they will need help from God to do all these things; but Augustine was convinced that such help will not be denied to one who, by the grace of God, sincerely wants it.

Concluding Thoughts

It seems to me that there are important practical implications of Augustine's somewhat abstruse theory of knowledge.

First, the fact that we imperfect humans can come to know some perfect things suggests that there is something in this universe bigger and better than we are. Despite our pretensions, we are not "the best that is."

Secondly, the presence of the fundamental ideas in the fabric of the rational soul demonstrates the high value placed on human beings. Rather than treating humans like incompetent babies, pouring knowledge into them, God plants seeds of knowledge in humans by imaging himself in them and then gives them the power to make this knowledge real and actual. God leaves it up to the individual to choose to think, to choose to know.

Thirdly, the human being needs help to do this. It is absolutely necessary that there be illumination of mind and grace to support purification of will. Also, in most cases, there is need for a good teacher to direct the mind of the ignorant and an environment to support them in their quest.

4. Finally the need for experience in order to know places humans firmly in their present condition. It points out the importance of this life. Completely withdrawn humans cannot know or successfully make their way down the pilgrim road to heaven.

Once knowing what this universe is like, the human has a chance of choosing the goods that will bring everlasting happiness. The power of choice that makes this possible is the topic for the chapter that follows.

Notes

1. See *DGL*, 12.10.21, PL 34, 461.

2. *DT*, 14.14.19, PL 42, 1051.

3. *DT*, 14.8.11, PL 42, 1044.

4. *DT*, 11.5.8, PL 42, 991; *DT*, 12.14.22, PL 42, 1010; *DT*, 12.13.21, PL 42, 1009.

5. See *DT*, 12.14.23, PL 42, 1010; *DT*, 12.3.3, PL 42, 999; *DT*., 12.4.4, PL 42, 1000; *DT*, 12.15.25, PL 42, 1012.

6. See *DT*, 15.12.21-22, PL 42, 1073-76. In a letter written to Nebridius in 389 (*E* 7, 2.4, PL 33, 69) Augustine distinguishes three types of mental image: [1] those formed of actual sense impressions (for example, Carthage); [2] those images of fancy that we create through the exercise of creative imagination (for example, Alexandria); [3] those "images" of numbers, dimensions, and other pure abstractions.

7. *DT*, 15.12.22, PL 42, 1075. The Latin text for this important passage reads as follows: Haec igitur omnia, et quae per se ipsum, et quae per sensus sui corporis, et quae testimoniis aliorum percepta scit animus humanus, thesauro memoriae condita tenet, ex quibus gignitur verbum verum quando quod scimus loquimur, sed verbum ante omnem sonum, ante omnem cogitationem soni. Tunc enim est verbum simillimum rei notae, de qua gignitur et imago ejus, quoniam de visione scientiae visio cogitationis exoritur, quod est verbum linguae nullius, verbum verum de re vera, nihil de suo habens, sed totum de illa scientia de qua nascitur.

8. *DT*, 15.12.22, PL 42, 1075.

9. *DT*, 15.10.18, PL 42, 1070-71. Augustine gives an extended discussion of these internal words in *DT*, 15.11.20, PL 42, 1071.

10. *DT*, 11.3.6, PL 42, 989.

11. See *DT*, 10.12.19, PL 42, 984.

12. *DT*, 15.15.25, PL 42, 1078. In many places Augustine points out that there is a similarity between sensation and thinking. Thus, the three relationships that make sensation possible:

1. the relationship between the an object seen and the external eye;

2. the relationship between the "vision" of the one seeing and the ontological form of the object which "informs" the sense-power;

3. the relationship between the object seen (or "vision" of the act of sensation) and the will-intention that brings them together;

are mirrored in analogous relationships which make thought possible:

1. the relationship between the image of the object "remembered" and the "eye of the mind";

2. the relationship between the "vision" of the one thinking and the "image" in memory which "informs" the "eye of the mind";

3. the relationship between memory-image ("vision" of thought) and the will-intention that brings them together.

See *DT*, 11.4.7, PL 42, 989-90. See *DGL*, 12.11.22-23, PL 34, 462, where Augustine uses the example of how we come to understand the meaning of words.

13. *E 7*, 1.2, PL 33, 68. See *DT*, 12.14.23, PL 42, 1010-11, where Augustine discusses the learning and forgetting of the principles of science.

14. See *DT*, 14.3.5, PL 42, 1039. Here Augustine gives an interesting example of "recalling" a faith now past.

15. See *C*, 10.14.21, PL 32, 788; *DT*, 12.14.23, PL 42, 1010-11; *DT* 15.12.22, PL 42, 1075. O'Daly agrees with Bubacz that for Augustine: "An a priori functioning of memory is the prerequisite for the simplest perception and the most complex mental activity alike." Gerard O'Daly, *Augustine's Philosophy of Mind* (Los Angeles: University of California Press, 1987), p. 143.

16. See "Ideas," *Encylopedia of Philosophy*, ed. Paul Edwards (New York/London: Macmillan Pub., 1967) vol. 4, pp. 118ff.

17. *DDQ , 46.2*, PL 40, 30.

18. *Ibid.* Augustine says in another place that the only reason why created beings can be called chaste, beautiful, good, or wise is because they participate in chastity, beauty, goodness, wisdom. Those who are chaste, beautiful, etc. by participation, could be otherwise. But chastity, beauty, goodness, wisdom, themselves are unchangeable, eternal, and perfect (*DDQ*, 23, PL 40, 16). God's personal involvement and plan for each individual is reflected in many passages from Augustine. For example, he will write that "since the network of the universe is so perfectly ordered in time and place, where not even one leaf of a tree is superfluous, it is simply impossible that any human being should be created and be superfluous" (*DLA*, 3.23.66, PL 32, 1303). See *ENN 262*, 18, PL 36, 208

where Augustine speaks about God being both father and mother to every individual human being.

19. *DDQ*, 46.2, PL 40, 30.

20. Augustine explains God's creative action as an "inserting" of a form in the thing made which thereafter "forms" the thing from within. This is quite different from the action of a potter who imposes a "form" on a vase by a purely external shaping. It follows that when we come to know part of creation, the principal ideas are present by participation in the knower and the thing known since neither would exist unless this reflection of God's nature was present in them. See*DCD*, 12.26, PL 41, 376.

21. *DT*, 4.1.3, PL 42, 888. In a letter to Nebridius Augustine clearly states that he believes that each individual has her/his own idea contained in the Word from all eternity. He writes: "You ask whether . . . that highest truth, that highest wisdom, that 'form' of all things through which is made everything that is made, that which our faith professes to be the one and only Son of God, not only contains the ground (*rationem*) of humanity in general but also contains the ground for each human being. . . . (Well, I would answer) if you consider the flow of history, the ground for the variety of the human race can be found in that holy place." *E, 14*, 4, PL 33, 80.

22. *DGL*, 1.18.36, PL 34, 260. In another place Augustine suggests that the reason why the angelic spirits understand the cosmic order is because in the Word of God they are able to see the eternal causes . . . "those hinges, on which history hangs." *DCD*, 9.22, PL 41, 274.

23. *DT*, 12.14.23, PL 42, 1010. See *DIA*, 6.10, PL 32, 1026. In the *Confessions* (and in other places) he notes that we can recall the innumerable concepts and laws of mathematics, ideas which in no way could be perceived by sensation. (See *C*, 10.12, PL 32, 787).

24. *DCD*, 8.6, PL 41, 231-32.

25. *DT*, 8.3.4, PL 42, 949.

26. *DDQ*, 46.2, PL 40, 26.

27. *DDQ*, 46.4, PL 40, 27.

28. *DT*, 12.12.22, PL 42, 1009.

29. Thus, Augustine writes: "Our mind sees in that truth eternal [the being of God], which is the source of all temporal things that have been made, that perfection ['form'] which makes us to be what we are and which gives us the power to act in a rational way on material nature and on ourselves." *DT*, 9.7.12, PL 42, 967.

30. Portalié believes that this is the position that Augustine takes. He writes: "Our soul cannot attain to intellectual truth without a mysterious influence of God which does not consist in the objective manifestation of God to us (as in ontolog-

ism), but in the effective production of a kind of image in our soul of those truths which determine our knowledge. In scholastic language, the role of producing the impressed species which the Aristotelians attribute to the agent intellect is assigned to God in this system. He is the teacher, who speaks to the soul in the sense that he imprints that representation of the eternal truths which is the cause of our knowledge. The ideas are not innate as in the angels, but successively produced in the soul which knows them in itself." Eugène Portalié, *A Guide to the Thought of Saint Augustine* (Chicago: Henry Regnery Co., 1960), pp. 112-13. Nash calls it the "Franciscan theory" since it was held by Bonaventure and his disciples in later medieval times. If the force of this position is that God in some way "implants" ideas or "writes" truths in the mind, I do not believe that Augustine would agree. It seems closer to his position to say that God has "made" the soul in such a way that knowledge is passively contained always in the fabric of the soul. "Primed" by some experience of the world and itself and under proper illumination [perhaps also with some grace-filled divine help] the soul is able to make such passive knowledge active by looking at itself and expressing in a mental "word" what it finds there. See Ronald H. Nash, *The Light of the Mind: St. Augustine's Theory of Knowledge* (Lexington, Kentucky: The University Press of Kentucky, 1969), p. 97.

31. Nash (*op. cit.*, p. 98) notes that some interpreters of Augustine (Gilson, Copleston, and Bourke) believe that this approach comes close to what Augustine was trying to say with certain important modifications. Without denying the real existence of the principal ideas and necessary truths in God, Augustine (they say) was not interested in the explaining the "content" of ideas or judgments. He was only concerned about explaining their formal qualities. He was not (for example) interested in explaining the content of the principal idea of beauty so much as he was concerned to explain its "eternity," its "unchangeableness," its "perfection" . . . qualities which were not special to itself but were shared with all the other principal ideas. My own view is that it is correct to say that the problem for Augustine was not the source of the "content" of the ideas so much as the formal element of "perfection," "unchangeableness," "eternity." To say this, however, still does not explain how these formal elements came to be in the mind. I, for one, would not be prepared to say that Augustine maintained that these characteristics have no foundation in the reality described, that they are "forms" imposed by the mind." As we have seen, the primary "place" of the principal ideas is the nature of God and it is from that really existing source that they derive their perfection, immutability, and necessity. I further would not agree with Gilson that the issue is only about judgments. We have an idea of "perfect justice" before we express its meaning in a judgment. But before we make the judgment, the meaning of the

idea must be understood. We understand what perfect justice is before we connect it to other ideas. Its definition is contained in the mental word we make of it. See Etienne Gilson, *The Christian Philosophy of Saint Augustine* (New York: Random House, 1960), pp. 90-91.

32. This is the position of those whom Bubacz calls "concordantists." It includes Aristotle, Aquinas and other members of the Aristotelian-Thomistic tradition. Nash notes that Boyer gives this interpretation to Augustine's position. See Bruce Babacz, *St. Augustine's Theory of Knowledge: A Contemporary Analysis* (New York: Edwin Mellen Press, 1981), p. 136. See Nash, *op. cit*, p. 95.

33. See Nash, *op. cit.*, pp. 121ff. It is in this sense that one can interpret the text of Augustine from the *De trinitate* where he makes the following points. The law of justice is transcribed and transferred to the heart of the person who acts justly, not by the person reaching out and discovering it, but rather by the law being "impressed" upon the person's heart. The process is much like that of pressing the seal of a ring into soft wax. The impression in the wax lasts long after the ring has been removed. Even the person who is not just but who yet knows what the law of justice demands is somehow "impressed" by the law even though he has turned away from it. *DT*, 14.15.21, PL 42, 1052.

34. *DT*, 12.2.2, PL 42, 999; *DCD*, 8.6, PL 41. 231-2. See also *DLA*, 2.15.39, PL 32, 1262. This argument that the principal ideas are different from the mind, and, more importantly, superior to it, is crucial for Augustine's "empirical" argument that the human being is not the "best" thing in the universe. As we shall see in a later chapter, it will be the foundation for his proof for the existence of God.

35. *DT*, 9.11.16, PL 42, 969-70.

36. *DVR*, 30.55, PL 34, 146; *DLA*, 2.8.22, PL 32, 1252.

37. *SO*, 1.4.9, PL 32, 874; *DLA*, 2.8.20, PL 32, 1251; *DLA*, 2.10.28, PL 32, 1256. See Nash. *op. cit.*, p. 81.

38. See *RET*, 1.8.2, PL 32, 594; *DQA*, 20.34, PL 32, 1054-55.

39. *DT*, 12.15.24, PL 42, 1011.

40. *RET*, 1.4.4, PL 32, 590.

41. Some of the texts bringing out this reflection of God in the rational soul include the following:

"The image of the creator . . . must be found in soul of the human being, that is, the intellect and reason." *DT*, 14.4.6, PL 42, 1040.

"Although the human mind is not of the same nature as God is, yet the image of his nature, which is better than any other nature, ought to be sought for and found there in us, where there is also the best thing that our nature has." *DT,* 14.8.11, PL 42, 1044.

"The mind is an image of God especially in its activity of contemplating eternal things." *DT*, 12.4.4, PL 42, 1000.

"Men and women, since both share a common human nature, have been made in the image of God." *DT*, 12.6.10, PL 42, 1003.

42. *RET*, 1.8.2, PL 32, 594.

43. See *DT*, 14.15.21, PL 42, 1052. Since even the most undeveloped or retarded mind is still made in the image of its creator, it would follow that all humans receive the impression of the principal ideas but not all can see them. This is so because to receive the ideas all that is necessary is that one be a human being. To have the intellectual vision of them one must have a developed mind, pay attention, and have the mind illumined.

44. *C*, 10.21.30-1, PL 32, 792-93. For an extended discussion of how the mind moves from the "latent" knowledge in memory to the "actual" knowledge of "recalling and paying attention to it" See *DT*, 14.7.9-10, PL 42, 1042-44.

45. *DGL*, 4.32.49, PL 34, 316-17.

46. See *DT*, 11.8-10.15-17, PL 42, 996-98.

47. *DT*, 11.10.17, PL 42, 997-98.

48. *DT*, 12.14.23, PL 42, 1010-11.

49. See *DDQ*, 46.2, PL 40, 30-31.

50. *DCD*, 11.27.2, PL 41, 341.

51. *DT*, 12.15.24, PL 42, 1011-12.

52. *E 120*, 10, PL 33, 457.

53. *CA*, 3.6.13, PL 32, 940-41.

54. See *SO*, 1.6.12, PL 32, 875-76; *ibid.*, 1.8.15, PL 32, 877.

55. *CFM*, 20.7, PL 42, 372. Other texts seem to suggest that this light *is* God. See *DGL* 12.31.59, PL 34, 479.

56. *E 147*, 18.45, PL 33, 617.

57. *DGL* 12.31.59, PL 34, 479-80.

58. See *E 120*, 2.10, PL 33, 457.

59. *DDQ*, 46.2, PL 40, 31. See *SO*, 1.13.22, PL 32, 881.

60. Bubacz, *op. cit.*, p. 149.

Chapter 7

Free Will and Grace

General Introduction[1]

Augustine believed that the question of whether or not human beings were capable of free choice had important ramifications for human happiness. He took it as a fact of experience that all humans desire happiness and spend most of their waking hours trying to achieve it. He was also convinced that perfect happiness could only be achieved by the possession of that good which would satisfy all innate desires. Many human desires are acquired and therefore can be done away with, but there are some [for example, the desire for life, meaning, and love] which flow from human nature itself. These cannot be eliminated, only satisfied; and, until they are satisfied, a human being cannot be perfectly happy.

Our desire for such natural goods is infinite. We do not want simply a long life. We want immortality. Perfect happiness means possession of all good, and for Augustine this meant possession of God. For humans who are able to make responsible choices, the way to possess God is to choose to do so by choosing day by day to act like a human being. But this demand only makes sense if human beings are able to make responsible, free choices. The purpose of this chapter is to examine Augustine's views on the important issues that are the pre-conditions for establishing the possibility of happiness: namely, the nature of the will, freedom, and the place grace plays in choosing to do good.

The common understanding of will is that it is the power whereby a person moves toward (or "chooses") something presented by the intellect as being "good" (that is, "desirable"). Will is said to be free if it has the power to act or not act even though all the necessary conditions for acting have been fulfilled. A free act is thus one whose implementation and direction are caused by the person doing the act. Assuming that I have eliminated internal compulsive neuroses and external overpowering forces "pushing" me to choose, it is reasonable to describe my act as being free, that is, an act which proceeds from my unimpeded rational desire. If I am free, then the reason why I choose "this" over "that" [indeed, the reason why I choose at all] is simply because I want to choose.

Since freedom is a self-determined choice of goods revealed by the intellect, there are certain situations where free choice will be impossible. For example, the will cannot choose if the intellect does not present a desirable good. The will is a blind faculty. It can only move toward something that is revealed by intellect. We cannot desire what we do not see. Furthermore, the will cannot be free when it is dominated by overpowering passion or disabling psychosis. In such situations people cannot control their choices. They must be "cured" before they can choose well. Acting under such compulsion "pushing" the will this way or that, people cannot reasonably claim that the action is "theirs." The act flows more from their compulsion than from rational choice. There is no question that such compulsive activity sometimes occurs. A more critical issue is whether human beings are ever free. What is the dominant factor in any action? How [for example] to explain the "evil that human beings do"? Do humans do evil because of their nature or their nurture or is it because of their unfettered [though not uninfluenced] free choice?

Those who opt for "nature" as the determining agent in human choice claim that the reason why I choose a particular good is because it is in my nature to do so. I am programmed by my genetic make-up to seek certain things and reject others. I move purely by blind instinct. My actions of choosing this or that are no different than a flower always turning toward the sun or a bee always building its hive in the same way. The cure for evil is through medicine correcting the bad gene that makes me do the bad. There are no "evil" people. Some are just morally "disabled."

Those who hold that "nurture" governs our choices argue that we are made good or bad because of our environment. I am what I am and act the way I do because this is the way I have been brought up or because this is what my society has made me to be. Human behavior is "learned" and ingrained by a subtle system of rewards and punishments. Just as a chicken can be trained to play a little piano in a shopping mall stall, so I can be trained to do the good by "education" in schools and (if needed) by re-education in prison.

Those who defend "freedom" as the explanation of much of human activity will not deny that our choices are influenced by nature or nurture. Indeed, they will even allow that in some isolated cases "nature" or "nurture" will determine the decision. However, they will insist that in most cases I am the one responsible for what I do. When I move toward some "x" as a desirable good, it is because I have decided to do so. I could have decided otherwise, but I did not. I may be influenced by the way I am built and the place and people where I live, but the choice to do or not to do this or that is ultimately my choice and I must take the blame or credit for it.

No one denies the existence of will. Those who are able to use reason do in fact make choices. A coercive argument for freedom is more difficult. This is so because the strongest evidence is "private" rather than "public." I know that I make free choices (for example, to rewrite this dull paragraph on this dull Sunday morning) but there is no way to communicate this direct experience of my freedom to someone else. My freedom is something like my love. Just as I can tell friends "I feel love for you," I can tell them "I freely choose to do this." But I cannot show them my love or my freedom. My love and my freedom must be "believed" by others. It cannot be experienced by them in the way that I experience it.

Of course there are some bits of "public" evidence which can support the claim to this necessarily "private" experience of freedom. We can, for example, point to the unpredictability of human activity. There always seems to be a "wild-card" present in each of us that makes it difficult for others to say for sure what we will do next. Every once in a while this unpredictability explodes in a "converting choice," a choice which changes the whole direction of a person's life in one dramatic moment. Thus, the persecutor Paul falls off his high horse and rises up a missionary. The despairing sinner Augustine reads a phrase in the Bible and begins his hope-filled climb to sanctity. An alcoholic, after years of denial, stands up one day before strangers and says, "Yes, I am an alcoholic too!" and begins a radical change of life. In these and similar cases there seems to be no reasonable explanation for the choice from what has gone before. The person somehow or other has simply decided to do something different . . . indeed, to be something different.[2]

The "how" and "why" of such converting choices puzzled Augustine for most of his mature life. Specifically he wondered at his own conversion, concluding finally that God must have intervened in some extraordinary fashion. Though he had been free, at the same time he had been compelled by the grace of God to choose the path of righteousness. His explanation of this mysterious process will be examined in the following pages.

Augustine on Free Will

Introductory Clarifications

Augustine describes the will [*voluntas*] as the unforced reaching out of the rational soul toward something that it wishes to possess. For Augustine the experience of his will is just as immediate as the experience of his existence. He is certain that he exists. He is also certain that he wants to exist. He perceives that he has a power which reaches out to an object of desire and this is all that is meant by the assertion: "I have a will."[3] The fact that Augustine describes the will as the "unforced reaching out" suggests that he believes that "to be free" is part of "having a will." If freedom is not present, the movement toward an object may be instinct pushing from within or some sort of gravity pulling from without, but it is not will. He does admit that the will in fact is drawn irresistibly but freely toward God when the person finally comes to see that infinite good, but he denies that such infinite attraction could ever exist in this life. Moreover, even in the case of this heavenly beatific vision, the will is still moved by motives. The motivation comes from outside, but the driving force for the action, the motive, is still internal to the one acting.[4]

Augustine makes a careful distinction between "free choice" (*liberum arbitrium*) and "liberty" (*libertas*). Free choice is simply the will choosing something under the influence of motives. As such it may be bad or good. It always contains the possibility of choosing evil. "Liberty" excludes that possibility since it is specifically the use of "free choice" to choose good effectively. Under the influence of "liberty" the will not only chooses the good; it also carries through that choice into action.

Certainly the human power to choose freely (*liberum arbitrium*) is a great benefit, but it is still only an intermediate good.[5] Even from the beginning it was a power that could be used badly. The first innocent humans were able to choose good or evil. Even now, our wounded will still has some control over itself. Just as it can command other parts of the body, saying "walk here," "eat this," "pay attention to that," so too it can move itself toward or away from a perceived good or evil.[6] When a person misuses something in the universe, it is thus not the thing that should be blamed; rather it is the fault of the person himself.[7] Humans were created with a nature that enabled them, with little help, to turn toward God or to choose themselves and things of earth. How they decide determines their destiny.[8]

This is the way humans were made, but is it the condition of the human race now? Unfortunately Augustine does not answer this question in any one place in his works. His thoughts on grace and freedom were developed over a lifetime of controversy with those who (in his opinion) either made too little or too much of human freedom.[9] One thing is certain: We are not now the way we were. Therefore, to understand Augustine's words on grace and freedom we need to examine his description of those two moments in human history: the way we were at the beginning of time and the way we are right now.

"The Way We Were": Eden

Reading the story of creation in Genesis, it was clear to Augustine that the central characteristic of the human condition in Eden was peaceful love of God.[10] Those first humans were subject to God, but they found it easy to obey the divine commands. They were not distracted by unruly passion. They were not tempted (at first) by outside influences. They had each other and their God and for them that was more than enough to be happy.[11] They were as perfect as they could be as human beings, with no defects in body or soul. They had everything that was "due" human nature and much more. They had those extraordinary extensions of their natural powers that have come to be known as preternatural gifts.

For example, it was natural that their body should be subject to the rule of their soul, but in Eden this subordination was the rule of friend over friend. It was as though the body loved to be ruled by the soul and the soul ruled the body as a lover might guide its love.[12] That body should be subject to soul was natural. That they should be related as lovers was more than nature could expect or even hope for. Again, it was natural that humans should have the power to "know." Creation gave them powers of sensation and powers of mind, but above and beyond this those first humans had an extraordinary clarity in their perceptions. They understood themselves and they understood the universe around them. Genesis tells us that Adam was even able to "name" the animals with a name which captured exactly what they were. The first humans, indeed, were masters of science, but they were much more. They were wise, able to fit particulars together in one unified whole.[13]

As beings of body it was natural that they should experience growth, a flourishing, and then inevitable deterioration. At some point in their lives they could expect that catabolism would become the dominant force in their metabolic processes. But in Eden this natural process of degradation was put on "hold." The first humans did not need to worry about growing old with dignity because they were not destined to grow old. Like the blessed in heaven they could have remained forever in the prime of their lives. They were able to live well, to flourish, without working at it. Though it was in God's plan that humans should continue the race through physical procreation, the first humans were able to bear children without the pain of giving birth.[14] They could enjoy without difficulty the pleasures of eating and drinking. Food and drink were readily available and were matched exactly to their finely tuned "concupiscence" which would never have desired too much or taken too little.[15]

Best of all, they were destined never to die. By nature they should have. Though their soul was spirit and therefore intrinsically immortal (it could not "fall apart"), they themselves were composites of body and soul. With the natural collapse of the body they could reasonably expect that someday their two parts would separate and that they would cease to exist as human beings. Moreover they were contingent in both body and soul. It was not "necessary" for them to exist. Even the soul's intrinsic immortality could not have protected it from going out of existence if the power that supported its contingency suddenly ceased. The soul, even though it was the best thing in creation, was still like a fragile balloon. There was no guarantee that it would not suddenly lose its breath of being if the support of God was withdrawn. The first humans did not face this terrifying prospect. They had been created mortal but they then received both intrinsic and extrinsic immortality as an extraordinary gift from their divine lover.[16]

In their original condition humans lived in a divinely enhanced way. They lived at their level of being with a perfection that could not have been expected. They were naturally and preternaturally gifted. But they had even more. They had supernatural gifts which allowed them not simply to operate at the level of human beings but to live as true friends of God.[17] As a result of this extraordinary gift, the first humans were able to live and "operate" in an environment totally above their natural possibilities. By this gift of "supernaturalness" they were raised up to a point where it now became possible for them to receive a reward far beyond the hopes and dreams and powers of a created being: the beatific vision, the face to face contact with the Infinite Being. It was something like (but much more) a plane figure being made able to live the life of a cube. Humans were raised to an entirely new dimension. Once this divine condition was lost by the first sin, it was not to be restored until Christ redeemed the human race by his death.[18] This too was a miracle, God now making humans not only his children but also his brothers and sisters.[19] Indeed, Augustine remarks that the reason for God becoming human in the person of Jesus Christ was in order to remedy the sin of humans trying to be their own God.[20]

There was a difference in degree between graces given in the beginning and the graces needed now. In their days of innocence human beings did not need grace to "reacquire" supernatural life and activity. They had been given it in the beginning and they had not yet lost it. However they did need grace for maintenance of their life with God. Since it was not natural for them to be in such elevated positions, they needed the support of grace to preserve their blessed condition.[21] There was no necessity driving Adam or Eve to fail in virtue. In their state of innocence they were "able not to sin" (*posse non peccare*). Their condition may not have been as secure as the blessed in heaven who are "not able to sin" (*non posse peccare*), but it was infinitely better than the condition of humans after sin. Humans now are "not able not to sin" (*non posse non peccare*) if left on their own. Indeed, Augustine strenuously argues against the Pelagians that, with the exception of Mary (whom he places in a separate category), there is no human who has the use of reason who has not been touched by sin in some way. Now no one can persevere in virtue without grace. In Eden before sin the human race was able to persevere without any extraordinary help beyond the "cooperating" graces mentioned above. In Eden humans possessed "liberty" as an ongoing condition; now they must pray constantly for divine help in recovering their ability to choose the good.[22] In Eden humans lived at peace with themselves and their surroundings; after Eden they needed grace to overcome rebellion from within and temptation from without.[23]

Before sin humans had every possibility, indeed they had the likelihood, of always choosing the good. Physically and mentally and spiritually they were better than they deserved to be and they had divine support to keep them in that happy condition. All they had to do was to continue to realize that God was the source of their strength to choose rightly, just as he was the source of their being and their power to choose at all. One can only wonder why those first innocent gifted humans would turn their backs on that friendly God of Eden. It was so easy for them not to sin. They had everything they could possibly want . . . everything, that is, except for one thing. They were not God. They were not in charge of the universe and this they apparently wanted to be. The first human fault was not one of lust or intemperance or cowardice, those pedestrian vices of the weak. The sin of these perfect humans had its source in pride, the haughty vice which made them want to be better than the one person who was above them: God himself. Their pride expressed itself through an act of disobedience, the pretense of an inferior to be superior.[24]

Augustine considered their disobedient pride to be the most horrific sin possible. It was the sin that made hell for the angels. It was a sin whereby those first humans, lovingly created more perfect than they had any right to expect, threw that love back into the face of their creator. By their actions they said to their God: "There is no need for you anymore. We are as good as you. We can achieve our destiny on our own, thank you very much." And they said such things and did such things with a clarity of mind and a freedom of will that we cannot even imagine now. They were the best of any of us and in trying to be better than they were, they made themselves and their offspring worse than God ever wanted them to be. The idyll of Eden and of the "way we were" became the tragedy of the "way we are." At one time the human race was happy and free; now it spends its days struggling against despair and confusion and compulsion. Now it has become terribly difficult to do those righteous acts which had been done with such ease during the brief shining days of Eden.

"The Way We Are"

The effect of that first bad choice by human beings was disastrous. Since they had decided to separate themselves from God, to withdraw themselves from divine dominion by a calculated act of rebellion, they received their just deserts. God allowed them to live their lives at the level they had chosen for themselves. Since humans had freely abandoned God, they became liable to just judgment.[25] Justice was exercised not through some terrible revengeful act of a furious God. Justice was served by a disappointed God permitting recalcitrant humans to suffer the natural effects of their rebellion. As night follows day and morning succeeds night, radical separation of creature from creator resulted in a human nature that was damaged and changed.[26] Now there was a quasi-genetic defect in the human spirit and the wound was passed on to everyone conceived and born thereafter. The "bad blood" of the parents poisoned the children.[27]

The damage coming from this first sin manifested itself in various ways in Adam and Eve. They fell from the supernatural level and became incapable of "seeing" God. They lost that special divine support which had empowered them to choose and do the truly good. The "gates of heaven" were closed to them. No longer could they dream of being with God for all eternity. Now fallen from grace, they lost all their hopes for a good future. They also lost the perfection of their present. Their wonderful preternatural gifts disappeared and they became liable to the death and dissolution that was proper to their contingent nature. Someday they would die and in the meantime they had to work to make a living.

And more, like bandages ripped from delicate skin, the tearing away of these preternatural "additions" left behind a tenderness, a sore spot in human nature. When the special gifts of clarity of mind and easy freedom of will and friendly subordination of body to soul disappeared, they left behind a gap, a depression. Human nature was not destroyed but it was damaged. Fallen nature was not depraved, but it was deprived. Humans were subject to unaccustomed pains in body and debilitating wounds in spirit.[28]

The spirit-wounds were the most tragic. Now humans experienced a blinding ignorance and compulsive desires (concupiscence). It would have always been a task for humans to learn things, but now sin made discovery of the truth a project rather than simply an adventure. It was as though the mind's eye had been covered with a cataract that made even the most brilliant colors, the most dramatic truths, gray and distant and unimportant. Though truths such as "I am," "I think" retained their clarity, eternal truths lost their luster. Why bother with eternity when time was so interesting? After Eden the human mind was consumed with trivial pursuits. It lost sight of the lasting forest in its enthusiasm for the crash and thunder of falling trees. Humans found it difficult to pay attention to anything beyond the passing scene. Disorder infected those natural desires which in Eden had driven them into the arms of God. They seemed to lose the will to choose anything beyond the immediately satisfying and the crass. The order of being was thrown upside down as the demands of the vegetative and animal nature took precedence over the needs of the spirit. Humans ate and drank enthusiastically with the hope that such excess would indeed "make them merry." A consistent choice of higher goods over lower goods, spirit over matter, became a problem. Indeed, it was even difficult to desire any good in a balanced, controlled way. After the first sin humans still had the capacity to love but love became disordered in its choice of object and sometimes uncontrolled in its ferocity. Humans did not lose free will (*liberum arbitrium*) when they left Eden. They could still choose between "this" or "that." But they lost the ability to effectively choose good (*libertas*) on their own.[29]

Still, though the condition of fallen humanity was sad, it was not without some bright spots. Humans were not annihilated. They continued to exist. Surely this could be taken as a sign that there was some good left in them.[30] Moreover, God allowed them to continue the race. He did not take from them the great gift of being able to cooperate with him in the creation of children.[31] God also left with humans that extraordinary "light of reason" by which even the most lowly is a true image of the divine. The light may have been dimmed by sin but it was not altogether extinguished.[32] When we are born, the fire of intelligence seems banked, almost negligible, but as we grow our minds waken. We begin to see what is true about our world and ourselves. With effort our minds can develop the discipline of virtue, that mental structure which can lead to wisdom. Day by day we discover various arts and skills which allow us to use and enjoy the wonders of this world.[33]

Even in their limping powers of choice, humans retain an autonomy which sets them apart from and above the rest of creation. They did not become automatons driven by internal forces they could not understand or control. They were not made into stones driven to their destiny by external forces. Even after the terrible wounding of sin, humans are moved by motives, not gravity. Whatever bad things can be said about the way humans now sometimes act, it remains true that they are mostly responsible for their actions.[34]

The one great difference in the power of will now is that (to use Augustine's terminology) free choice is no longer capable of liberty without outside support. Without exception, every good use of free will comes from God.[35] Of course we don't need special help from God to perform every act of choice. As Augustine wryly observes, we are perfectly capable of choosing evil without anyone's assistance;[36] but when we speak the truth and act righteously, this must be attributed to the gushing grace-giving waters coming from the fountain that is God.[37] Without such help a human can neither see nor choose the good.[38]

Fallen humanity would indeed have been in a sorry state if they had been left on their own. Luckily, they were not abandoned. Unlike Satan and his cohorts, humans were given a second chance. They were left with a "thirst" for knowing how they should act in this imperfect world and were given divine law to quench that thirst. God himself came as teacher to individuals of good heart, telling them what their life was, what it could be, and what it should be.[39] Without such divine illumination, humans were unable to recognize the disorder in their lives. They lived complacently as animals, freely giving in to their lowest desires with no knowledge that anything was wrong.[40] The gift of law changed all that. Humans were able to recognize that the life proposed by God's commandments was indeed good and began to feel shame when they did not live up to its standards.[41] Their shame was well-deserved because God did not simply give them law to guide their minds. He gave them the grace to love it, to want to observe it, to bravely go ahead and choose the moral course proposed by it. Before the gift of grace humans were paralyzed by the wound of "difficulty" (*difficultas*), but with grace they acquired the strength they needed to overcome that difficulty and to make the good choices necessary to achieve the crown of glory.[42]

Grace thus restored liberty, overcoming the disorder in mind and will that was part of the wound of sin.[43] Once again humans were able to participate in the very life of God. They took up again their status as adopted children of God. They were able once again to hope for a day when they would possess that God who had been their creating parent, who was their maintaining power, who had become their suffering savior, and who now operated day by day as an energizing spirit deep within.[44] Such grace is a great gift, greater indeed than the law. Law gives only the power to know; grace gives the ability to love. Human love of righteousness is the effect of grace; divine love is its beginning. No one merits grace. It is always a purely gratuitous gift of a God who first loves us. We perform good acts only because grace has been given to us.[45] It was this conviction that led Augustine to compose the prayer that so infuriated Pelagius: "O God, give what you command and command what you will."[46]

The Pelagian Objection[47]

Augustine spent most of his life arguing about whether or not individual humans had the capacity to achieve perfection in their own lives.[48] As a young man he argued with the Manicheans who claimed that the human was simply a pawn of divine forces battling deep in the individual soul.[49] In his middle years he faced the challenge of Donatism which

insisted that the ministers of the sacraments had to be perfect and un-
stained for these major sources of grace to be effective. Finally, toward
the end of his life he was called to do battle with Pelagianism, a theological humanism which denied that any strengthening grace was needed
for a person to do good.

The three central claims of Pelagianism were these:

1. There is no great difference between Adam's condition before the
first sin and the way we are born today. Just as we are liable to sin and
death, so too was he.

2. There is no "hereditary" weakness of will coming to us because of
that first sin. Once enlightened as to what we should do, it is just as
easy (apart from environmental influences) for us to go ahead and do
it as it was for Adam. In sum, there is no "original sin" carrying its bad
effects to the rest of the race after Adam. We are not now "born in sin."

3. Though baptism may be necessary to unite us with Christ, it is not
needed to cleanse us from sin.[50]

Pelagius and his disciples believed that too much was made of
Adam's original condition and too little is made of our own. Adam by
nature was as liable to death and sin and illness as any human being since.
There was nothing infectious about his sin. Indeed, the sin of Cain his son
was much worse. Apart from a history of bad example from others and
bad habits built up by ourselves, we are in no worse shape than our ancestors. Of course we need the "grace" of God to be virtuous, but this grace
is nothing more than the nature that was created in us, the law that has
been revealed to us, the illumination given to us by the divine teacher, and
the forgiveness granted to us by the God who comes as judge. Grace is
needed to illumine our searching minds and to forgive our sinful hearts,
but it is not needed to strengthen our will to do the good nor to make us
repentant when we do the bad. We are called to perfection and we can
achieve it without extraordinary outside help. The church of Christ even
in this life is legitimately restricted to the perfect because if people choose
not to be perfect, it is literally their own "damning" fault.[51]

Augustine was upset by such rigor because he believed that it un-
justly limited the church to a few of the "best" people. His own view was
that the city of God on earth included all those poor wandering souls who
were predestined to ultimately persevere . . . those who, despite their
weakness and imperfection, would be able to avoid the death-dealing
vices of pride and despair and who would thus at least try to cling to God.
For Augustine true Christianity was not characterized by perfection but

by the readiness to say "I'm sorry" in humble and trustful expectation of forgiveness from a loving God.[52] Simple illumination of the mind is not sufficient to accomplish this. In order to do good one must not only know the law; one must also love the law. This is precisely the effect of the gift given by the Holy Spirit. The divine Spirit gives the gift of being able to love. For the Pelagian, instruction was enough for a person to do the right thing. Once knowing what to do, any human should be able on his own to go ahead and do it.[53]

Augustine believed this to be impossible. Only God can give the power to love rightly. Humans were still able to love after the disaster of original sin, but they could no longer love sensibly. They became like living magnets gone crazy, drawn toward everything except that for which they had been made. The remedy for such craziness could only come from God. This was the clear teaching of St. Paul that "The love of God has been poured out in our hearts by the Holy Spirit who has been given to us." (Rom 5:5) The meaning of this and similar passages was that in order to help humans pursue good, God gives not only free will and the commandments. He also gives the divine Spirit whereby the soul is so formed that it can now delight in and love the supreme and unchangeable good that is God. It is because of this gift that the human being can develop the burning desire (love) to become one with God. Left to themselves, humans can only sin. This is so not simply because they need instruction on what to do but even more because they need the power to delight in and to love the things of God. This is a completely gratuitous gift given even before we are able to want it.[54] It is by this grace that

> . . . we not only know what we should do but we also do what should be done; we not only believe what should be loved, but also that we love so powerfully that we become able to believe.[55]

We cannot claim to earn this grace. Merit comes only through proper loving, and we need grace to perform even that first act of efficacious love of God.[56]

The Pelagians reacted to such sentiments by declaring them to be destructive and dangerous. To blame Adam for our troubles is too easy an excuse. It leads to the self-fulfilling conviction that one must fail in trying to live a virtuous life. With such an attitude a person is likely to say: "Well, if I must fail, if despite all my efforts I must sin, why bother to try not to sin?" It seemed to Pelagius much better to give sin-filled humans at least a hope of doing good. With such hope they may end up with a somewhat better life and, even if they do not, at least they will not have failed for lack of trying.

The Augustinian response was that trying to be righteous on your own is a fruitless effort. It is analogous to saying to a person falling from a tall building: "Flap your arms and you will be better for the effort." This is simply foolishness. To save a falling human you must lift him up, and the same must be done to save a human already fallen. Human beings can no more do good on their own than they can fly, and all the instruction in the world will not change that. Perhaps it would have worked in the beginning when we were able not to sin, but now something more is needed.[57] We have lost our wings, the love which carries us to God, and this must be restored. We are not able to avoid sin without some repairs. Only when healed can we fly to the sun and enter the heavenly city where we need never fear dying or losing our wings again. Then we will not be able to sin.[58] Just now we are far from the glory of that ideal state. Indeed we cannot even recover the powers of innocence enjoyed in Eden. We are no longer able to avoid sinning without grace. And that simply is a fact.[59]

Human Freedom under Grace

Augustine recognized that there is deep mystery in the interplay of grace and freedom in the human spirit. When you proclaim one, you seem to deny the other.[60] It is therefore not a matter to be passed over or dealt with carelessly.[61] For all it will be difficult to understand and for most it will be impossible. Approaching the topic one should begin with an act of faith and then pray for wise understanding,[62] always careful to preserve both the power of God and the freedom of the individual.[63]

Despite the mystery involved, Augustine consistently maintained that only by the grace of God could any individual choose the good and, at the same time, the choice must be free if free choice is to have any meaning.[64] If God wills the salvation of Peter, necessarily it will happen, but the salvation will not be Peter's unless he freely chooses it.[65] In a sense Peter is compelled to be saved; but he must be compelled freely for his choice of God to be truly an act of his love.

But is not the phrase "compelled freedom" an oxymoron, a union of hopelessly contradictory concepts? How can one be compelled by an irresistible force and still be free? Augustine hints at the solution to this paradox in his famous principle: "My love is my weight; wheresoever I go, it is my love that takes me there.[66] This is more than a pious thought. It is a factual description of how and why humans choose anything. For choice to occur there must first of all be love, a love which is drawn out of us by the presence or promise of delight. We love because we are pleased to love, pleased either because we see that the object of our affection is good in itself or because we experience some benefit from it.

There are three elements in any act of love: [1] the intellect that knows; [2] the goodness of the object known; [3] the delight that such known goodness creates. All love must begin with intellectual activity. We are drawn to certain objects only because the intellect presents them to us as goods, that is, objects worth loving. Our delight in an object is directly proportional to the clarity of our perception and such perception can be affected by various factors. Internally the health of the mind and the length of one's attention-span can increase or decrease clarity. Externally, perception is diminished by distance. It is difficult to perceive as desirable an object that is far away in time or space. Past loves fade unless special effort is made to recall them from time to time. "Absence does not make the heart grow fonder" when extended over great spaces for an extended time.

Just as distance from the object affects the intensity of our love, so too does the degree of goodness in the object. When we are surrounded by more or less equal goods, we become indifferent to any one of them. We are not drawn irresistibly to choose "this" over "that," nor indeed to choose at all. It is easy for us to withhold choice, taking longer [as we say] "to make up our mind." This momentary abulia comes not from having nothing good to choose but from having so many somewhat delightful options that we are not driven to choose any one. If the mind is able to perceive an object and that object has a goodness that could be the source of desirability, then it may become an object of choice for us. But this will happen if and only if we delight in it. We are delighted by the prospect of making it our own, of being united to it, of possessing it, indeed even perhaps of being possessed by it. Only the presence of delight [or the promise of it] will make us choose the good perceived by the mind. Only then do we begin to be "drawn toward" it, that is, love it.

In the natural exercise of free choice, then, there are three factors at work: knowledge, delight, and love. This being the case, it would seem reasonable to conclude that to give or enhance these factors is not to destroy freedom; it is to empower it. This is important for understanding Augustine's equanimity about freedom under grace because he firmly believed that this is exactly how grace operates on the power of choice.

Grace empowers us to freely choose the good because it illuminates our minds, gives us delight, and draws our love.[67]

Augustine saw no conflict between this irresistible grace and human freedom. Thus, at the very beginning of his debate with Pelagius, he insists that there is no threat to freedom in preaching the need for grace.[68] In 412 he tells questioners from Carthage that reason demands that neither grace nor free will should be sacrificed.[69] In the same year he writes to his friend Marcellinus that grace establishes free will by curing it of the disability which prevents it from loving righteousness.[70] Finally, toward the end of his life he devoted an entire book [*De gratia et libero arbitrio*] to proving that the testimony of sacred scripture demands acceptance of both the power of grace and the freedom of the individual.[71] It is true that in all of these works he spends little time explaining how grace and freedom work together, but at the same time he insists that an understanding of their interaction is not impossible.[72]

Given our present powerlessness, there is no doubt that we need grace. But it is also certain that for any of us to responsibly do a good act, we must truly want to do the good act. To have a good act credited to our account, we must do it knowingly and willingly. But to do anything "knowingly" and "willingly" is problematic in our present "cracked" condition. Just now it is difficult for us to always do "the right thing" because our desire to do anything is dependent on the depth of our understanding and the warmth of the satisfaction or delight that such perception gives us. Our only hope is found in God's promise that he will come to even the least and lowest of us to prepare [and "repair"] us so that the desire for the truly good will take over our lives.[73]

But what does this "preparing" entail? If it only "helps" us to choose good, it obviously does not take the place of our freedom. It supports it. It is like a prosthesis which strengthens our crippled legs. It is a necessary support for our walking but we are the ones who do the walking. Even with a brace strapped firmly to our leg, even after having been given a cane, we still can decide "not to walk." If this were all that grace does to our spirit, it would not interfere with our freedom. We may [through grace] have been lifted up to that path that leads to heaven, but still we are the ones who must choose to walk down it.

It is clear that Augustine's vision of God's graceful support goes far beyond the literally "pedestrian" image of a helpful cane given on our limping way to heaven. Grace does much more than simply strengthen our powers of choosing to walk the right path. It makes us walk. It not only "lifts us up" to that high road to heaven. It makes us run down that path. Grace, in sum, not only enables us to choose and do the good; it compels us. But how can it be that such grace-generated compulsion does not destroy freedom? Augustine answers: "Because grace compels through freedom, not in spite of it."

An example of the process can be found in the way God brings a person to faith. Augustine admits that a person's coming to faith is a mysterious and personal matter, but two facts are certain in every case: (1) No one believes except by free choice of the will; and (2) In every case the will must be prepared by God (Prov. 8.35).[74] Within these parameters, the preparation for faith involves three distinct divine actions:

1. illumination of the mind;

2. assisting the will to control its untoward desires;

3. strengthening the will so that it is able to persevere in the midst of the trials that will come with faith.[75]

Illumination of the mind is essential because to believe is "to think with assent."[76] Faith has an intellectual component. One cannot believe what is not known and to "know" implies at least a minimal understanding of what one knows. Put simply, one must think before one can act. Just as we must think before we speak, so too we must think before we can believe. In everyday life we are sufficient to think for ourselves; but when it comes to matters of knowledge and worship of God, our sufficiency comes only from God.[77]

Grace acts on the mind of the potential believer in various ways. It must reveal content and this involves more than simply arranging circumstances so that the person hears the word preached. Grace must also give understanding of what is being said. Thus, God works on the potential believers externally through the persuasive force of the evangelical exhortations that they hear, and internally at the very doorway of mind where no person has control over what shall enter or be retained.[78]

Augustine fervently agrees with the sentiments of his mentor, St. Ambrose, that neither our heart nor our thoughts are in our own power.[79] God gives our human hearts whatever pious thoughts we possess, those thoughts which are the foundation of a faith that works by love.[80] Once one believes, God then continues teaching through the ear of the heart,[81] showering the mind with light that is eternal.[82]

Such illumined understanding of the things of God is an important part of the free choice to be righteous. But it is only a part. Understanding must be combined with delight before one can be drawn by love to choose. The person must experience a heavenly delight sufficient to off-set the competing delights of earthly desires. This giving of delight/love is the most important function of grace. Knowledge and love are both gifts of God but knowledge is the lesser gift. One can be saved without much knowledge but heaven is denied to those who put limits on their love.[83]

It is for this reason that Augustine became so upset with the Pelagian Julian for teaching that simple knowledge of God's law was enough for salvation. Julian provided an extensive list of the ways in which grace affects humans by commanding, blessing, sanctifying, compelling, pro-voking, and illuminating. But this was not enough in Augustine's view because the most important effect of grace was left out: namely, the giv-ing of love.[84] We become believers by coming to love what we believe. We become doers of the good when we come to love observing God's law, and we come to this love only because God's grace brings it about that we begin to "delight" in doing God's will. Just as illumination is the crucial element in the mind's coming to "see," so too delight is the crucial element in our coming to "love" what we now see and understand.

The way to greater holiness is not to study more books but to gradu-ally come to such great delight in "the things of heaven" that we are able to control the powerful earthly delights that enchant us with the "here and now." At the end of our time, we will be saved if we have that love for God and delight in heavenly things that impels us to choose the "path of righteousness" revealed by God's law. With such love and delight, "do-ing good" is easy. Indeed doing the opposite becomes truly unthinkable.[85]

The delight given by God through grace makes us love what we should love. But is such love truly our love? If our knowledge of the good and our delight in the good and our love of the good are all caused by God's grace, is the act of choosing the good still our action? There seems to be no reason for saying it is not. God intervenes in our choosing, to be sure, but the intervention is internal rather than external. Grace affects our knowledge, delight, and love. God's intervention is no more invasive than the intervention of a clever teacher who makes a student understand, delight in, and finally love a foreign discipline. The only difference is in the power of the intervention. When we act for the good under the influ-ence of grace, we are still exercising our ability to do something, that is, our ability to do what we like to do and not do what we dislike to do.[86] We do freely the good because now we like to do it. The fact that this "liking" comes from the effect of grace seems irrelevant. As long as the will is not "pushed" to do "x," it may be said to be free with respect to "x." To be "drawn" by "x," attracted by "x," does not destroy freedom. It establishes its conditions.

This image of "being drawn" is precisely the image that Augustine uses in describing the action of grace on the will. For example, when he considers the scene in the Old Testament where God influenced the fierce warriors of Israel to choose the young David as king, Augustine points out that God did not induce them by tying them up in chains until they decided correctly. Rather he worked inside them, moving their hearts and drawing them to choose David by their own free will.[87] If God has such power over humans in the choice of a king, it would seem reasonable to say that God should have like power in bringing a human to conversion.

The conversion of Peter is a case in point. Peter came to Christ [Augustine says] by having Christ "revealed" to him by the Father. Did this do injury to Peter's freedom? Augustine argues that it did not because it used the natural processes whereby a human (and, for that matter, any higher animal) is moved in one direction rather than another. A sheep will follow after a green branch, a child will reach for delectable chestnuts, not because they are forced to or pushed to. They are drawn by their love for the delightful treat before them. Freedom is not destroyed; it is overridden. It is a principle natural to humans that "everyone is drawn by what pleases him." Cannot God, the creator of this nature, use this principle to draw humans toward heaven?[88]

The sensible answer can only be to ask "Why not?" Since God has created the person who is Peter to be a free being, it certainly is not beyond possibility that he should be able to work "through that free will" to move Peter from being unwilling to being willing.[89] The tools for such influence are present in the knowledge, delight, and love that fuel the engine of free choice. One cannot infallibly attract sheep or children. A blind sheep will not be drawn by a green branch that it cannot see. A child will likely turn away from chestnuts if it has already gotten sick from eating too much. But is it remotely possible that Peter would turn his back on Christ once Christ illuminated his mind to see and moved his heart to delight in that eternal good which Peter had been created to achieve? It is extremely unlikely. Indeed, Augustine would say that it is simply impossible. But this impossibility of choosing otherwise under the influence of compelling grace does not make Peter's conversion any less free. The illuminated knowledge remained his; the enhanced delight was still his;

and the love that resulted drawing him irresistibly to Christ was without a doubt still his. Thus, it was under the influence of his knowledge, delight, and love that Peter gave up his nets and ran down the path after Christ, drawn irresistibly by the grace of God.

Concluding Reflection

Augustine certainly did not think that God's grace-filled intervention lessened in any way the dignity of the human being. In his last years, perhaps remembering his days of being driven by his pride in himself and ambition for power and desire for sexual satisfaction, he wrote these words: ". . . our free will can do nothing better than to submit itself to be led by him who can do nothing wrong."[90]

Considering the alternative of being driven by earthly desires, Augustine felt that there was nothing to lose in having our wills "drawn" by the will of God. Indeed, at the end of time when finally we see God face to face, we may come to realize that the heavenly delight by which God "pulled" our free choice toward heaven was the best thing that could have happened to us. Even now with our wounds of mind and will still plaguing us, we should be able to see that it is better to put our faith, hope, and love in God rather than in ourselves. It just makes good sense to depend on the will that is stronger.[91] It is rational to submit oneself to one who loves us infinitely more than we can ever love ourselves, one who created us with the intention that someday we might all be together in a land where love and delight are unending and where we are finally and forever free . . . free to choose that one and only infinite good whom we now see clearly for the first time.

Some have suggested that Augustine's increasingly harsh language against Pelagianism was due to his being an "old man" who had fought all his life for orthodoxy only to find in the end that his fidelity to Christ's teaching was being questioned. He was accused by some Pelagians of being a "closet Manichaean" (denying human freedom) and accused by some in the church of Africa of being a "closet Pelagian" (because of his gentle treatment of Pelagius in some of his earlier writings).[92] Some elderly do have a tendency (sometimes rightfully so) to be impatient with those who disagree and Augustine's last opponent, the young bishop Julian, certainly left much to be desired when it came to civility. However, there may be another reason for Augustine's vigor in this last great battle of his life.

Perhaps as he grew older Augustine became less concerned about personal autonomy in this life and much more concerned about his salvation in the next. Looking at his own past indiscretions, he was perfectly pleased to transfer the responsibility for his salvation into the hands of God. To be sure, he was probably tired and perhaps a little depressed that problems and debates never seemed to go away. But also, as he perceived the gradual weakening of his powers, he came to rejoice more and more in the assurances he found in scripture, assurances to humans trying to be faithful as they wandered through the desert of this life. Perhaps he read God's words to Israel as applying to all members of the human race:

> You have been my burden since your birth, you whom I have carried from your infancy. Even to your old age I am the same; even when your hair is gray I will bear you. It is I who have done this, I who will continue, and I who will carry you to safety (Is 46:3-4).

As an old man who probably found it difficult to walk, he did not mind being carried the rest of the way. The predestination that seemed to be implied in such "carrying" did not bother him a bit. As we shall see, it did bother others, even some who had been his staunch supporters against the Pelagians. Predestination was the final triumph of grace but it raised many questions and seemed to present the most difficult challenge to the human freedom and divine fairness. These are matters for discussion in the chapter that follows.

Notes

1. As a general introduction to the issue of will and freedom, the following articles from *The Encyclopedia of Philosophy* (New York: Macmillan, 1967) are helpful: "Freedom"; "Determinism"; "Volition"; "Choosing, Deciding, and Doing."

2. William C. Tremmel, "The Converting Choice," *Journal for the Scientific Study of Religion* Religion, vol. 10, n. 1 (Spring, 1971) pp. 17ff.

3. See *DDA*, 10.13-14, PL 42, 104-05.

4. Augustine remarks that just as now we cannot will to be unhappy and yet are still free in our choice of happiness, so too in heaven when we are face to face with God we will be free and yet be unable to choose evil (*ENC*, 28.105, PL 40, 281). This infallible choice of God under the influence of the beatific vision is an interesting example of how the will can be compelled to choose a good and yet still be free. In the presence of the infinite good, the will is drawn by its proper object. It can no more "not choose" than the eye can "not see" when it is functioning normally and is presented with a colored object. As long as the will is "drawn" by a good presented to it, rather than "pushed" by some internal addiction or psychosis, it can reasonably be said to be "motivated" (moved by motives) which for Augustine is the distinguishing mark of a voluntary action. The love of the saints for God revealed before them is still truly their love even though they could not do otherwise since there is no other good to be desired. It would seem to be as unreasonable to call a person "unfree" because he cannot choose the "not good," as it would be to describe a person as blind who cannot see in the dark.

5. *DLA*, 2.18.50, PL 32, 1267-68; See *RET*, 1.9.6, PL 32, 598.

6. *DLA*, 2.19.51, PL 32, 1268.

7. *Ibid.*, 1.16.34, PL 32, 1240.

8. See *ibid.*, 2.19.53, PL 32, 1269.

9. *RET*, 1.8.3-4. After repeating many of his statements from *De libero arbitrio* defending freedom, Augustine points out that his lack of emphasis on the need for grace has a very simple explanation. It was not the purpose of the book. As he remarked to Pelagius, this absence was more than remedied by his later voluminous writing insisting on the need for grace. Augustine always maintained that through all his controversies he never changed his view that human beings were free and that grace was necessary to effectively choose good. (For example See *ENC*, 9.32, PL 40, 247-48.) However there was a change in his emphasis over the last thirty years of his life. For an examination of this development See J. Patout Burns, *The Development of Augustine's Doctrine of Operative Grace*, (Paris: Études Augustinienne, 1980).

10. Augustine writes: "The love of those first humans for God was perfectly peaceful and their mutual love for each other was that of a true and sincere friendship. It was a love that brought them great joy because they were always in the presence of their loved one." *DCD*, 14.10, PL 41, 417. See *ibid.*, 14.26, PL 41, 434.

11. *DCG*, 11.29, PL 44, 934.

12. *OIJ*, 5.1, PL 45, 1432.

13. *Ibid.*

14. *DCD*, 14.10, PL 41, 417. See *ibid.*, 14.26, PL 41, 434.

15. *DCD*, 13.20, PL 41, 394.

16. *DGL*, 6.25.36, PL 34, 354.

17. These supernatural gifts were literally graces in that no human being had a claim on them. In later times two types were distinguished: "sanctifying grace" and "actual grace." Sanctifying grace was described as a supernatural quality residing in people as a continuing condition of their life whereby they were made participators (*consortes*) in divine nature. (See A. Tanqueray, *Brevior Synopsis Theologiae Dogmaticae* [Desclée & Socii: Paris, 1931], 7th ed., # 886, p. 512.) Sanctifying grace thus gave a condition of being. Something more was needed to support action. This was the function of actual grace. This was an aid to action that would come and go as needed. It both enlightened the human mind to see what should be done and gave the human will the strength to do it. It supported that elevated level of activity which led to the truly "supernatural" reward of seeing and possessing God. [See *ibid.*, # 898, p. 518.] As Gilson and many others have noted, Augustine made no explicit distinction between sanctifying and actual grace. He did however recognize that by the gift of God [that is, grace] we are both made "sharers in divine life" and are supported in our attempts to do good actions. See Etienne Gilson, *The Christian Philosophy of St. Augustine* (New York: Random House, 1960), p. 150. See Jaroslav Pelikan, *The Christian*

Tradition, (Chicago: University of Chicago Press, 1971), vol. 1, p. 292. See Bernard J.F. Lonergan, S.J., *Grace and Freedom*, ed. by J. Patout Burns (London: Darton, Longman & Todd, 1971), pp. 2-3.

18. *DGL*, 6.24.35, PL 34, 353; *ibid.*, 6.27.38, PL 34, 355.

19. *CFM*, 3.3, PL 42, 215.

20. *E 140*, 4.10, PL 33, 542.

21. *DGC*, 11.32, PL 44, 936; *ENC*, 28.107, PL 40, 282.

22. *DCG*, 12.33, PL 44, 936.

23. *Ibid.*, 12.35, PL 44, 937-38; 12.37, PL 44, 938-39. See Eugène Portalié, *A Guide to the Thought of Saint Augustine* (Chicago: Henry Regnery, 1960), p. 207. See Paul Lehmann, "The Anti-Pelagian Writings," *A Companion to the Study of St. Augustine*, Roy W. Battenhouse (ed.) (New York: Oxford University Press, 1955), p. 226.

24. *DCG*, 11.29, PL 44, 933-34; *DCD*, 14.13.1, PL 41, 420-21. See Gilson, *op. cit.*, p. 150. See also John M. Rist, "Augustine on Free Will and Predestination," *Journal of Theological Studies*, vol. 20, pt. 2 (October 1969), p. 430.

25. *DCG*, 10.28, PL 44, 933. See *RET*, 1.15.2, PL 32, 608-09.

26. *OIJ*, 4.104, PL 45, 1400-01.

27. *DPM*, 1.16.21, PL 44, 120-21. See *ibid.*, 1.15.19, PL 44, 119; *CEP*, PL 44, 614. See Pelikan, *op. cit.*, p. 299.

28. *DLA*, 3.19.53, PL 32, 1296. It should be noted that by "carnal concupiscence" Augustine means any earthly desire which interferes with our desire for God and heavenly things.

29. *DQS*, 1.1.11, PL 40, 107. See Gilson, *op. cit.*, p. 151.

30. *DNG*, 53.62; 3.3; *DGC*, 19.20; *DCD*, 19.13.2, PL 41, 641. See Pelikan, *op. cit.*, p. 300.

31. See *DCD*, 22.24.1-2, PL 41, 788-89.

32. *Ibid.*, 22.24.2, PL 41, 789.

33. *Ibid.*, 22.24.3, PL 41, 789.

34. *DLA*, 3.1.2, PL 32, 1271.

35. *RET*, 1.9.6, PL 32, 598.

36. *SER* 156, 11.12, PL 38, 856.

37. See *IJE*, 5.1, PL 35, 1414.

38. *DLA*, 3.18.52, PL 32, 1296.

39. *Ibid.*, 3.20.57, PL 32, 1298.

40. *DQS*, 1.1.4, PL 40, 104.

41. *DQS*, 1.1.12, PL 40, 107. See Gilson, *op. cit.*, pp. 153-54.

42. *DLA*, 3.20.58, PL 32, 1299. See Pelikan, *op. cit.*, p. 301.

43. See *DQS*, 1.1.7-14, PL 40, 105-08; *DGA*, 4.7, PL 44, 886.

44. See *RET*, 1.9.6, PL 32, 598; *DSL* 28.48, PL 44, 230.

45. See *DGA*, 5.11-12, PL 44, 888-89.

46. *C*, 10.29.40, PL 32, 796; *ibid.*, 10.31.45, PL 32, 798; *ibid.*, 10.37.60, PL 32, 804.

47. For general information on the Pelagian movement See Gerald Bonner, *St. Augustine of Hippo: Life and Controversies* (Philadelphia, PA: The Westminster Press, 1963), pp. 312-52.

48. See Peter Brown, *Augustine of Hippo* (Los Angeles: University of California Press, 1967), p. 348.

49. See Pelikan, *op. cit.*, pp. 279-80.

50. The points of controversy are summarized by the six propositions attributed to Caelestius and condemned by a gathering of North African bishops in late 411:

1. Adam was created liable to death and he would have died even if he had not sinned.

2. Adam's sin affected only him. It had no effects inherited by the rest of the human race.

3. The moral law leads humans to the kingdom of heaven in the same way that the gospel does.

4. There were some sinless human beings even before the coming of Christ.

5. Newborn infants are born in the same state of innocence possessed by humans before Adam's first sin.

6. The whole human race did not die in and through the death and sin of Adam; nor does it rise again in and through Christ's resurrection.

See *DGP*, 11.23, PL 44, 333; *DGC*, 2.11.12, PL 44, 390-91. See Pelikan, *op. cit.*, p. 316; Gerald Bonner, *op. cit.*

51. See *OIJ*, 3.13, PL 45, 1252. Since humans were able to obey the commandments if they so chose, they were personally responsible when they did not do so. Indeed, even the least infraction of the law was serious since it was an act of disobedience toward God. Portalié gives a fair summary of this rigorist position when he says: "Every man who could have acted better than he did is going to hell." Portalié, *op. cit.*, pp. 188-89; See Pelikan, *op. cit.*, p. 314.

52. For Pelagius, the only true Christian was the here and now saint. Augustine gives quite a different picture of the "ordinary" Christian . . . the one who is likely to be saved (See *CEP*, 3.5.14, PL 44, 598). Bonner sums up the difference between Augustine and Pelagius by remarking that if Pelagius had had his way, the Catholic Church would have been turned into a tiny assembly of saints. This was far from Augustine's vision of the church as a rather large school for sinners.

Gerald Bonner, "Pelagianism and Augustine," *Augustinian Studies*, vol. 23 (1992), p. 34.

53. Augustine agreed with Pelagius that there were three factors in the process of free choice: nature, decision, and execution. In order for people to do a good act, they must first of all possess a nature which has the possibility of free choice (the *posse*). Then they must decide to do the good act (the *velle*). Finally they must carry through this decision by actually doing the good act, making the good act exist (the *esse*). For example, to do the good act of giving alms to a poor person, one must (1) have a nature which is able to choose (*posse*), (2) make the choice (*velle*) and then (3) actually give the alms (*esse*). Using these terms, the difference between Augustine and Pelagius on our ability to choose the good can be explained as follows:

a. Pelagius' position was that God gave the nature, but the power to choose and the power to carry the choice into action remained in the individual even after sin. God obviously was the source of the *posse*, the free nature formed at creation. But after that no special divine intervention was needed for the individual to accomplish the choice (*velle*) and the execution (*esse*) which flow naturally from free human nature.

b. Augustine countered by arguing that indeed humans still possess the free nature given by God (*posse*) but now because of the wound of sin God must also give the *velle* and the *esse* for a person to effectively do a good act. This God does through the gift of grace which helps the individual delight in and desire the doing of the good.

54. *DSL* 3.5, PL 44, 203.

55. *DGC*, 1.12.13, PL 44, 367.

56. *DGA*, 22.44, PL 44, 909.

57. *DCG*, 12.33, PL 44, 936.

58. *Ibid.*, 11.32, PL 44, 935-36.

59. Augustine bases this view on his reading of St. Paul where for example Paul writes to the church at Philippi: "Work with anxious concern to achieve your salvation. . . . It is God who, in his good will toward you, begets in you any measure of desire or achievement" (Phil 2:13-14, NAB trans.)

60. *DGC*, 1.47.53, PL 44, 383.

61. *IJE*, 41.1.1, PL 35, 1692.

62. *E 214*, 7, PL 33, 970.

63. See *IJE*, 53.1, PL 35, 1778.

64. Augustine writes: "There is no doubt that once people have achieved the age of reason they cannot believe, hope, or love unless they will. Nor can they

attain the prize of God's call to heaven unless they run to it voluntarily." *ENC*, 9.32, PL 40, 247-48.

65. ". . . necesse est fieri si voluerit." *Ibid.*, 103,27, PL 40, 280. See John M. Rist, *op. cit.*, p. 437.

66. *C*, 13.9,10, PL 32, 849.

67. Augustine was of the opinion that the grace given to fallen humanity is much more powerful than the grace given to humans before original sin. Those first humans had possessed grace which gave them the possibility of persevering in good if they so chose. Those now who are the predestined elect are given perseverance itself . . . by means of which they "cannot help persevering" (*DGC*, 12.34, PL 44, 937). It would seem that the only true freedom with respect to good and evil (that perfect indifference to alternative courses of action that would make the agent fully "responsible" for the direction of the choice) existed only in Eden. Once humanity was weakened by sin, it was determined by its wounds to do evil. It could not do good. After healing, those elect chosen to be flooded with grace could do nothing else. The problem that this raises about human freedom comes not from the need for the will to have alternative choices in order to be free. Augustine makes clear that this position is simply absurd. To maintain it is to deny freedom to God who certainly and above all has no option to choose evil (*OIJ*, 1.100, PL 45, 1116). But it is absurd on the human level also. Are we to deny freedom to humans in heaven who have no alternative but to choose the infinite good present before them? Evil, after all, is an absence, a lacking of good. It would make no sense at all to say that we cannot choose freely unless the good before us is imperfect. If the good presented is indeed perfect and infinite, the will must choose it because it is its proper object. To say that the will could be indifferent to such an overpowering good or could only choose freely if presented with a lesser good is as absurd as to say that the eye can see only when colors are dim or that the ear can hear only when sound is muffled.

68. *DNG*, 32.36, PL 44, 264.

69. *DPM*, 2.18.28, PL 44, 168.

70. Augustine writes: "Do we destroy free will by grace? Far from it! We rather bring it into being. Grace makes the will healthy so that it can love righteousness freely." *DSL*, 30.52, PL 44, 233.

71. *DGL*, # 1-6, PL 44 881-886.

72. *CJH*, 4.8.47, PL 44, 761-62. See *DGC*, 1.47.52, PL 44, 383.

73. *OIJ*, 6.11, PL 45, 1520.

74. *Ibid.*, 6.10, PL 45, 1518.

75. *CJH*, 5.3.9, PL 44, 788.

76. *DPS*, 2.5, PL 44, 962-63.

77. *DDP*, 13.33, PL 45, 1013. See *DPS*, 2.5, PL 44, 963.

78. *DSL*, 34.60, PL 44, 240. In one of his sermons Augustine describes how God can affect both our environment and our reaction to it. Speaking to his people about adultery, he makes a list of how God protects a person from falling into this sin. God says to the human being: "You were not an adulterer. . . . I ruled you for myself. I preserved you for myself. There was no companion lest you commit adultery. I brought it about that there was no companion. The time and place were not suitable. I brought it about that this was so. A companion was present, the time and place were apt, but I terrified you lest you consent" (*SER 99*, 6.6, PL 38, 598). The conclusion is clear. We owe God thanks not only for the good we do but perhaps even more for the evils we do not do.

79. *DDP*, 8.19, PL 45, 1002.

80. *Ibid.*, 8.20, PL 45, 1003. See *ibid.*, 13.33, PL 45, 1013.

81. *DPS*, 8.13, PL 44, 970.

82. *DPM*, 1.35.37, PL 44, 130.

83. *DGC*, 1.26.27, PL 44, 374.

84. *OIJ*, 3.106, PL 45, 1291-92. See *ibid.*, 3.114, PL 45, 1296.

85. See *DNG*, 57.67, PL 44, 280; *OIJ*, 1.107, PL 45, 1121; *DSL*, 16.28, PL 44, 218; *DNG*, 69.83, PL 44, 289.

86. *DSL*, 32.53, PL 44, 235.

87. *DCG*, 14.45, PL 44, 913.

88. *IJE*, 26.6.5, PL 35, 1609.

89. *CEP*, 1.19.37, PL 44, 568.

90. *DGP*, 3.5, PL 44, 323.

91. *DPS*, 11.21, PL 44, 976.

92. See Gerald Bonner, *Augustine and Modern Research on Pelagianism*, St. Augustine Lecture (Villanova, PA: Villanova University, 1970), p. 58.

Chapter 8

Human Destiny

Introduction

A human being who lives in these days after Eden can only live by hope. In our "cracked" condition we lack perfect control over our present and find it difficult to erase memories of our somewhat tarnished past. Only the future holds the promise of infinite possibility, perhaps even the possibility that someday everything will be just fine.

Looking deep into ourselves we know for certain that we want to live, that we want to live forever at the peak of our powers, that we want to live forever the "good" life which brings us happiness. Most humans can resonate with the response given by the young Augustine to the question: "What above all do you wish to know?" Without hesitation he answered: "I want to know if I am immortal."[1] In truth, all of us would like to live happily "forever after" but it seems that the only certain fact in our future is that we shall someday die. Augustine used the powerful image of a river to represent the story of human life. He writes:

> As a torrent is formed from the rains and eventually breaks through its narrow banks and runs roaring down the slopes until it finally finishes its course, so it is with each of our lives. Indeed, the whole human race, gathered together from hidden sources, rushes through time until it dies, falling again into a hidden place. Thus, this passing state that we call our life roars and rushes away.[2]

The dominant fact of our lives is that we are rushing toward the end of our river and, if we paid attention, we could even now see the mist and hear the crash of the great falls ahead that marks our end. We are not especially happy about the prospect. No one likes to plummet into an unknown. As a consequence we waste much precious time in the hopeless task of trying to slow our pace, dreaming of finding some quiet eddy where we can rest and watch the passing tide. We may be restless (because of the sweeping current that tumbles us along) but like hummingbirds we are constantly in search of some sweet nourishment that will stay our journey, something to hold onto that we can love and call our own. When we find such a lovely thing, some blossoming twig or other, we reach out to grasp it hoping that it will hold us in place so that we can enjoy the delight of the present forever. We try to ignore the persistent pull of the current of time that calls us to move on. It is a dangerous dream because we can become so entwined in present joys and nostalgia for an unrepeatable past that we ignore our future.

This would be a terrible mistake. Like it or not the great falls await us. We, like the rest of the human race, must someday plunge over the brink of this life into the "hidden places" beyond . . . a land (we are told) of quiet pools, brilliant rainbows, and soft refreshing mist. Since this future is inevitable, how much better is it for us to let go of our past and present, to stop fighting the current, and to plunge bravely toward our destiny! How much better is it to face this death in an authentically human fashion, to recognize it as a fact of our future and to accept it as a free being!

Later on in his life, Augustine's faith gave him the certainty about immortality that he had sought in his early years. Although he did dabble in arguments from reason for life after death, the fullness of that life was only revealed to him after he came to believe in Christianity. The bible then became his main source of information about the nature of life beyond death. It also helped him answer the question: "How should I live now facing my future death?" His response to that question is the first topic for our consideration.

The Authentic Response to Death[3]

In this discussion the phrase "authentic response" shall mean a response that is generated by the existential condition of the one making the response. An authentic response is therefore a realistic response because it flows from the essential and relevant accidental characteristics that go to set the individual in her/his place in the actual world. If there are any characteristics that are common to all human beings, the response to death flowing from them is an "authentically human" response in that it can be reasonably expected from every human being. Thus, if humans are beings who have a mind that naturally seeks truth and a body that naturally falls apart, it would be "non-authentic" to blissfully sail through life "not thinking" about at least the possibility that life might come to an end.

Accidental characteristics of individuals or groups may also play a part in determining an "authentic" response for them. For example, if I believe in a religion that teaches reward or punishment in an afterlife, this should have some impact on how I face death. Of course, some accidental characteristics (for example, being bald or not being bald) should have no impact on how I face death. If I yearn for death because of hair loss, I may deserve sympathy but I need therapy. My thirst for death is not a reasonable response to my hairless condition.

The importance of determining the "authentic" response to death and making it part of one's life is evident. If the perfection of the human being demands living an "examined" life, basing one's actions on "what one is" rather than "what one pretends to be," then one should take into account every aspect of one's existence. On the basis of what one is, one can build reasonable hopes for the future and make realistic plans. If death is to be a fact for me, it certainly will be an important fact, one that I must reasonably take into account in my day by day living. To do otherwise would be to live a fantasy, a fantasy which may be comforting but which adds little to the quality of my life as a human being.

Augustine's thoughts on the authentic response to his own death are based on facts, facts about his human nature and the inevitability of his death. For him the first fact was that the same rational soul that gave life to his body also gave his mind a thirst for knowledge. Humans need to know, to understand, to be conscious of their situation. As Augustine urged his sometimes puzzled listeners: "Use your brains! Every human wishes to know what is going on. There is no one who does not wish to understand."[4] The point that he was trying to make is that we humans are meant to be conscious of who and what we are; we are meant then to use that information in an intelligent consideration of our future.

But what are we? For Augustine, a second fact that forces itself upon us is that we are composites. We are not a unity. Rather, we are a thing of many parts. Specifically we are combinations of matter and spirit, body and soul, and there seems to be no absolute necessity why these parts cannot someday fall apart. This, indeed, is the normal meaning of death: our parts fall apart. When that happens both body and soul are in an imperfect condition. The body, no longer with a principle of unity holding it together, continues to dissolve into its material elements until there is little or nothing left of it. The soul, though perhaps surviving, is now incomplete. Its natural desire to be united with body goes unfulfilled. Though it may be "at rest," it cannot enjoy the level of happiness that comes only to a complete human being of body and soul.

These two facts about being human are certain: We are meant to understand our condition and our condition is one of radical contingency. Unfortunately a third fact is equally certain. There will come a time when we will fall apart. Death is much more than a possibility for us; it is certainty. Over and over again throughout his long life, Augustine comes back to this point: death is the common lot for us all.[5] This life is nothing other than a "race toward death." We all move toward it at the same speed even though for some the goal is closer than for others. A human being is "in death" from the moment of birth,[6] and our increasing day by day feebleness is but the extension of our future death into our present moment.[7] The attempt to avoid it is in vain. As Augustine told his friends: "Humans fearing death weep and moan and plead and curse but all they accomplish is to die a bit later. . . . They cannot stop their dying."[8]

Faced with the fact of our mortality, how should we respond? Augustine answers by saying that we must begin by facing up to this fact of life and planning accordingly. He expresses amazement that most humans do not seem to take death more seriously. We become so involved in our present that we seem to have no time left for our future. We prove by our actions the truth of the principle that Augustine learned from personal experience over a busy lifetime: "Familiarity with the thought of death is hardly compatible with noisy and busy meetings or with endless running to and fro."[9] Even when we see others die, we do not identify the sad event with ourselves. We say: "Well, they are dead and gone but we are alive and here."[10]

To face death authentically we must face up to it, but this does not mean that we need to rejoice at the prospect. There is nothing "unauthentic" in having an aversion to death, in wishing that it would not happen to us. Augustine was speaking from personal experience when he remarked: "Death is not able to be loved; it can only be tolerated. By nature not only humans but indeed every living thing abhors death and fears it."[11] He goes so far as to suggest that a person who does not fear death may already be dead.[12] Admittedly, a person can gain merit from a noble death but the dying process in itself is good for no one. It would have been a much happier situation if those first humans had not sinned and thereby made death a necessity for all the rest of us.[13]

At every stage of his life Augustine admitted to his own fear of death. As a young man of thirty-three, he tells God: "I think I can be disturbed by only three things: the fear of losing those I love, the fear of pain, and the fear of death."[14] As an old man of seventy-six, facing the threat of death from the barbarians at the gates of the city, he prayed: "Lord, save this city if it is your will. But if not, then give me the strength to endure and to die in your arms."[15] At this last stage of his life he was willing to die; but he still saw it as something to be endured. He had lived through the various ages given to a human being. The only thing he had to look forward to was death. He was at the end of his river and heard the crashing waters of the great falls ahead. He hoped against hope that he would be able to accept this last stage of his life with the equanimity of his mentor Ambrose or with the sentiments of that unnamed friend who, facing death, prayed: "If I should never die, it would be very good. But if I must die sometime, why not now?"[16]

Augustine treasured those words because they represented for him a truly authentic response to death from a human being who believed in Christ. There was a recognition of death. There was a wish that "things could have been otherwise," that humans could enter eternity in some other way. And finally, there was willingness to accept it with high hopes for the good things that awaited on the other side of the falls.

Life after Death

Introduction

That the river of this life will someday end is certain. We know that there is a great falls called "death" ahead of us. It marks the end of our time. We hope that it will mark the beginning of something new. But of this we cannot be sure, at least not as sure as we are of those events that we experience. We have not experienced death in ourselves as yet, but we have seen it in others and we know that this experience will someday be ours. We have hints about immortality, testimony that it will indeed be part of our future, but we would like to be sure with the certainty that comes from experience or from incontrovertible proof. We would like to be as certain that "Myself + death = life" as we are that "2 + 2 = 4."

Augustine shared such sentiments. In his earliest writings [*Soliloquies, De immortalitate animae*] he was driven by a desire to be certain about his immortality and he somewhat vainly tried to prove it from reason.[17] One of the great gifts of his eventual faith in Christ was that not only did it finally convince him of immortality, it also revealed to him something about what life beyond death would be like. His faith told him that life beyond the great falls would fulfill his deepest desires. Put simply, his faith promised him perfect happiness.

Such happiness in life after death was for him an important element in any theory of immortality. Even before his conversion he had been aware of many theories of immortality but he found none of them satisfying. Like the rest of us, he knew what he wanted out of immortality. Any immortality worthy of the name must involve individual, conscious life after death. I want "Donald" to survive the plunge over the falls, and I want to be conscious of that fact. To be told that I will continue as part of the eternal fabric of reality, that I will be absorbed into the infinite being of some everlasting mind, is truly not an inviting prospect. Indeed, faced with such a nebulous existence, the Epicurean assurance seems more attractive . . . the assurance that whatever waits for me on the other side of death, I will not be conscious of it.

The conviction that "I" shall survive forever after death must overcome formidable obstacles: namely, my intrinsic and extrinsic mortality. Intrinsically I am made up of parts. There seems to be no good reason why I will not fall apart. My life is characterized not by stability but by change. My being seems to be constantly coming and going and the radical change that occurs at death points to the final going of "me." Furthermore, even if I were one seamless whole, my existence is not self-supporting. I am contingent. There was a time when I did not exist. This proves that I am not "necessarily so." There seems to be no compelling reason why I should "be so" forever. At very least I need some support for my fragile existence that comes from a power beyond myself.

Historically three different theories have tried to respond to such objections.[18] The first of these, the *immortal soul doctrine*, maintains that the human being is really a spiritual soul which is temporarily encased in a material body. I am my soul and it is this that will survive the body's corruption. The body is indeed made up of parts and it will fall apart in death, but the soul is so radically different from the body that it should be able to survive the disaster. At death the soul will be able to move on to another life either as pure spirit or as a resident in another body. Of course the soul is still contingent but this can be overcome by positing a benevolent God who "holds" it in existence, or [more simply] by simply declaring it to be eternal.

The *shadow-man doctrine* of immortality found in the religions of Greece and Rome does not depend on the existence of a spiritual soul. It holds that the "real" human being is an ethereal "shadow man" encased within the fleshy body of our experience. At death this external body does indeed corrupt but the real "shadow-me" continues to exist in another land beyond death. It is a land of sadness because its inhabitants are literally only "shadows" of their former selves. Augustine suggests that this is the reason why ancient mythologies are so filled with stories of the dead desperately trying to come back to this life. They want to escape the diminished life of their shadow-land and return to the lusty life that they so enjoyed in their flesh and blood bodies.

A third theory of immortality, the *reconstitution doctrine*, starts with the assumption that "I" am the composite of spiritual soul and material body. Though the soul may indeed survive death, my body does not. Therefore, my true immortality as "person" begins when at the end of time I am "reconstituted" by reuniting my soul with my restored body, now perfected and free from the ills and weaknesses of this life. This solution thus asserts a future resurrection of the body, an event that can only be hoped for or believed because of the testimony of reliable witnesses.

Augustine on Life after Death

As might be expected of a believing Christian, Augustine firmly maintained the reconstitution position on immortality. Although he was convinced that the soul is immortal in its own right, for him this was not enough. The human being "Augustine" is not the soul; it is the union of body and soul and any sort of life apart from this composite had to be incomplete. Torn apart by death, the individual person could never be "perfectly happy" even though their salvation was assured. The basic desire of any human is to be perfectly happy and such perfection can come only when the person whole and entire is in peaceful unending possession of God.

Since the soul is spiritual, there is no absolute necessity for its sharing in the body's destruction at death. Physical death (what Augustine calls "first death") is caused by the separation of body from soul, that spiritual principle which had maintained the ever-changing body as an integral unit. Once that principle of unity is withdrawn, the unity from multiplicity which is the body disappears and the body, made up of parts, begins to fall apart. However, the soul is spirit and has no parts. Furthermore, since it is so radically different from the body, there is no compelling need for it to be dragged down by its quickly corrupting partner.

In his youth, Augustine tried (somewhat unsuccessfully in his view) to prove the immortality of the soul from arguments based on reason and experience. Later on, after his conversion, he ceased to consider it an issue that needed argumentation. Thus in 412 he writes to his friend Volusian that he cannot imagine anyone, even the most feeble-minded, doubting the immortality of the soul or the fact of life after death.[19] In 415 he tells Jerome that he personally is convinced that the soul is immortal, not in the way God is immortal having no beginning or end, but in its own fashion, that is, having a beginning but no end.[20] Faith had given him the conviction that he had so earnestly sought by rational argument.

Still, these early attempts at "proving" the immortality of the soul remain interesting because they clearly show the Platonic influence (through Plotinus) on his early writings. As a young man he was still entranced by the unaided mind's capability of discovering any truth, including the truth of the immortality of the soul. Much later on he will admit that a purely reasoned approach to such a difficult problem was a foolish venture for the ordinary human being.[21]

Although Augustine himself did not think much of the effectiveness of his arguments from reason, two of them give an interesting "window" on his mind. The first of these was developed in his *De immortalitate animae*. It argues from the content of the mind to its nature, and it reflects Augustine's continuing wonder at the mind's ability to know the eternal and immutable even though it itself is enmeshed in time and is ever-changing. Later on he will use this mystery as a foundation for his unique argument for the existence of God. Here he uses it as an indication of the soul's immortality. If the soul were totally limited by time (he argues), how could it ever recognize truths that go beyond time? It would seem improbable, if not impossible, that a one-dimensional power should be able to perceive realities beyond all dimensions.[22] The argument is persuasive. A container must to some extent share the qualities of that which is contained. As the classical principle states: "Everything is received in accordance with the mode of being of the receiver." One cannot capture quicksilver with a sieve nor can one perceive an idea with one's eyes.

One weakness of the argument is that, taken to its logical end, one could conclude that the soul is eternal and unchangeable. This conclusion

Augustine rejects since it bestows on the soul a characteristic of God. God alone has such perfect immortality, life that it is immutable with no beginning or end. To assert this of the soul is contrary to both faith and experience. The soul is evidently changeable and scripture clearly teaches that it had a beginning. Therefore, the most that can be said of the soul is that it is not wholly contained by time.[23]

A second argument for the immortality of the soul points out the centrality of happiness in Augustine's world-view. An incontrovertible fact about human beings is that we want to be happy. We want to be satisfied. We want all of our desires fulfilled. A second incontrovertible fact is that such perfect happiness does not occur in this life, if for no other reason than that everyone's "river of life" is destined someday to plunge over the great falls. No matter how pleasant our river excursion may be, there is always a tinge of sadness mixed in because it will some-day end. As Augustine observes: "No end is enough for us except that of which there is no end."[24] Happiness must be unending to be perfect. Temporary ecstasy literally leaves much to be desired and in that sense it is not as satisfying as it could be. It is not perfect.

For some philosophers (for example, Unamuno) this universal thirst for perfect happiness is sufficient to prove the case of "unending" human life. However this approach rests on the unsupported assumption that if all humans desire something, the reality must exist and be achievable. Such an assertion can certainly be questioned. Humans create all sorts of imaginary goods as objects of desire, objects which exist only in their fantasies. A sad truth about life is that "Wishing does not make it so." However, Augustine's argument is not affected by this objection. His conviction that the universal desire for happiness implies immortality rested on his recently acquired belief in the God of faith, a God who is the creator of human beings and who is all-knowing, all-powerful, and [most importantly] all-good. It is simply unthinkable that such a God would give humans a thirst for unending life without such life being a possibility. If the truth "I exist" is the most certain truth an individual perceives about this actual world, the truth "I will exist forever" is equally certain once one is convinced of the existence of an infinitely perfect, benevolent creator in this actual world.[25] This argument from the desire for happiness has the added merit of being an argument for the immortality of the whole person and not simply the soul. Human beings desire happiness for their whole person and the person does not exist when body and soul are separated.

Such arguments for the immortality of the total person thus avoided the problems which Augustine perceived in the classical descriptions of life after death. Most did not seem to take into account the need for happiness in the afterlife. For some immortality meant an endless recycling of this life with all of its miseries. For others who saw the passage of death as a "one-way" trip, immortality meant either life as a disembodied spirit sometimes devoid of individualized personality or a life in a dull, dark land populated by shadow-people, half-humans filled with nostalgia for their former earthly life. Not exactly a hell, this Hades was far from being a heaven of everlasting delight. It was more like a hospital for the terminally ill, populated by walking skeletal figures with wan, gray faces and bulging distress-filled eyes. It was far less than the fullness of life promised by the Christian description of a life after death populated by bright pure spirits and smiling flesh and blood embodied souls.[26] For Augustine, there could be no perfect happiness without resurrection. To live beyond death is only worthwhile if one can live like a true human being: that is, a being of spirit and body.

The doctrine of the resurrection of the body has special importance for one floating down this river of life, perhaps already hearing the distant thunder of the "death falls" that threaten to end life forever. Resurrection promises the unending life of the person I perceive myself to be. The promise of resurrection tells me that life beyond the falls will be something like the life I have now but much better. It takes away some fear of the unknown. I don't know how it is to live as pure spirit. Contrary to some who claim that they would gladly discard all bodily experience if they could, most of us could put up with it only for a short while if promised that someday we would be "all back together again" and be just fine.[27] Resurrection to heaven promises me that the natural desire of my soul for its no longer obstreperous material partner will be fulfilled.[28] I will have no desire to wander further looking for some "greener meadow." I will be at home with my flesh and blood.

Resurrection of the body will also restore to reality for all eternity that special reflection of God that can be found only in the human composite of body and soul. Through resurrection each human will reflect in a special way the person of Jesus Christ who became a being of soul and body because he saw some good in it. In sum, resurrection will make the individual truly happy as "person" and will restore to the universe that order that can be fulfilled only by a created being of spirit and matter.

Considering its importance for most humans now moving toward death, it would be advantageous if there were a coercive argument from reason proving resurrection. Unfortunately there is none. There is nothing in the nature of the body that promises resurrection. Indeed, just the opposite. The body by nature falls apart. It decomposes. To be alive as body depends on a delicate balance between catabolism [breaking down] and anabolism [building up] and the testimony of both science and personal experience is that there will come a time when the body can no longer repair itself.

Even if I know that some humans have come back to this life after dying, this is not the same as resurrection to new life. No reasonable person would be satisfied with coming back to the same life he had left. The story of Lazarus tells of a human who came back over the "death falls" to this same rushing river. This cannot be completely satisfying because the resurrection we yearn for promises life on the other side of death. Even if I know that someone indeed made that trip and now lives on the "other side," this fact taken by itself gives no assurance that I will someday have the same experience. At best such events argue for the possibility of my resurrection, not that it will actually happen.

Augustine knew that he could not prove his future resurrection from reason but he also knew that it was a necessary corollary of his faith in Christ. He believed completely in the sentiments expressed by St. Paul: "If there is no resurrection of the dead, Christ himself has not been raised. And if Christ has not been raised, our preaching is void of content and your faith is empty too" (1 Cor 15:13-14). The resurrection of Christ and its implied promise of resurrection for ordinary humans is the basis of hope for a happy future life.[29] A person with firm faith is gifted with an absolute certainty that Christ indeed rose. The story of his post-resurrection days records that he "showed" himself to his friends, that they "touched" him, that they "ate" together: these were all signs that the resurrected Christ was no "shadow-man." Rather he was a flesh and blood human being, different to be sure, but still flesh and blood.[30] And, just as clearly, scripture records that Christ promised that this resurrected condition will be ours also at the end of time.

Though Augustine could not use reason to prove resurrection, it was a useful weapon in responding to objections. Thus, to those who objected that the decomposition of the body makes resurrection impossible, Augustine answers that if God can create from nothing, it would seem to be possible for God to restore what has fallen apart.[31] Against the objection that Christ's resurrection was a singular event with no application to other human bodies, Augustine points to the intimate union between Christ and his disciples. If we are united with Christ as our head, it would seem to follow that we can share in his experiences, at least those that pertain to his human nature. Furthermore it does not make sense to doubt my resurrection when Christ went through his death and resurrection specifically to guarantee my successful resurrection into the city of God.[32]

Furthermore (he continues) we should not overly mystified by human resurrection. The world is filled with analogies for the phenomenon. Life coming from death is not an unusual event in the world of nature. A seed must be buried before new life can be produced.[33] We sleep each night and wake to a new day. The moon wanes only to appear again in its fullness. The sun sets at night but rises each morning. Trees lose their leaves in autumn so that they can be reborn in the spring. Even the rotting leaves discarded on the ground are nourishment for new growth.[34] The message of nature is clear. On this river that is our time, death is just the beginning of life. Should we wonder that the end of our time gives way to a new beginning? Nature tells us that it is a possibility; faith assures us that it is a fact. At the end of our river we shall rise whole and entire to a new life in an eternal sea beyond.

The Nature of Life after Death

After this life we shall rise to a life without death. But what will that life be like? The first thing that must be said about it is that it will be fixed. Human history is linear. There is no going back, either in life on the river or in going from the other side of death back to this life. Upon death one's eternal destiny is fixed and the place of that destiny will be in one of two eternal cities: heaven or hell. From the time of the first angelic turning against God through endless eternity, all rational creatures [angels and humans] are divided into two communities or "cities" by their love.[35] We are drawn toward the earthly city or toward the heavenly city by what we now love. At the end of our lives, each of us plunges over the same great "death falls," but there we are divided into two streams, one falling into the dark pool of "second death," the other falling into that bright eternal sea where God waits for us. Our ultimate destiny is not fixed until the moment of death. Consequently no living human can be certainly identified with either city. Even the supposedly best may end up with wills fixed against God and even the worst may, like Dismas on Calvary, be called to final conversion. The virtues of river people must therefore be tolerance of others and prayerful humility for self. The vices that must be avoided at all costs are pride and despair, thinking before our final plunge that we are irretrievably saved or lost.[36]

The first citizen of the city of God is God, the infinitely perfect being. Since God always was and always will be, the city of God is truly eternal with no beginning or end. Other members of this heavenly city are those created pure spirits (angels) who from the first moment of their existence made a free and final choice of God over self, and those human beings who by the grace of God have received or will receive the gift of final perseverance in love of God. The city of God is thus the community formed by God, the "good" angels, and the "the assembly of the saints." It is that invisible, mystical body where Christ is the eternal head and the members are those who remained faithful to him in time.[37] Truly united with Christ in love, the "good" angels and the human "blessed" share with him the eternal life of heaven. It could not be otherwise. Members of a body must be where their head is.

A natural question for one still on the river side of death and hoping someday to be with God is: "What will life in heaven be like? What are its characteristics?" Augustine's people apparently asked the question frequently and he tried to satisfy their curiosity in his sermons and writings. Of course he had no direct experience of such a life, but using scripture and common sense he was able to offer his friends some "educated guesses" about the nature of heavenly life. For example, one absolute certainty was that life in heaven is beyond anything that we can experience on earth. Augustine told his listeners: "Please do not think that you will see in your eternal life anything like what you now see!"[38]

The reason for his warning is obvious. The fundamental characteristic of life in heaven is the vision of God, a face to face contact with infinite being that can never be described, much less replicated, in this life.[39] This vision of God will surpass even our most ecstatic experiences of earthly beauty:

> . . . the beauty of gold and silver, of groves and fields, of sea and air, the beauty of angels. It will surpass the beauty of any earthly thing because we shall see the one from whom the things of earth derive their beauty.[40]

This direct experience of God will bring perfect satisfaction. We shall ask for nothing more because nothing more will be left to be desired, nothing more will be left to puzzle us.[41] Our happiness will be complete because not only will we see God; we shall possess and be possessed by God. In Augustine's words:

> Your God shall then be everything for you. God whole and entire shall possess all of you. Though with God you will possess everything, you will still have enough room to live with him. You will contain all of God and he will contain all of you. You shall be one.[42]

The natural result will be ecstasy:

> In heaven we shall see, we shall love, we shall praise. What we see will never fade away. What we love will never leave us. Our songs of praise will never cease.[43]

"Exhilarating peace" is perhaps the best phrase to describe how we will feel. There will be absolutely no contrariness. We will have true concord with God, with other humans, and with ourselves. We will experience that eternal sabbath rest that can be given by God alone.[44] At the same time we shall be vigorously active, constantly praising God with shouts of "alleluia" and "amen" without tiredness or boredom. We shall sing "Amen" because we will be constantly learning the answers to questions that have bothered us in this life. Heaven will be an everlasting revelation of the secrets of the universe. We shall know the answers and cry in discovery "So that's what it means! Amen!" The beauty of the reality that we now see clearly for the first time will so overcome us that we will not be able to stop shouting over and over again: "How wonderful! Alle luia!"[45] Our praises will be without clatter because we shall be singing deep inside our spirit. We shall be

> . . . silently absorbed by the most pure and most fierce contemplation of that triune God which we now proclaim so loudly in faith with clacking words and syllables.[46]

We shall be at peace because internally there will be no tension between body and soul. We shall be friends with our body.[47] We will have no enemies within or without. We shall have "oneness of heart" with all around us, those humans we have loved in this life and those we have come to know on the other side of death. There will be no secrets. We will feel secure in being open to others. There will be no need for trust because we shall see each other as we are and love each other for what we are.[48]

Finally and most importantly, there will be no tension between ourselves and God. Face to face with God's infinite goodness, we will find it impossible to love anything or anyone more than him. We shall be "glued to God by love and intoxicated by the fullness of God's house." We shall finally and forever be safe and will never become satiated with praising and loving God.[49]

Sadly, the idyllic heavenly city is not the destiny of every rational creature. Some angels and some human beings will spend an eternity separated from the one being whom they were created to embrace. Augustine firmly believed that hell exists and it is not without inhabitants. It includes Satan and other fallen angels as well as those humans who have freely chosen non-God [themselves or other creatures] over God.[50] These, because their wills were fixed at death in rejection of God, are forever denied entrance to the city of God, the kingdom of God and the blessed. Augustine rejected the theory of Origen and his followers that hell was only temporary. In his view, to say such things was to go against the clear teaching of sacred scripture.[51] The message of Christianity is that hell is eternal. Once one has died with will turned against God so it shall ever be.[52]

Hell is a place of punishment and the most terrible aspect of this punishment is but the natural effect of the crime committed. Since the creature has fixed its will against God, they must be separated from God forever. The punishment of hell may sometimes be less and sometimes more; but the sense of "alienation from the life of God" will be forever.[53] This is that "second death" which is the ultimate failure for human beings. Just as death comes to the body when the soul departs, so death comes to the soul when God departs.[54] The death of the soul from the separation caused by grave personal sin becomes at death the fullness of "second death." Augustine warned his friends again and again that they should fear second death much more than physical death. The reason is obvious. Physical death lasts but a moment but there is no end to that dark existence that is separation from God.[55]

After the resurrection of the body there will be only heaven and hell, but between death and resurrection there will be an interim state where the separated soul waits for its reunion with the body. For the blessed it will be a place of rest where they wait out the days till the end of time. For them, death will be like a sleep, a restful time during which they can "burn off" the residue of their imperfect life in preparation for the fullness of life that awaits them at resurrection. During this time they can profit from the prayers and good works of those left behind. Though infallibly saved, they need purification and this can be helped by the charity of others.[56] For those who die rejecting God, the damnation and the pain of loss begin immediately. However, just as the souls of the blessed do not yet experi-

ence the fullness of their joy, so the souls of the condemned do not experience the fullness of their pain. This "fullness" comes to both only after
the resurrection of their bodies. Indeed, compared to what happens after
resurrection, the joys and sorrows of the separated soul are like dreams.[57]

The river of our life ends in the same way for all. We plunge over the
same "death falls" but then we separate. Some fall into a place of damnation; others are raised up to a place of eternal joy. The prospect is daunt-
ing because we never know how we shall die until we die. Will we be
friends of God or enemies at that last moment? Will we have control over
"how" we shall decide? Augustine addresses these disturbing questions
in his discussion of predestination.

Predestination

Looking at an as yet unrealized future, we can dream that our most
basic desires will be fulfilled: that we will indeed live forever, that our
"forever" will be happy, that at very least we will have some control over
what that "forever" will be like. Even if our future ends up to be bleak and
dark and bad, we can take some consolation if we are the ones who made
it so. We can hardly complain if our future hell is self-created. Our desire
to be in control of our future, whatever its quality and however long it
may be, is the reason why any mention of a predestined or fated future is
so terrifying. That there will be a city of the damned and a city of the
saints is not disturbing if we are in control of our travel plans. To hear that
we are predestined to be in one or the other, that even now someone
somewhere can "foresee" which city will claim us as its citizen, is dis-
heartening at the very least. We say: "How can there be a future possibility for me if someone can see my future with the clarity equal to my vision
of my present or past? How can I hope for an already foreseen future, a
future that will be infallibly actual someday?" Hope depends on possibility. It is useless to hope about an actuality; all one can do is endure it.

Augustine believed that we must live our lives with hope but he also
believed that our destiny is foreseen and predestined by God. This is the
clear teaching of scripture, suggested by one story after another, and confirmed explicitly by Paul in his letter to the Romans where he writes:

> We know that God makes all things work together for the good of
> those who have been called according to his decree. Those whom he
> foreknew he predestined to share the image of his Son. . . . Those he
> predestined he likewise called; those he called he also justified; and
> those he justified he in turn glorified (Rom 8:28-30).

The story of predestination reads as follows. After the fall from grace in Eden, humanity was truly without hope. It was literally a "damned lump" . . . a community which on its own was irretrievably lost. No one could be born of the race of Adam without being subject to damnation and no one can escape that damnation without being reborn in Christ.[58] Augustine was convinced that some in fact are so "reborn" and that their salvation was predestined by God from all eternity. Predestination for him meant only one thing: the predestination of the *saints*, those who in fact will be saved at the end of time. He explains the *meaning* of predestination in the following words:

> This is the meaning of "predestination of the saints": It is God's fore-knowledge of those who will be saved and the preparation of the gifts whereby they will be saved. As for the rest, they are left as part of that mass that, in accordance with the just judgment of God, is forever lost.[59]

His explanation of the *process* of predestination follows closely the steps outlined in the text from Romans 8:28-30 cited above:

1. *"All things work together for the good of those who have been called according to his decree."*

> This general principle is the foundation for the positive spin that Augustine puts on predestination. It is a process that brings good. Its goal is salvation and not damnation. The fact that it is not extended to everyone is not as important as the fact that it is extended to some, since no one deserves it. The last phrase suggests that not everyone who is "called" will in fact be saved. Only those are saved who are "called according to his decree," that is, receive faith, love, and perseverance.

2. *"Those whom he foreknew he predestined."*

> The first step in predestination takes place in eternity. God looking out over the multitude of creatures who will actually exist sees those who will be saved and makes the choice to give them the grace needed to guarantee that they will be saved and thereby "share in the image of his Son."

3. *"Those he predestined he likewise called."*

> This call is a call to faith, the recognition in some way of the person of Jesus Christ. This calling is completely gratuitous. It cannot be earned. It cannot be merited. It depends in no way on what the person did or did not do before. It is purely a gift of God given to some and not to others for reasons hidden in the mystery of God's wisdom. For those

who die in infancy, this "calling" comes through the sacrament of baptism. For adult unbelievers it comes through conversion and baptism. For those martyred for the sake of Christ, it comes from their act of martyrdom. This "calling" is absolutely essential for salvation and Augustine had difficulty in seeing how it could be extended to others outside of the categories above [for example, unbaptized infants who die without baptism].

4. "Those he called he also justified."

Once called to faith, the person receives an outpouring of love through the Holy Spirit. This love inclines them to choose to do the good and gives them the strength to overcome concupiscence and thereby effectively do the good. Under the influence of the Holy Spirit, the person is now able to acquire merit by doing acts which have a truly supernatural effect. Thus, for example, under the influence of this God-given power to love, a person is able to pray for the souls in purgatory and thereby better their lives.

5. "And those he justified he in turn glorified."

The final grace which insures glorification in the heavenly city is the grace of perseverance, the grace to remain a friend of God till death or to repent of one's sins and become a friend of God at death. This grace, like that of faith, is completely gratuitous. It is not merited. It is not earned. It may be given at the moment of death to one [like Dismas on Calvary] who has spent a lifetime in unbelief and criminal acts. It may be denied to a fervent believer who has spent a lifetime in good works but who in the end falls away from God. Only those who are "called according to God's purpose" receive this gift of perseverance. Those who have received faith and the "heavenly delight" in doing good but who do not persevere are indeed "called." But they are not among the "chosen."[60]

Augustine's doctrine on predestination was one that developed over his lifetime. Although he always insisted on the need for grace in determining human destiny, in his earlier writings he placed more emphasis on the place of freedom than he did in his later writings against the Pelagians and semi-Pelagians. Reacting to the latter's insistence on individual control over destiny, Augustine emphasized more and more the power of God in determining who would be saved and who would be lost. He argued that just as there is no way a person can merit coming into existence on this earth, there is no way a person can merit the gifts of faith and final perseverance that guarantee existence in heaven.[61]

Augustine would be the first to admit that the whole subject of predestination involves mystery. He frankly declares that he does not know
why some are chosen and others are not. God's judgments are always
unsearchable but in the giving or denying of perseverance they are "even
more unsearchable."[62] He waXrned his questioners about spending too
much time in investigating that which is inscrutable and trying to find out
things which simply cannot be found out.[63] No Christian who follows the
teaching of scripture can deny the fact that God gives perseverance to
some and not to others, that some are predestined to glory and others are
not. Does it make sense to deny the fact simply because we cannot understand it? Does it make sense to deny the "what" because we cannot understand the "why"? The only sensible answer to such questions is a
resounding "No!"[64] The only consolation he offers to those who continued to puzzle over the mystery is that someday, assuming they are among
the "predestined saints," they will come to know not only "who" is in the
city of God but also "why" some have been saved and others have been
lost.[65]

Predestination is indeed a great mystery, but there are some aspects
of it that are worth examining further. For example, *"How can a person
be truly free and yet predestined?"* How can a being claim to be free
when someone else "brings it about that" his future shall be thus and so?
The phrase "brings it about that" contains the central difficulty. Predestination accomplishes its purpose by infallibly "bringing it about that" the
wills of those who are chosen by God will freely choose conversion to
faith, will freely choose to do good acts thereafter, and will freely choose
to persevere in doing good even till death. Those not chosen are abandoned and left powerless to come to faith, do the good, or persevere to the
end. They may have the natural power to believe, to choose, to persevere
but these powers are rendered inoperable because they never receive the
divine energy to activate them. They are made insensible by neglect.
They are hardened by not receiving the shower of grace that has softened
and changed those who are to be the saints.[66]

The process of salvation for those who die in infancy is similar but
simplified. For them too the future is foreseen and some are "called" to
and "chosen" for salvation through baptism or martyrdom. The grace of
perseverance is not required. Once made a child of God by baptism, it is
impossible for them to turn away. Their salvation consists simply in being released from the burden of original sin inherited from their ancestors.
In a sense these "innocents" who are called and chosen are compelled to

be saved by the first grace given in baptism. For adults called and chosen, additional graces are necessary, graces which enlighten their mind to the law of God and impel their will to delight in and do the truly good.

For adults and infants alike, it is grace alone that separates the saved from the lost;[67] but even so, Augustine insists that those able to make free choices must exercise their freedom. The grace driving the saints to salvation is truly irresistible, but still their conversion to faith, their delight in doing God's will, their perseverance till the end, must come from their free choice for it to be described as their faith, their delight, their perseverance. If God wills the salvation of Peter, necessarily it will happen;[68] but the salvation will not be Peter's unless he freely chooses it. The paradox of predestination thus comes down to this: the "saints" must choose their salvation but they cannot choose otherwise. They are free in their choice but it is a *compelled* freedom.

The previous chapter on grace and freedom discusses how one can freely choose to do the good under the influence of grace. Predestination introduces only two new elements: namely, how the specific good acts of faith and perseverance can be both "compelled" and "free." It would seem that the process is no different than that previously described. God's action of irresistibly bringing faith and perseverance to those he chooses does not seem to be any different from his action of making those selected delight in doing good. God saves the blessed by making them delight in believing, delight in doing the righteous act, and seeing to it that the delight is so powerful and permanent that it lasts even till the last moment of life. There is still mystery in this process, but Augustine remained certain about two truths: "If a person is saved it is because of God's grace; if a person is lost it is because of human fault." There the matter must rest until all things are made clear in the city of God.

A second puzzling aspect of predestination has to do with *God's foreknowledge*. How can God know before time what we are going to do in time? If God knows what we are going to do before we do it, how can our action be said to be free? Augustine considered both of these to be legitimate questions, but (he adds) having questions should not weaken a believer's certainty about the fact of God's foreknowledge:

> It is just silly for a person to admit the existence of God and then deny his foreknowledge. . . . If we profess belief in the supreme true God, we must likewise confess his will, his supreme power, his foreknowledge. Anyone who does not know the future is most certainly not the God we worship.[69]

If God is truly perfect, no limitations can be put on his powers beyond the limits imposed by impossibility or contradiction. God cannot
make a being more powerful than himself or a stone which is impossible
for him to move. God cannot make a world where the principle of non-
contradiction ("A" is either "X" or "not-X") is false. But knowledge of
the future is neither impossible nor contradictory. Prophecy is not self-
contradictory any more than memory is.

How God foreknows our future will remain forever hidden from us
because we exist in an entirely different context. We cannot even understand the time in which we live; how can we hope to understand the eternity which is the place of God? We move through our lives experiencing
an "is," remembering a "was," and hoping for a pleasant "will be." Our
knowledge is limited by those parameters. How can we possibly understand the working of a God in whom there is no "was" or "will be" but
only an "is"?[70] It is clear that God's absolute immutability of substance
demands a similar immutability in action. Nothing can change in God's
knowledge of our lives even though our times constantly come and go.
We cannot hope to understand this way of knowing. It is simply too radically different from our experience.[71] In God's eyes what we call past and
future is always present. He can know with certainty what we only con-
jecture. The unfathomable aspect of all this is not so much God's foreknowledge as its certainty. Even we can "see ahead" with some degree of
accuracy. We know, for example, that we shall die. Indeed, in some
strange way we constantly "live" in the future. Augustine notes that we
could not sing a song if we did not in some way foresee what comes next.
We come close to combining past and future into the present. In our present singing we foresee what comes next because we remember.[72]

It is difficult for us to understand even our own stream of time: how
we can exist in a continuity where the past "is no longer," the future "is
yet to be", and the present is a flickering instant that quickly disappears
even as we try to grasp it. No wonder, then, that we cannot comprehend
God's life beyond time. However we should be able to understand that
there is no contradiction between God knowing beforehand what we shall
do and the freedom we exercise when we actually do it. This was the
mistake that led Cicero to deny God's foreknowledge. He thought that he
was faced with two choices: deny human freedom or divine foreknowledge.[73] But why say that foreknowledge causes the future? Remembrance
does not create the past. Our almost certain knowledge of a future eclipse

does not cause it to happen. Why claim that God's absolutely certain knowledge of our future makes it to be that way?[74]

In his debate with the Stoic philosophers, Augustine agreed that they were right in believing that God orders everything in the universe and that he knows beforehand everything that happens. God is the cause of all causes (including human free choice) but he is not the cause of all choices. He knows them but does not cause them. Indeed, he knows them precisely as being free. God knows the full extent of history, not because it is cyclic, but because he is God.[75]

The issue of God's foreknowledge of our future remains an enigma but it is not bothersome. The issue of the *fairness of predestination* is quite a different matter. Given that the purpose of human life is "happiness," how can it be fair to predetermine only some to glory? Is not the selection of only some from the "damned lump" that was humanity after Adam equivalent to the "abandonment" of others. And does not such "abandoning" of the helpless violate some moral principle that should guide a noble life? Is God not bound to the same rules of nobility as we are?

Moreover, if God has the power to actualize any possible world and if he knows that in this world some will be saved and some lost, is it not unfair to those lost for him to choose a world which contains their damnation? When God made Lucifer [the best of the angels] and made the first innocent humans, he *knew* that they would fail.[76] Would it not have been better "not to create them" or to "create" only angels and humans who would freely choose not to fail? There is no question that God can bring good out of evil, success out of failure, but is not more good derived from good, more success derived from success? It is certainly true that human and angelic sin proved that they were free. It is also true that God's rescue of some proved his mercy and power. But are there not better ways of teaching than through the mistakes of others?[77]

Predestination will ever remain beyond our understanding, but would it not be a happier prospect if everyone were saved? We would not mind "not being able to earn" gratuitous gifts such as faith and perseverance if at least we all got them. The story of humanity's rise and fall and rise again would not be a terribly sad tale if only everyone would achieve eternal life sometime. Universal salvation is a pleasant dream but Augustine sadly could not see it being part of the real world. His reading of sacred scripture forced him to the conclusion that God will save some by a positive grant of grace and others will not receive such grace. God predestines some for glory by doing something; others are fated for damnation because they are left to their own resources.[78] Hell was created to house Satan, but Augustine was of the opinion that quite a few humans were destined to end up there also. As far as he could see, the ranks of the blessed in heaven were restricted to those baptized infants who died in infancy and adults who had been called, justified, chosen, and glorified by the grace of God, that is, those who in some way received the gifts of faith in Christ, divine love through the indwelling Holy Spirit, and perseverance.[79]

He was firmly convinced that no one is saved except by the mercy of God and it seemed to him that this grace was not in fact given to everyone. For example, Augustine was convinced that Judas was damned because of his betrayal and despair.[80] The number of the condemned included infants who died without baptism and adults who never came to faith and divine love, or, if they did, did not persevere. The number of the saved was fixed and was not much more than the number of the angels who had failed at the beginning of time. The sad fact is that a majority of humans will never become citizens of the city of God.[81]

The conclusion follows that "God does not will all human beings to be saved." Though some statements from Augustine's earlier writings seem to suggest the opposite,[82] Patout Burns points out that by the time Augustine came to battle the semi-Pelagians he was not able to affirm this universal will of God to save all.[83] God clearly chooses not to give to some the graces that are necessary and necessitating for escape from that damned lump that is the condition of the human race after Adam. Infants without baptism, adults who never come to faith, those who try but do not persevere . . . all of these are lost forever because they were not rescued. The various passages in scripture (for example, 1 Tim 2:4) that seem to say that God does indeed want all to be saved can only mean that God selects his saints from all kinds of human beings and that Christians should work for the salvation of all regardless of class or condition.[84]

The troublesome aspect of this saving some and abandoning others is that some are lost through no fault of their own. There can perhaps be some personal responsibility placed on adults who never come to faith or do not persevere. They at least (in Augustine's view) have done something evil in their lifetime. But what about the infants who die without baptism? They are excluded from heaven simply because they are part of the *massa perdita* and have not been rescued. Augustine was not happy about their fate but he could find no persuasive argument for their salvation. There were only two eternal cities and he could find no indication in scripture of any "key" other than baptism or martyrdom that would allow pagan innocents to unlock the door to heaven.[85] Through no fault of their own they are left "not rescued" from that "lump of perdition" that is the human race after Adam.[86]

If God is to be accused of unfairness in the abandonment of the lost, a violation of moral principle must be proven. Can one, for example, argue that God's action in "choosing some and not others" is unjust in that it violates commutative justice? It would seem not. No creature has a "right" to live the life of the blessed any more than one has a "right" to exist in the first place. Furthermore it can be argued that the punishment of separation from God is something that the human race justly received because of Adam's rejection of God in Eden. Those who are in a damnable condition are there because of human fault. Their sentence matches the crime and there can be no violation of rights in that. No criminal has a "right" to an executive pardon and that is precisely what the gift of grace amounts to. It is an amnesty freely given to quite undeserving creatures.

But is there something unfair in some receiving amnesty and others being passed over? The selection seems arbitrary and thus an unfair distribution of the burdens and benefits of the society that is the human race. If so, it is a violation of distributive justice which demands such fair distribution. However, here again it would seem that since salvation is "owed" to no one and since "punishment" is owed because of the freely chosen malicious acts of human beings, the fair principle for giving salvation (amnesty) can only be "freedom." This is the principle of distributive justice which makes it fair to give Christmas gifts or send Valentine cards to whomever we wish. If salvation is truly unmerited in and of itself and, because of sin, even more undeserved, then the giving of it cannot be "owed" under any aspect of justice.

However there is more to morality than justice. A human being who guides her/his life only by the principles of justice would be something of a monster. Our actions must be regulated by charity also, that virtue which demands a beneficence by which we are concerned about the welfare of others and do our best to promote that welfare. One corollary of beneficence is that we must try to "rescue" others from harm unless we have a legitimate excusing reason. If such beneficence is demanded of humans, it seems appropriate to expect the same beneficence in God . . . to expect that God will "rescue" us from harm when it is possible and when he does not have a good reason for not rescuing. The excuse of impossibility may be ruled out immediately. God is omnipotent and can do anything that does not involve a contradiction. The fact that he saves some demonstrates that there is no impossibility in giving salvation. The issue thus comes down to questions like the following: Does God have a good reason for not rescuing all? Does God have a good reason for rescuing the specific ones that he rescues (for example, Dismas) and a good reason for not rescuing others who on the surface at least seem more worthy? Did God have a good reason for choosing Peter for perseverance and allowing Judas to remain in despair? On the face of it, their cases seem similar. They both came to Christ at about the same time and walked with him for the same three years. Peter denied Christ and Judas betrayed him. Why was Judas "not rescued" while Peter was?[87]

Augustine would have liked to answer such questions, but he could not. Predestination in all of its aspects remained filled with unfathomable mysteries, perhaps the greatest being why anybody was saved. All he could say about the mystery of selection is that by choosing some to be saved God shows his mercy and by allowing some to remain damned he shows his justice. He also believed that having a majority damned made the minority appreciate their salvation even more. Augustine believed that the selection process had to be fair because it was done by an infinitely good God. God must have good reasons for not rescuing some, but what those reasons are will be forever hidden to humans this side of death. Augustine advised his friends that they should not let the mystery of predestination come to dominate their lives. Better by far for humans to thank God that they are able to puzzle over the mystery. This at least means that they have heard of Christ and have come to some belief in a good God who rules the universe. That in itself is a sign that God's grace works in them.

Notes

1. *SO*, 2.1.1, PL 32, 885.

2. *ENN 109*, 20, PL 36, 1462.

3. For a more expansive discussion of this topic See Donald Burt, "Augustine on the Authentic Approach To Death," *Augustinianum* 28 (Institutum Patristicum "Augustinianum," Rome, Italy, 1988) 527-63.

4. *SER 265F*, [Lambot 25] in *Revue Bénédictine* (1957), 101-03. Translated by Quincy Howe, Jr., *Selected Sermons of St. Augustine* (New York: Holt, Rinehart and Winston: 1966), p. 190.

5. *DCD*, 1.11, PL 41, 25. In another place Augustine writes: "To be born and to die, the beginning and the end: these are the two facts of our lives. By being born we begin our labors, by dying we move on to an uncertain future. These two facts we know. They are the constant facts we must face in this our land" (*SER 229E*, [Guelferb. 9], 9. in *Miscellanea Agostiniana*, vol. 1, p. 467). Augustine uses the analogy of the lamp to explain this inevitability. A lamp is filled with light only because it is constantly burning off its resource of oil. If it burns a long time, the light begins to flicker and die as its source of energy is used up. The light can be kept burning only by supplying new oil. Eventually, however, the light dies forever because the wick deteriorates. Even at its brightest moments the essential element of the lamp is slowly being eaten away by time and by use. We humans are like living lamps. We must take nourishment over a lifetime in order to maintain our vital activities. It might seem to the simple that as long as we have enough to eat and drink our life can go on forever. But this cannot happen. The very vessel in which the vital activity is carried on is itself corroding, wearing down, and wearing away. The day will come when it can no longer support the flame of life no matter how much nutriment is poured into it. When that day comes, the body falls apart, the soul escapes and the human is dead. To put it simply: our "wick" wears out (*SER 362*, 11, PL 39, 1617).

6. *DCD*, 13.10, PL 41, 383.

7. *ENN 84*,10, PL 36, 1076.

8. *SER 161*, 7, PL 38, 881.

9. *E 10*, 2, PL 33, 73.

10. Augustine remarks: "We think of the dead when they are carried out to be buried and say: 'Poor fellow, only yesterday he was walking around!' (or) 'I saw him less than a week ago and he spoke to me of this and that . . . and now he is no more.' This is what we say. But we think this way only as we weep for the dead and are busy about the funeral and prepare the procession and carry out the body and bury it. Once the body is buried, we bury the thought of death with it. The thought of following our dead friend ceases. We return to our life of fraud, stealing, perjury, drunkenness, and to endless pleasures of the flesh" (*SER 361*, 5, PL 39, 1601).

11. *SER 299*, 8, PL 38, 1373.

12. *SER 348*, 3, PL 39, 1529.

13. *DCD*, 13.8, PL 41, 382; *ibid.*, 13.11, PL 41, 384.

14. *SO*, 1.9, PL 32, 877.

15. Possidius, *Vita S. Aurelius Augustini*, c. 29, PL 32, 59.

16. *Ibid.*, c. 27, PL 32, 56-57.

17. Looking back on these arguments at the end of his life, Augustine admits that he can scarcely understand them himself (*RET*, 1.5.1, PL 32, 590). But if one is certain of immortality, arguments become irrelevant. Augustine wanted to be certain of his immortality. Once he achieved that, he lost interest in trying to prove it to someone else. Indeed, it is not too much to say that he would feel comfortable with the following sentiments of Unamuno: "And if I grapple myself to God with all my powers and all my senses, it is that he may carry me in his arms beyond death looking into these eyes of mine with the light of his heaven when the light of earth is dimming them forever. Self-illusion? Talk not to me of illusion. . . . Let me live!" Miguel De Unamuno, *The Tragic Sense of Life*, trans. J. Flitch (New York: Dover Publications, 1954), p. 47.

18. For a full treatment of these solutions See *Encyclopedia of Philosophy*, Paul Edwards, ed. (New York: Collier-Macmillan, 1967), vol. 4, 139-50.

19. *E 137*, 3.12, PL 33, 521.

20. *E 166*, 2.3, PL 33, 721.

21. Referring to the trouble that ancient philosophers had with immortality, Augustine writes: "With regard to those who have endeavored to discover these things from human reason, scarcely a few have been able to arrive at the investigation of the immortality of the soul alone, and they were men endowed with great talent, had sufficient leisure, and were trained in the most subtle learning. And even for the soul they have not found a blessed life that is stable, that is, a

true life, for they have said that it returns to the miseries of this life even after its blessedness" (*DT*, 13.9.12, PL 42, 1023).

22. See *SO*, 2.19.33, PL 32, 901-01; *DIA*, 2.2, PL 32, 1022.

23. See *ibid.* See John A. Mourant, *Augustine on Immortality*, St. Augustine Lecture, 1968 (Villanova: Villanova Univ. Press, 1969), p. 6.

24. *IJE*, 101.5, PL 35, 1895.

25. See *DT*, 13.8.11, PL 42, 1022-23; *DCD*, 14.25, PL 41, 433.

26. See *DT*, 13.9.12, PL 42, 1023-24. See Mourant, *op. cit.*, pp. 14-15.

27. Mourant points out the benefits of seeing life after death as involving resurrection. He says: "The soul is no longer a 'ghost in a machine' nor even more significantly a 'ghost outside the machine' pursuing an insubstantial existence, an ever-wearying and unceasing peregrination and metempsychosis, so typical of Greek eschatologies" (Mourant, *op. cit.*, p. 46). Augustine criticizes both Plato and Porphyry for their views on life after death in *DCD*, 13.19, PL 41, 392-93.

28. See *DCD*, 22.21, PL 41, 783-84. In a somewhat poetic fashion, Augustine speaks about another important form of resurrection, the resurrection of the spirit which occurs in this life and is a necessary condition for eternal happiness. He says: "Death according to the spirit is to believe no more the vain things which were believed and to do no more the evil that one did. Resurrection according to the spirit is to believe that saving truth which was not believed and to do the good that one did not do" (*SER 362*, 20.23, PL 39, 1627).

29. See *SER 361*, 2.2, PL 39, 1599; *ibid.*, 3.3, PL 39, 1600; *SER 214*, 12, PL 38, 1072. Augustine suggests that one of the purposes of Christ's resurrection was to give us hope for our own (*SER 362*, 12.12, PL 39, 1618-19).

30. See *SER 361*, 8.8, PL 39, 1603.

31. *SER 361*, 12.12, PL 39, 1605. See *DCD*, 21.7, PL 41, 718-20; *ibid.*, 22.4, PL 41, 754-55.

32. *SER 361*, 13.14, PL 39, 1606; *ibid.*, 16.16, PL 39, 1607-08.

33. *SER 361*, 9.9, PL 39, 1603-04. Augustine also compares resurrection to birth and remarks that the latter is a daily testimony to our future resurrection (*SER 242a*, 2 [Mai serm. 87], *Miscellanea Agostiniana*, p. 328).

34. *SER 361*, 9.9-11.11, PL 39, 1603-05.

35. Augustine writes: "Two cities have been formed by two loves; the earthly by the love of self, even to the contempt of God; the heavenly by the love of God even to the contempt of self" (*DCD*, 14.28, PL 41, 436). And again: "What is the city of God? . . . It is composed of those who love each other and love their God dwelling in them. . . . Those who are full of love are full of God and when you have many together filled with love, they make the city of God" (*ENN 98*, 4, PL 37, 1261).

36. See *DGL*, 11.15.20, PL 34, 437. See *DCD*, 14.6-7, PL 41, 409-11; *ibid.*, 14.28, PL 41, 436.

37. Augustine writes: "These children of God are the members of God's Son. The person who loves them, by loving becomes himself a member. Through love he becomes a part of the structure of Christ's body" (*IEJ*, 10.3, PL 35, 2055).

38. *SER 4*, 8, PL 38, 36.

39. Augustine says: "What can be said about our future? John says: 'Most beloved, we are now children of God but what we shall be is not all that clear. We do know that on some future day we shall become like God. We shall see the Lord as he truly is.' (1 Jn 3.2). There is then being prepared for us a wonderful surprise that is simply beyond imagining! Now we may get some vague hint of what that present shall be but the vision is no better than trying to solve a puzzle reflected in a darkened mirror. No one could ever describe in words the sweetness and the beauty of the gift that our Lord is preparing for those who care about him and hope in him. . . . You are preparing yourself to receive something simply beyond wonder, something that prompted Paul to cry out: 'The dark times of this life cannot be compared to the future glory that will be revealed to us' (Rom 8:18). What in the world can this glory be? Nothing else than to be like angels and to truly see . . . for the first time to truly *see* the Lord our God" (*ENN 36/2*, 8, PL 36, 368. See *DGL*, 13.26.54, PL 34, 476).

40. *IEJ*, 4.5, PL 35, 2008.

41. See *IJE*, 101.6.2, PL 35, 1895-96.

42. *ENN 36/1*, 12, PL 36, 362-63.

43. *SER 254*, 6.8, PL 38, 1185.

44. See *DCD* 19.20, PL 41, 648; *ibid.*, 22.30, PL 41, 801-04. See *E 55*, 9.16-17, PL 33, 318.

45. *SER 243*, 9.8, PL 38, 1147; *SER 362*, 28.29, PL 39, 1632-33.

46. *DCR*, 1.25.47, PL 40, 343.

47. *SER 155*, 14.15, PL 38, 849. The people of Augustine's day, being mostly earthy folk, were much interested in the nature of the body in heaven. Augustine tried to satisfy their curiosity as best he could. Thus, in *Sermon 362* he makes the following points.

1. The essential characteristic of the resurrected body will be that it is no longer corruptible (18.21, PL 39, 1625-26).

2. Our life will be like that of the angels (25.27, PL 39, 1630-31).

3. We will retain the power of eating and drinking but there will be no need for it (12.12, PL 39, 1618-19).

4. There will be no need to marry and have children because there will be no death, neither will there be growth nor aging. There will be no need to do business

because all wants will be fulfilled by God. There will be no doing "corporal works of mercy" because there will be no one in need. (26-27.28, PL 39, 1631-32. See *Sermo 242a*, 3 [Mai serm. 87], *Miscellanea Agostiniana*, pp. 329-30).

In the *City of God* he becomes even more specific. He writes that no matter how old or young or deformed we are at death, we shall rise in the prime of our maturity. We shall have the beauty and stature appropriate to our person [that is, the tall will still be tall, the diminutive will still be diminutive] but if we are too scrawny or too obese this will be corrected. Moreover, our complexion will have no blemishes since we will be in the kingdom of our Father where "The just will shine like the sun" (22.20, PL 41, 782-83). Finally all those parts of the body which in this life contribute to beauty as well as function (here Augustine uses the beard of a man and the breasts of a woman as examples) will continue to be part of the resurrected body since the body will lose nothing that enhances its beauty even though the function is no longer required (22.24, PL 41, 791).

48. See *ENC*, 22.91, PL 40, 274; *SER 243*, 5, PL 38, 1145-46; *SER 306*, 9.8, PL 38, 1404-05; *CEP*, 4.10.28, PL 44, 632; *DCD*, 19.27, PL 41, 658.

49. *ENN 35*, 14, PL 36, 351; *ENN 83*, 8, PL 36, 1061-63.

50. See *DCD*, 14.1, PL 41, 403; *ibid.*, 15.4, PL 41, 440-41. See *DCR*, 19.31, PL 40, 333-34.

51. See *ENC*, 29.112, PL 40, 283; *DCD*, 21.17, PL 41, 731; *ibid.*, 21.27.6, PL 41, 751; *DFO*, 14.27 - 21.49, PL 40, 211-30; *DOD*, 1.1-13, PL 40, 149-57.

52. See *DCD*, 19.28, PL 41, 658; *ibid.*, 21.17, PL 41, 731-32; *ibid.*, 21.23, PL 41, 735-36; *ENC*, 29.111-113, PL 40, 284, *E 102*, 4.22-26, PL 33, 379-81.

53. *ENC*, 29.112, PL 40, 283.

54. *DCD*, 13.1, PL 41, 377; *ibid.*, 13.12, PL 41, 385-86; *SER 344*, 4, PL 38, 1513-15.

55. See *SER 335B* [Guelferb, ser. 31], 5, *Miscellanea Agostiniana*, vol. 1, p. 562. See *DCD*, 13.12, PL 41, 385-86.

56. See *ENC*, 29.110, PL 40, 283; *DCD*, 21.13, PL 41, 728; *ENN 37*, 3, PL 36, 397.

57. See *DPS*, 12.24, PL 44, 977-78; *ENC*, 29.109, PL 40, 283; *SER 280*, 5.5, PL 38, 1283; *SER 328*, 5-6, PL 38, 1454; *SER 281*, 5, PL 38, 1283. Although Augustine is ambivalent about purifying fire in purgatory, he seems to have no doubts about burning fire being part of the punishment of hell. However, he remained in doubt about its exact nature, (See *DCD*, 21.26.4, PL 41, 745; *DGL*, 7.28.42, PL 34, 371; *ENC*, 18.69, PL 40, 265).

58. *ENC*, 14.51, PL 40, 256. Augustine uses various phrases for this "damned mass" . . . *massa perditionis, massa luti, massa peccati* (See *EER*, 62, PL 35, 2080-81). The basis for the concept comes from St. Paul (Rom 9:16-17). Augus-

tine writes: "Out of that lump, which totally perished in Adam, were formed vessels of mercy in which is found the world that belongs to reconciliation" (*IJE*, 87.3, PL 35, 853). For those who question the fairness of taking only part of the "lump" to make vessels of mercy, Augustine responds with the words of Paul (Rom 9:20-21): "Can a potter be blamed for using his clay in any way he wishes?" (See *ENC*, 25.99, PL 40, 278; *DDQ*, 68.3, PL 40, 71-72).

59. Haec est praedestinatio sanctorum, nihil aliud: praescientia scilicet, et preparatio beneficiorum Dei, quibus certissime liberantur, quicumque liberantur. Caeteri autem ubi nisi in massa perditionis justo divine judicio reliquuntur (*DDP*, 14.35, PL 44, 1014). J. Patout Burns comments that Augustine never developed a doctrine of predestined damanation to match predestined glorification. Indeed, he "discussed failure and condemnation as little as his opponents would allow." See J. Patout Burns, *The Development of Augustine's Doctrine of Operative Grace* (Paris: Études Augustiniennes, 1980), pp. 177 & 180.

60. See *DCG*, 14 & 16 & 21, PL 44, 368-71.

61. Bonner notes that the beginning of Augustine's emphasis on the absolute need for grace can be found as early as 397. "In responding to Simplicianus Augustine suddenly came to comprehend, with an absolute clarity, what he believed to be the full significance of 1 Corinthians 4:7. . . . He came to perceive that the elect are not chosen because they believe, but in order that they may believe." Gerald Bonner, "Augustine and Pelagianism," *Augustinian Studies*, vol. 24 (1993), pp. 35-36.

62. *DDP*, 9.21, PL 45, 1004-05; *SER 165*, 7.9, PL 38, 907.

63. *DDP*, 11.25, PL 45, 1007-08.

64. *DDP*, 14.37, PL 45, 1015-16.

65. See *ENC*, 9.29, PL 40, 246; *ibid.*, 24.95, PL 40, 275-76. Lesousky correctly notes that Augustine was not terribly concerned about the "why" and "how" of predestination. His main concern was to insist on the reality of predestination and God's control of the process. Only thus could one insure the preeminence of God's will and the absolute dependence of human beings on that will. See Mary Lesousky, O.S.U., *De Dono Perseverantiae*, Patristic Studies # 91 (Washington, D.C.: Catholic University of America Press, 1956), p. 89. It should also be noted that Augustine and his age were not as overwhelmed by mystery as some today seem to be. They did not expect to understand everything (not even the everyday mysteries of growth and death) and were satisfied to sit back and wonder at the grand events around them.

66. In Romans 9, St. Paul gives various examples of this gratuitous selection of the "chosen" and the "hardening" of those not chosen. For example, he says that not all of the Israelites were true Israelites, though they were said to be a "chosen" people

(v. 6). Again, God determined that of Rebekah's twin sons, the older [Esau] should serve the younger [Jacob] (v. 12). Commenting on Exodus 10.1, Paul notes that Moses was moved to do the will of God while the Pharaoh remained obdurate (vv. 15-18). In none of these cases was God's decision based on merit. The only principle guiding decisions was that: "He has mercy on whom he will and whom he wills he hardens" (v. 16). See *ENC*, 25.98-99, PL 40, 277-78. Augustine goes on to explain the "insensibility" of those who rejected Christ as a hardening of heart caused by God not giving the grace to enable them to do otherwise. God hardens the heart of a person only in the sense that he does not "soften" a heart already hard. He "abandons" by "not helping" (See *IJE*, 53.6, PL 35, 1777).

67. *ENC*, 25.99, PL 40, 278.

68. ". . . necesse est fieri si voluerit." *ENC*, 27.103, PL 40, 280.

69. *DCD*, 5.9, PL 41, 149.

70. *IJE*, 99.5, PL 35, 1888; *DT,* 15.13.22, PL 42, 1075-76; *ibid.*, 6.10.11, PL 42, 931-32. Some theories explained God's foreknowledge by asserting a cyclic theory of history. Having witnessed one cycle, God would know infallibly what would happen in every repetition. History would just be "déjà vu all over again." Augustine saw no need for such strained explanations. In fact history is linear and God knows the unrepeated future simply because he is God (See *DCD*, 12.19, PL 41, 368-69).

71. *DCD*, 11.21, PL 41, 334. Translated by G. Walsh & G. Monahan, *The City of God* (New York: Fathers of the Church, Inc., 1952), pp. 217-18. In another place Augustine writes: "In God's sight there is nothing that exists as past and future; everything is now" (*DDQ*, 17, PL 40, 15).

72. See *DT*, 15.7.13, PL 42, 1066-67.

73. See *DCD*, 5.9-10, PL 41, 148-53.

74. *DLA*, 3.4, PL 32, 1275-76.

75. *DCD*, 12.19, PL 41, 368-69; *ibid.*, 5.8, PL 41, 148.

76. See *DCD*, 11.17-18, PL 41, 331-32; *ibid.*, 22.1, PL 41, 751; *DLA*, 3.5.15, PL 32, 1278.

77. Augustine suggests a reason why God chose this actual world over other possible worlds that seem to us to be better. Speaking about the failure of the first humans, he writes: "God was in no uncertainty regarding the defeat which man would suffer; but, what matters more, God foresaw the defeat which the devil would suffer at the hands of a descendant of Adam, and with the help of divine grace this would be to the greater glory of the saints. Now, all this was so accomplished that nothing in the future escaped the foreknowledge of God, yet nothing in the foreknowledge compelled anyone to sin. God's further purpose was to reveal to all rational creatures, angelic and human, in the light of their own experi-

ence, the difference between the fruits of presumption, angelic or human, and the protection of God. For of course, no one would dare to believe or declare that it was beyond God's power to prevent the fall of either angel or man. But, in fact, God preferred not to use his own power, but to leave success or failure to the creature's choice. In this way, God could show both the immense evil that flows from the creature's pride and also the even greater good that comes from his grace" (See *DCD*, 14.27, PL 41, 435-36).

78. The current position of the Catholic Church on predestination, salvation and condemnation is summarized by Sachs as follows: "The position held by virtually all Catholic theologians who have recently written on these themes may be summarized under five propositions:

1) Because human beings are free, they are able to reject God. Therefore hell is a real possibility.

2) Hell is, therefore, the self-chosen state of alienation from God and not an additional punishment inflicted by God upon the sinner.

3) Though final damnation remains a possibility with which every individual must reckon, neither scripture nor church teaching claims that anyone in fact has been or will be finally lost.

4) The real possibility of hell must be understood in terms of the gospel of God's universal saving will, which is revealed and effected in Jesus Christ. Thus heaven and hell are not to be considered equally possible outcomes, either for humanity as a whole or for individual human beings. . . . Greshake concludes that because the human person is innerly equipped and oriented to choose God and finds his or her appropriate place only in heaven "hell is not only that which should not be, but also, so to speak, that which is much more difficult to attain" (241).

5) Certain knowledge about the final outcome of judgment for individuals is impossible, but because of Christ's victory over sin and death, we may and must hope that all men and women will in fact be saved. John R. Sachs, S.J. "Current Eschatology: Universal Salvation and the Problem of Hell," *Theological Studies*, June 1991, vol. 52, no. 2, pp. 233-41.

79. Augustine does hint at exceptional ways in which "being called, justified, chosen, and glorified" could be accomplished. Thus he says that Dismas the good thief and others as well received the Holy Spirit in a way other than through baptism. Saintly humans were able to possess the Spirit even before the coming of Christ (See *DDQ*, 62, PL 40, 53-54; *RET*, 1.26, PL 32, 627; *DA*, 3.9.12, PL 44, 516-17). The heroes of the Old Testament (for example, the prophets) were gifted with a faith in a Christ who was yet to come (See *DCD*, 18.47, PL 41, 609; *IJE*, 109.2, PL 35, 1918). Salvation was given to some Jews of antiquity and other non-Jews who were "partakers of his worship" (See *E 102*, 12, PL 33, 374-75;

DPS, c. 17.34, PL 44, 985-86). Even toward the end of his life he suggests that although hearing the preaching of the gospel is indeed the ordinary way of coming to faith, this does not preclude the possibility that a few may receive the doctrine of salvation through God himself or through angels from heaven. See *DDP*, 19.48, PL 45, 1023.

80. *IJE*, 107.7, PL 35, 1914; *DCD*, 21.24, PL 41, 736-41.

81. See *ENC*, 24.97, PL 40, 276-77; *ibid.*, 9.29, PL 40, 246; *ibid.*, 16.62, PL 40, 261. See *DCD*, 22.1, PL 41, 751-52; *DCG*, 13.39, PL 44, 940; *E 186*, 7.25, PL 33, 825; *ENN 68/2*, 13, PL 36, 862-63. Augustine was of the opinion that the greater number of the damned has the therapeutic effect of convincing the minority who are saved that they had little to do with their salvation, ". . . thus discouraging anyone from taking pride in his own merits." *ENC*, 25.99, PL 40, 278.

82. See *DCR*, 26.52, PL 40, 345-46; *DSL*, 33.58, PL 44, 238-39. See Lesousky, *op. cit.*, pp. 89-90.

83. See Patout Burns, *op. cit.*, p. 178. See *DCG*, 10.27, PL 44, 932-33; *OIJ*, 2.220, PL 45, 1238.

84. See *ENC*, 27.103, PL 40, 275; *DCG*, 14.44, PL 44, 943; *ibid.*, 15.47, PL 44, 945.

85. Patout Burns suggests that perhaps these infants did not suffer the pain of loss even though they did not have the vision of God. He writes: "Augustine did use the natural image of God in the human spirit as a basis for arguing that exile from the kingdom of Christ constitutes a punishment which must be justified by sin. Still, he did not indicate that the exile frustrates any desire and thereby torments the unbaptized infant." Patout Burns, *op. cit.*, p. 185, fn 3. Some places where Augustine discusses the unbaptized infant are *DLA*, *DPS*, chaps. 23-25; *DDP*, 11.25; 12.30-31; *DPM*, 1.30.58; 3.3.6; *CJH*, 3.3.9, 3.12.25, 5.1.4, 5.11.44.

86. See *IJE*, 53.6, PL 35, 1777.

87. There are many other puzzles. For example: Why is it that one infant is chosen to receive baptism and another is not? Why was the message of Christ preached to towns which would not believe but was not preached to towns (for example, Tyre and Sidon) that would have believed if given the opportunity? (See *ENC*, 27.94-5, PL 40, 275-76). Augustine answers by citing analogies from scripture with similar unanswerable questions: for example, the choosing of Jacob rather than Esau (*ENC*, 25.98, PL 40, 277-78); giving laborers the same salary no matter how long they worked (*DDP*, 8.16-18, PL 45, 1002-03). In the end he simply says: "Whom he draws and whom he does not draw, why he draws one and does not draw another, do not wish to judge unless you wish to be wrong" (*IJE*, 26.2, PL 35, 1607).

Chapter 9

Origins

Introduction

The preceding pages have addressed Augustine's answer to the question: "What is it to be a human being?" This chapter will examine his answers to the questions:

1. Where did we and the world of our experience come from?

2. What are the essential components of the world of our experience, that is, those components that are characteristic of everything in the actual world?

Augustine believed that the process whereby the universe was formed will always be beyond human understanding.[1] Many elements will remain mysterious and confusing, grudgingly yielding glimmers of the truth. Even so, he was convinced that the effort to discover the nature and origin of the universe is a worthwhile endeavor. Indeed, it is for many humans the first step in the discovery of God. As Augustine remarked in one of his sermons:

> I can't see God just now as he is in himself. I can only search for him
> in his works, first through an examination of this material world and
> then through an examination of my own soul.[2]

We humans must begin our search for God with the physical universe because we cannot understand ourselves unless we know something about the context of our lives. We do not live independently of the world around us and what we see there can have important implications for self-understanding and our happiness. The world around us has a crucial part to play in whether we live out our lives in hope or despair. It is hard to be happy in a world of chaos existing only temporarily on the brink of nothingness.

Various theories have been offered to explain the world of our experience. Some (like Marx) have maintained that it is eternal and that the order that we perceive is the result of a evolutionary process that is driven by laws of nature. No one and no thing is responsible for the origin of the universe. It simply always "was." Only change needs explanation and such explanation can be found in the unthinking and uncaring laws of nature. There is no great "mind" behind the existence of the changing universe. It simply *is*, and was so and will be so eternally.

Others will agree that the universe is eternal but maintain that order is not. At one time all things existed in a state of chaos (a not surprising condition for such a conglomeration of disparate things). Order came about over time either as the result of chance encounters and bondings, or because of the purposeful action of some powerful independent mind (*nous*). Among those holding this opinion, some maintain that the movement from chaos to order is linear. Once ordered, the universe will never again be chaotic. Others argue that the process is cyclic, that the universe will go through an eternal repetition of states of chaos and order.

As we have seen in Chapter 2, the Manicheans of Augustine's day offered a different and much more imaginative explanation. They taught that the universe of our experience is nothing more than the temporary battleground of cosmic forces of good and evil. The world did not exist eternally nor was it brought into existence *ex nihilo*. It came about by the mixing together of the primordial good and evil "gods" that had existed eternally. Their conflict will not be forever. The time will come when once again the forces will be separated. The universe (including humans) will cease to exist, and for the rest of eternity the two "gods" will exist separated in an uneasy balance of power. In the Manichaean scheme of things, as in many of the other ancient theories, individual humans live out their temporary existence as helpless pawns moved by forces beyond their control.

In stark contrast the Christian explanation of the universe's origin, the one defended by Augustine and examined in this chapter, is one that is centered on a creative act motivated by love. This ordered world was brought from nothing by an infinite being who even now must hold it in existence by continuing concurrence with the original creative act. The universe thus came into existence as the result of the free act of an infinitely perfect person [as opposed to some blind "force"] who knew what he was doing, who freely chose to create, who created to accomplish some purpose, and who cared about the result. The universe is not haphazard, and humans (created and conserved by an all-knowing, all-powerful *person* who cares about them) have a reason for living and hoping.

Creation ex Nihilo

Augustine saw reality as diversity, a combination of lesser and greater beings. It includes non-living material things (earth, water, air, fire), corporeal beings enlivened by a material principle of life (plants and animals), unified composites of matter and spirit (human beings), and pure created spirits (angels). Each level of being is good in its own way and together they constitute the "splendor of order" that makes the universe beautiful.[3]

The common characteristic of all these beings is that they are mutable. Both the world of matter and the world of spirit is ever-changing. Bodies deteriorate; minds flit from this to that. All of them seem ephemeral, as delicate as an angel's breath. Given the transient nature of the universe, the questions Augustine had to consider were:

1. How could such passing things come to be at all?

2. What is the source of the characteristic of mutability that all share?

3. What is the source of their differences, the reason why they exist at differing levels of being?

In addressing these questions, Augustine depended on two sources: faith and experience. Through faith he was able to receive information about the beginnings of things from the pages of sacred scripture, especially the book of Genesis. Through experience he was able to see that reality was characterized by change and that time was nothing more than the measure of that change. By experience he was able to perceive the specificity of existing things which demanded that each being be set apart from every other by individual perfections which determined that it be this and nothing other.

His knowledge of the writings of those who had gone before, both Christian and non-Christian, introduced him to various theories describing the origin of the universe, but the final and most powerful influence on him was the story of creation told in the Old Testament book of Genesis. Over the course of his long life, Augustine wrote five lengthy commentaries on that story, culminating in the twelve books of the *De Genesi ad litteram*.[4] Even after so much time and effort, he recognized that many of his conclusions were open to objection.[5] For example, he notes that there are at least six different interpretations of the very first lines of Genesis ["In the beginning God made heaven and earth"] and none of them contradict any certain truth of the Christian faith. The possibility of so many interpretations of the same text did not surprise him. He recognized that it was the divine teacher within each reader that revealed the "truth" which God wished to communicate at that moment, a "truth" that the sacred writer probably never suspected.[6]

Because of his own experience of the world and the testimony of scripture, Augustine was certain that the world had been created. This fact was not only the clear message of Genesis; it was also proclaimed by the things he saw each day. As he wrote in his *Confessions*, "We look upon the heavens and the earth, and they shout to us that they were made."[7] He argues that it could not be otherwise. If this changing world were *not* made, then there could be nothing in it now that was not there before. The phrase "not being made" connotes an independence in existence, to exist necessarily, to have always *been* what one *is* now. The fact that creatures change indicates that this permanence in existence is not part of their being. "To the degree that anything is no longer what it was, and is now what it once was not, it is in the process of dying and beginning anew."[8] Changing things are transients in the kingdom of being. They need to be *made* in order *to be* and it is impossible that they could have *made* themselves. Their very visible changing present proclaims a fact about their past. It is a voice that whispers, "We were made by someone else!" This quiet message from experience is confirmed by the clear proclamation of Genesis that the existence and order of the universe was brought about by God's creative act *ex nihilo*.[9]

The Genesis report of the fact of creation implies other truths. The *first* truth is that before the creative act there was absolutely nothing in existence except God. Therefore, God's "making" of the universe was far different from the way in which an artist builds a statue. There was no pre-existing matter in creation, no "stuff" that could be molded and formed into the shape of creatures. Before creation there was only God.[10]

A *second* truth is that God did not use intermediate agents in creation. God did not delegate the creative act to some lesser god or spirit. Creation was the direct act of God, making and maintaining all that there was to be from the highest to the lowest. God is thus intimately involved in the "being" and "support in being" of every existing thing. Each creature is "known" by God and touched directly by his omnipotent power.[11]

A *third* truth is that although God is intimately involved in every aspect of creation, creatures are not eternal emanations of God's substance. Reason makes clear why this must be the case. It is of the essence of God to be unchangeable. It is of the essence of creatures to be changeable. Since only God is immutable and since only the immutable is eternal, creatures being changeable must have a beginning. To assert that they are eternal emanations of God is to equate them with the Word and Holy Spirit, the second and third persons of the Holy Trinity.[12]

A *fourth* truth is that God was not in any way forced to create. The universe was formed purely and simply because God freely willed to bring it about. In the triune God the relationships are necessary and eternal. The divine Word and the Holy Spirit flow necessarily from the very nature of God. Creation flows from a quite different source: the divine will freely choosing to bring into existence something that did not exist before. To ask "Why did God choose?" is to try to find something greater than God's will, something that would move it to choose. But no greater thing exists. Thus, the only answer that can be given to question "Why did God create?" is the same answer explaining any free choice: "The act was chosen because the person loved what was chosen." If it is true that *Bonum diffusivum sibi* (Good tends to diffuse itself), it is not surprising that the infinite good should wish to bring into existence other beings who could share in the divine goodness.[13]

Augustine was certain about creation *ex nihilo* and the four truths that followed from it. He was much less sure about the exact way in which various species of things came to be. The first verses of Genesis seemed to him to be open to the following interpretations:

1. There was only one act of creation. All individuals and species were created at one time, though some in "seed" form to develop fully sometime later on.

2. There was only one act of creation. All individuals and species that will ever exist were created either actually or in the ordinary power of nature to produce new species and individuals. After the first moment of creation no extraordinary divine intervention in the normal course of nature was required.

3. There is a continuing creation throughout history whereby God continues to create new species and especially souls of individual human beings.

Augustine subscribed to the first interpretation, maintaining that (with the possible exceptions of the souls of later human generations) all creation came existence "in the beginning."[14] Before that, all creatures existed in their "eternal reasons" (*aeternae rationes*), the various ways in which the divine nature could be reflected.[15] Before time nothing was yet made, but everything was possible. Through a single *"fiat"* particular beings either began to exist actually as fully formed creatures (for example, angels and the firmament) or potentially in their "causes." These causes were of two kinds. There were "primordial causes" (*rationes seminales*) which at the appropriate time would produce fully formed new species. There were also those ordinary causes imbedded in existing nature whereby, for example, species once established have the power of reproducing others of their kind.

The Process: Formlessness to Formed Being

Augustine saw in the first verse of Genesis hints about the process of creation. The verse reads:

> In the beginning God created the heavens and the earth. Now the earth was a formless void, there was darkness over the deep, and God's spirit hovered over the water (Gen 1:1-2).

He interpreted the passage as referring to two events separated conceptually but not in time:

> 1. the creation of the "formless matter" (*informis materia*) that is the root of all change and therefore the foundation of all created being;

> 2. the production of the first "fully formed" creatures by the imposition on "formless matter" of that measure, form, and order which constitutes created being as an individual, independent existent.

In his view "formless matter" had to be (logically) the first element in the creation of changeable being. It is a pure potentiality which as yet has not been specified by any particular form or perfection. This is the first element in the creative act, establishing the potentiality for whatever is to be formed afterward. It is the foundation for all mutable being, be it spirit or body. It is the support of passing thoughts, the metabolic processes of living bodies, and the entropic movement of all material things.[16]

In book 12 of his *Confessions* Augustine admits to an initial difficulty in grasping the concept of a "formless something." His perplexity is not surprising. By definition "formless matter" contains nothing positive to understand. A being becomes intelligible only through those particular perfections which make it to be this being and none other. It is through such positive characteristics that we can distinguish a human being from an oak tree. Formless matter is difficult to comprehend precisely because it is not "non-being" nor is it "being." It is something in the middle, the "condition" for being. Augustine says that when he first came to think of it, he thought of it as some sort of monstrous disordered thing. Since it had none of the form that makes a being a thing of beauty, it seemed to him to be some sort of terrible ontic horror. He finally came to realize that he was looking at the issue the wrong way. Formless matter does not stand for something with a deficient form, for something warped by imperfection. Rather, it is something with no form whatsoever, a pure potentiality to receive form, a "nothing/something" (*nihil aliquid*), an "is/is not" (*est non est*).[17]

All things created depend for their formation on this formless matter. However the sequence of "formlessness" to "formed" is not a temporal sequence. It is rather a mental ordering of the elements necessary for the origin of any created being. Logically the "capacity to receive form" comes before "being formed" but clearly this cannot involve a sequence in time. The roots of time are in change from this to that, but before a being receives a specific form there is no particular "this" which can be subject to change. Time did not exist before changeable formed matter began to exist. God did not create formless matter and then mold specific things from it. His creative act was more like the action of an orator or a singer who forms words or melodies in the very act of making sounds. Augustine explains:

> If someone were to ask: "Well, which comes first, the sounding voice or the words?" it would be hard to find someone so stupid as to deny that the words are produced by the sounding voice. Obviously the speaker creates both at the same time but a little reflection makes it plain which of the two is the thing produced and which is the matter from which it is produced.[18]

Like the singing of a song, creation is a one step process, not two. In the beginning, God created those "first things" by simultaneously creating and combining "formless matter" and those perfections [forms] which give specificity and existence to actual beings. Once existing as independent entities, creatures retain their common base in that formless matter that is the root of their mutability, a mutability that is a natural characteristic of something that is made from nothing.

Augustine's argument that this ephemeral "formless matter" logically had to be the first element in God's creative act comes from both faith and reason. He accepted without question and quite literally the text (Wisdom 11:17) where God's "mighty hand" is said "to have fashioned the universe from formless matter," and he believed that this scriptural testimony was confirmed by reason analyzing the nature of change.[19]

Created things are characterized by their mutability. Whatever else they are, they are beings subject to change. To understand the phenomenon of change, it is necessary to posit some substrate that continues through the change. When a created being changes [for example, hydrogen is combined with oxygen to form water], it does not seem sensible to maintain that the original beings are annihilated and a totally new being is instantaneously created from nothing. Water is not formed by the annihilation of H_2 and O_2 and the simultaneous creation of H_2O. Change is a continuous transition from "this" to "that." A live "President Lincoln" is radically different from a dead "President Lincoln," and yet it seems only reasonable to say that there is a continuity between the person who was enjoying the show in Ford's theater and the dead body that resulted from the nefarious assassination. It would be absurd to say that there is no connection between the two states of affairs, and the connection can only be a "potentiality" for change that endures through any transformation.

By reason of its roots in formless matter, every creature has two characteristics: (1) it is mutable and (2) it exists in time. However, for a particular being to actually exist, it must possess three more characteristics:

1. it must be individualized;

2. it must be able to be distinguished from other things by its own proper form (perfections);

3. it must take its proper place in the order of nature.[20]

Actual being can exist only if it is closed off from all other existing things. It must be "this" or "that" for it "to be" at all. It is separated from its immutable creator by its mutability, but it must also be separated from the other created beings by a unique definition at this time in this place. My distinction from you depends on our having separate existences which irreversibly close us off from each other. I exist and you exist separated by that existential perfection that later scholastics were to term "subsistence."

The second element in a created being's individuality is the specific set of perfections [form] which constitute its essence as different from all other species [for example, human vs. plant] and which set the being as a particular thing within that species [for example, the "I" which is not "You"]. It is in its "ideal form" that created being existed from all eternity in the infinite nature of God. It is through its "imposed form" that a created being begins to exist in its own individuality, mirroring in its own personal way some aspect of its exemplar: the nature of God as expressed in the person of the Word.[21]

A creature also needs specification through an individualized finality which drives it to seek its proper place in the universe, that one and only place where it can be at peace. Every being has a goal and in working to reach that goal it fits into the order of the universe. Every created thing is made with a specific weight or gravity which naturally draws it back to God. Just as bodies do not remain in place unless the force of their gravity [Augustine calls it "the appetite of their weight"] has brought them to their proper place of rest, so too spiritual creatures are "restless until they rest in God."[22]

Creation of individual existing things occurs only when these three defining elements are joined with the pure potentiality of formless matter. As sacred scripture testifies: "You (O God) have disposed all things by measure, number, and weight" (Wis 11:21). *Measure* establishes the limits of a particular being, as when plotting out a garden to be exactly six feet by eight feet. *Number* has to do with giving something a specific form since making something to be "countable" implies making it different from all else in its perfections. *Weight* stands for that internal gravity [finality] that draws a being to that particular goal which, when achieved, brings restful peace. God can be connected with these three characteristics in a most true sense since it is God who places limits on everything, gives each being its particular form, and arranges all created things in one universal order. In accord with this order every creature begins its existence with its own measure, number, and weight and is capable of change only within the confines of its own individuality in accordance with the divine plan.[23] To change beyond the limits of one's "measure, number and weight" is to cease to exist.

God imposes these three elements in every created being and through them each creature reflects in its own way the perfections of the Trinity itself. It is because of this that it is possible for humans to see the creator in the things that were made and even to see in the triadic foundation of individual things a hint of the Trinity itself. In a limited sense, it is possible to say of the three individualizing elements in creatures what is said of the persons of the Trinity: "Each is in each; all are in each; each is in all; all are in all; all are one."[24]

Since each created being reflects the infinite good to the extent that it possesses a degree of measure, number, and order, it follows that every part of creation must be called good. Of course there is a hierarchy of good since there are different levels of measure, number, and order in individual beings. Some things exist at a higher level than others. Some have higher perfections. Some have a higher degree of order. But it would be incorrect to describe those humble things at the lowest level of reality as being "evil." They may be "less good" but they are far from evil as long as they reflect even the smallest aspect of the infinite good. Evil is the corruption of a being's natural measure, form, or order and [as we have argued in our previous discussion of evil] can be only properly applied to the perverse decision of the human will to choose to act contrary to its "place" in the universe.[25]

Throughout his writings Augustine speaks of a threefold need in creatures for a *conversio*, a "bending back" to God. Angels and humans must turn their darkened minds toward God [in the person of the Word] for the illumination that will allow them to see the truth. Free beings must turn back to God [in the person of the Holy Spirit] so that they may be able to receive the grace of being able to love rightly. Finally, in every creature from the lowest to the highest, there is the need for a "turning back" of formless matter to God so that unformed creation can receive the specific form [perfection] by which it is to reflect in its own special way the nature of God manifested in the person of the Word. Put simply, not only must free beings be converted in order to know God and to love God, all created being must "turn back" to God in order to exist at all. As Augustine writes:

> Incomplete created being tends naturally to nothingness because of its formless condition. It does not begin to reflect the perfections of its exemplar, the Word [the second person of the Trinity inseparably united to the Father], until it turns back (*conversio*) in its own appropriate way to its creator and thereby receives that form which gives it its proper level of perfection.[26]

The history of creation is thus the story of a "going out" and "bending back." The power of God goes out to make from nothing a something, but that something in order to be perfected must constantly be "bending back" to the creator for continued support. The universe, always on the verge of "nothingness," needs constant support for the fulfillment of its existence. It is something like a "joey" (a young kangaroo) peeking out of its hiding place in the pouch of its nurturing parent. Seeing the terrifying "nothingness" beyond its creator, the universe quickly turns back to its source to gain more strength to face its uncertain future.[27]

There are many mysteries here. For example how can a created being "turn back to its creator" when it is still unformed? How can "it" be converted when there is yet no "it"? Perhaps the process becomes easier to understand when we remember that there is no time sequence between the creation of "formless matter" and the production of a "formed creature." The action is one. What the process does suggest is that the act of creation is a dynamic interaction between creator and creature, that the creature is never far from its creator. The power of the Father is constantly exercised in keeping fragile creation in existence; the power of the Word is constantly exercised in recalling imperfect being to itself so that it can be measured against its exemplar's perfections which it must reflect in order to be. And, finally, the power of the Spirit is constantly exercised by a kind of "brooding action" over the process not unlike that of a loving mother helping the development of her young. In sum, creation comes about because of the power of the Father, a "recalling" and perfecting of incomplete creatures by the Word, and the nurturing love of the Spirit overseeing the whole process . . . all three actions occurring in an instant and before time.[28]

In his *Confessions* Augustine points out that a phrase such as "*before* time" makes no sense at all. Consequently any speculation about what God was doing *before* time is a useless exercise.[29] Time began with creation and thus there was no "before or after" until the first fully formed creature began to exist. Time is the measure of change according to "before" and "after" and there was no change to be measured until the first fully formed mutable beings came into existence.[30] There is an objective basis for time in change, the movement from this to that. Such change would exist even if there were no mind to measure it. But time itself remains heavily subjective, existing only in a mind that recognizes the flow in changing things and measures that flow from its own peculiar perspective. All judgments about a "long" time or "short" time are relative to the one making the judgment. For some a century is brief while for others a day can be an eternity. Another's time is always a mystery for me and my understanding of even my own time is hard to put into words. As Augustine says: "If no one asks me what time is, I know; if I try to explain to one who asks, I don't know."[31]

The elements of time are puzzling in themselves. When we reflect on them we discover that what we call "past" no longer exists and what we call "future" does not yet exist. Only the present "is," but we can only understand it as part of time by seeing it as passing.[32] The measurement of time is thus unlike the measurement of a road where the beginning and end exist as truly as the "right here" at which we stand. When we measure time, only the "now" actually exists outside our mind. The past exists only in memory; the future only in expectation.[33] In a world where everything seems to be speeding by, the burden of living is that our present cannot be grasped and most of our allotted days exist only in remembered past or anxiously awaited future with all the finality and insecurity that those realms convey. Thinking about our time, we can understand why Augustine ended his own reflections with the prayer:

> Just now my years are filled with sighs as I am torn between times past and times yet to come. The course of my time is a mystery for me. My thoughts, indeed the very life of my spirit is tumbled this way and that in the vortex of change. And so it shall be, my God, until finally I am consumed by your love's fire and am melted forever in union with you.[34]

Creation of the Angels

The first creatures produced fully formed were the angels.[35] They were intellectual creatures characterized by a spiritual nature which was able to know and to love. It is unclear whether Augustine believed that they had some sort of "spiritualized" body akin to the resurrected bodies of human beings. John Hammond Taylor suggests that Augustine inclined to this opinion but refrained from asserting it with much vigor or conviction. O'Toole agrees with this analysis, adding that in his uncertainty Augustine reflected the ambivalence of both Latin and Greek fathers on the matter.[36]

It is clear that Augustine believed that the glory of the angels is in their spiritual powers and that because of these they can justify the claim that there is nothing better in creation. One other certainty is that they, like all other creatures, have at the foundation of their being a "formless matter" [in their case a "spiritual" formless matter] which is analogous to a wavering lightless existence needing to be confirmed and illuminated by a turning back to God in the person of the Word.[37]

In their case the move from "formlessness" to "being formed" has two aspects. The first is in the order of being as it moves from nothingness to formed existence. The second is in the order of knowledge and choice as it moves from "non-illuminated life" to an "illuminated life" through which it is able to see and choose its creator. Through the first movement angels achieve their existence as living beings; through the second they achieve existence as "happily living beings" now united to the infinite goodness that is their creator. It is their existential formlessness that makes them to be "changeable beings"; it is their moral formlessness [the ability to choose this or that] that gives them the possibility of being happy or unhappy. In both cases, "being" and "being happy" are dependent on God. In a sense both are movements *ex nihilo*. In coming to exist, the spiritual being is directly removed from nothingness. In coming to see and choose God under the illumination and support of divine grace, though the spiritual being is the proximate cause of the knowledge and choice, the ultimate cause is the creator who gave the creature a nature capable of knowing and choosing.

In the formation of angels there is no time sequence in their being created and their being illuminated. As pure intelligences, their turning back to the Word both confirms their existence and illuminates their mind so that they can know. The content of their knowledge is first and foremost knowledge of God. Here once again there is a mystery. All the angels were "illuminated" [since this went hand in hand with the beginning of their existence] but not all angels were moved by that illumination to choose God and thereby confirm their "happy existence" with God forever. Put simply, some rejected God and fell away. The initial illumination of the angels could not therefore have been the beatific vision. If they had had such face to face vision of God, they could not have fallen away. In the presence of the infinite good there is no alternative good to choose. Thus, even though all the angels were flooded with knowledge of the divine [Lucifer perhaps having the most] it was not so overpowering as to "force" them to choose God. The illumination of the angelic intelligence did not imply that all would receive the gift of love from the Holy Spirit which would move them to choose the good. Some did receive that grace and were saved; others did not and were lost. That it happened is clearly taught by sacred scripture. Why it happened remained another mystery for which Augustine has no adequate solution.[38]

After the "illumination of" and "choice by" the angels for or against God they became fixed in their destiny forever. Though by nature they remain mutable, they are no longer subject to time. For them there is no past or future, only the present timeless day.[39] However, since they continue to interact with the creation below them which is in time [for example, in their coming to know various things in themselves as these things come to be formed over time] they become participants in temporal affairs through their activity.[40]

The knowledge of those angels who are now eternally confirmed in union with God has four parts:

1. the direct vision of God;

2. indirect knowledge of all creation [including "self"] in its exemplar, the person of the Word;

3. direct knowledge of "self" as a being radically different from and subordinate to God;

4. direct knowledge of all other creatures "in themselves" as they become fully formed at the appropriate time throughout the course of history.[41]

It is this last sort of knowledge that Augustine sees symbolized in the various stages of creation. The "first day" spoken of in Genesis refers to the angels now fully formed, illuminated, and joined irrevocably to God. They now were able to see all of creation in its hierarchical order [arranged in "six days," if you will]. First, they saw all of creation in its exemplar, the nature of God in the Person of the Word. Then as individual parts of creation came into existence fully formed, the angels knew them in themselves now as individual creatures separate from the creator. Seeing creatures as they were in themselves, the brilliant "day" that was the angel did not remain focused on them but quickly turned back to the creator in an act of love. This progression in the angelic knowledge of creation is symbolized by the verses of Genesis recording the movement from an "evening" [knowing creatures in themselves] to a "morning" and "midday" [knowing creatures in God and as referred back to God].[42]

Corporeal Creation and the Rationes Seminales

As we have seen, Augustine believed that all of creation came into existence at the beginning of time through one instantaneous act. Part of creation existed fully formed from the first instant. This included the angels [the "first day"] and the firmament, the beginning of corporeal creation. Just as "spiritual formless matter" was the first element in the creation of the spiritual world, so too "material formless matter" established the foundation for the mutability of future fully formed corporeal beings.[43] Whether or not there was more to the corporeal world than bodies and material energy remained a matter of doubt for Augustine. He could find no coercive evidence one way or the other for a world-soul or for guiding spirits inhabiting the heavenly bodies. What was clear was that God was not the "soul" of the world nor could he be identified with any aspect of the world. He was however intimately involved in corporeal creation by his continuing support of its existence and activity.[44]

All creatures existed from the beginning but some only in *rationes seminales*, hidden and invisible "causes" of new species latent in the fabric of creation. It was from these primordial causes that later on crops first appeared on earth and the first human beings became fully formed. Once the first individuals in a new species appeared, they in turn began to produce others of their kind through their natural reproductive powers. They contained in themselves the "natural seeds" of all future generations.[45] The *rationes seminales*, the primordial seeds of things, are analogous to but quite different from the "natural seed" through which living things propagate others of their kind. The *rationes seminales* served to explain how different species of things appeared at different times.[46] They also helped to explain apparent inconsistencies in the creation story of Genesis. For example, the Genesis story has plants and herbs appearing on the third day while the sun is not formed until the fourth day. How can plants grow without sunlight? Furthermore Genesis (1:12) reports that:

> When day (that is, angels) was made, God made heaven and earth and every green thing of the field *before* (emphasis added) it appeared above the earth, and all the grass of the field *before* it sprang forth.

Augustine interpreted such texts to mean that the earth contained the *causes* which would produce the fully formed vegetative world at some future time determined by the providence of God. As he describes the process:

> From the very beginning God created in the earth, in what I might call the *roots of time*, all of those things which were to appear fully formed in the future.[47]

The Formation of the First Human Bodies

In seeking to explain when and how the first humans were formed, Augustine was influenced by the following factors:

1. his conviction that all of creation occurred simultaneously with the beginning of time. After that first moment there was no new creation.

2. the apparent contradiction between the descriptions of the creation of the first humans in Genesis. For example, Genesis 1:27 reads:

God created human beings in his image; in the divine image he created him; male and female he created them.

But in Genesis 2:7, which has to do with the formation of Adam, we learn that

. . . the Lord God formed a man out of the clay of the ground and blew into his nostrils the breath of life, and so man became a living being.

And in Genesis 2:22 which has to do with the formation of Eve, we read that:

The Lord God then built up into a woman the rib that he had taken from the man.

Augustine interpreted the first event [God creating humans in his image] as one that occurred at the very beginning of time. He interpreted the second event and third event [forming the bodies of the first humans] as happening sometime after the first moment of creation.[48] But how could this be? Were the first humans formed at the beginning of time or later on?

Augustine answered that in a way humans were made both in the beginning and sometime later. He explained this paradox by distinguishing between the creation of the souls of the first humans and the formation of their bodies. Human beings are the "image and likeness" of God primarily in their souls, and it was these rational souls that were created fully formed from the beginning of time. Their bodies were also created "in the beginning" but only in their causes. Under the direction of God [and most likely with his special intervention] the potentiality of matter to bring forth human bodies was actualized at a later moment in the history of creation, and at that time he had "breathed" into them their rational souls. At that moment the human species began to exist in a fully formed state.

The first humans existed in body from the beginning but only in their "primordial causes." There was no mature adult, or infant, or fetus, nor indeed the ordinary visible seeds [semen/ovum] through which future generations would be propagated. The bodies were "hidden" in their causes from the beginning much like plants are "hidden" in the tiny seeds which will produce them. When farmers sow a new crop of corn, the visible seeds they hold in their hands are quite unlike the mature growth that they will produce. The seeds store the future in a quite unlikely vessel. The difficulty in the analogy between seeds of corn and the seeds of the first human bodies is that the latter "seeds" were invisible entities hidden in the fabric of creation . . . what Augustine calls "primordial pods" [*involucris primordialibus*] that would develop into entirely new fully formed species.[49]

It seems that at least in the case of the formation of Eve's body a special divine intervention occurred. There are causes which are part of the very fabric of nature which determine what a thing can and cannot do. A grain of wheat does not produce corn and a pure animal cannot produce a member of the human species [or vice versa]. So too, despite the advances in the science of cloning, it is beyond the natural powers of a human rib to develop into a fully formed human being. And yet this is precisely what Genesis 2:22 reports happened in the formation of Eve. God "built up" from the rib of the man that woman who was to be his companion through life. Such extraordinary intervention in the processes of nature would not be unknown in the years that followed. The power of God reigns over all the natural processes of creation and that power will sometimes bring about effects which are quite unexpected but are yet consonant with those processes. That a barren woman should bring forth a child, that water be changed instantly into wine is not the expected effect of natural causes but it is not contrary to them. Augustine maintained that one such example of divine intervention occurred in the formation of the body of Eve from Adam's rib. Natural causes were not contradicted by such intervention; they were simply overridden.[50]

Augustine's view on the formation of the body of Adam is not as clear. O'Toole notes that there is some dispute about which of the following explanations was maintained by Augustine:

1. Adam's body was formed through the ordinary causation that occurs in nature as, for example, when water is converted into wine by being absorbed by the vine that will produce the grape which contains the elements of the wine;

2. Adam's body was formed through the blooming of "primordial causes" (*rationes seminales*) which had in them the potentiality to develop into the first human body at the appropriate time;

3. Adam's body was formed by a special divine intervention working with but supplementing and going beyond the ordinary causes contained in nature [perhaps somewhat analogous to a sculptor who works with a block of granite to form a statue].

An argument that Augustine opted for the third explanation can be made from his apparent conviction that Adam's body was formed as a mature adult, bypassing the normal stages of development through fetus, infant, child, adolescent, adult. Both ordinary and extraordinary processes were provided for in the "primordial causes" but the extraordinary could only be activated by God's special intervention. Though God implanted in creation firm laws for the production of beings, laws which rest on the specific "form" or "number" or "nature" of the being, his will is still supreme over all. Thus, although normally the making of wine from water is a natural process that takes some time, there is no reason why God cannot bring about the effect in an instant. So too, the "causal reasons" implanted in creation from the beginning will normally bring about the slow development of new fully formed beings, but this does not mean that God cannot speed up the process. God's spirit still moves over the world that was made by an exercise of his infinite power.[51]

The Formation of the First Human Souls

Augustine's attempt to explain the origin of the human soul was faced with the following questions:

1. How was the soul of Adam formed and how was it introduced into his body to make of him a human being?

2. How was the soul of Eve formed?

3. How were the souls of the generations that followed formed?

Augustine concluded that the most reasonable answer to the first question was that God created Adam's soul simultaneously with the rest of creation at the beginning of time. Thereafter, at the appropriate time, God "breathed" it into Adam's body. Both elements of the first human being were thus made "in the beginning": the body in its causes, the soul as fully formed.[52]

Augustine's conviction that "creation from the beginning" was the most reasonable explanation of the origin of the first human soul does not mean that he was not open to other solutions that were in accord with scripture and common sense. Indeed, he believed that the only *certain* facts about the soul were the following:

1. it comes from God but it is not part of the substance of God;

2. it is incorporeal;

3. it is not born of God's substance [as a child is born from the substance of its parents];

4. it does not "proceed" from God's substance [as the Word proceeds from the Father];

5. it is made by God;

6. it is not made from a body;

7. it is not made from an irrational soul;

8. it is made from nothing;

9. it is immortal in that it has a life it cannot lose;

10. it is mortal in the sense that it is changeable and can become better or worse;

11. since it is changeable, it [like the angels] has at its roots a "spiritual formless matter" which is the foundation of its mutability.[53]

Augustine believed that Genesis 2:7 ["God breathed into his face the breath of life"] records the moment when God inserted Adam's previously existing soul into his recently formed human body to make the first fully formed human being.[54] This new species of creature was unique in that it was both the image of God in its rational soul and a being of earth in that its body had been formed from the slime of the earth. As Augustine interprets it, the Genesis story . . .

. . . is meant to convey the message that when the first human was formed, he received a rational soul that was not produced from water and earth as were the souls of other animals, but rather was created by the "breath of God." The human was still made to live like the other animals in an animal body, but it was one which now had been vivified by a rational soul.[55]

One might very well ask: "Why would a previously existing rational soul [the very "image of God"] be mixed with a mortal body formed from earth-slime?" It cannot be that it was "forced" to be mixed in its lesser partner. Augustine argues that the union was willingly accepted by the soul and that this desire for the body was not surprising at all. In his opinion, it was just as natural for a human soul to want its body as it is for a human being to want its life.[56]

With respect to Eve's soul, Augustine saw no evidence in scripture that it came about in any way different from Adam's, that is, it was fully formed at the very first instant of creation and was "breathed into" her body when it was formed from the rib of Adam. Indeed, the very silence of scripture supports the "sameness" of the process. If her soul had come about in some radically different way, one might reasonably expect that something would have been said about it. As Augustine says:

> If God makes all the souls of human beings coming into this world as he made the first one, scripture was silent about the others because what is stated as having occurred in the first case could have been reasonably understood as applicable also to the others.[57]

For similar reasons he rejects the solution that Eve's soul was drawn out of or generated by the soul of Adam. If this had happened (he asks), why did not Adam say to her "this is now soul of my soul"? It certainly would have been a more tender description of his love than the earthy words that he did use: "This is the bone of my bone and the flesh of my flesh."[58]

The Equality of Man and Woman

Adam was the first man; Eve was the first woman. Were they equal? Their souls were both fully formed at the beginning of time by the direct divine creative action *ex nihilo*. Their bodies also were created then but only in their causes. Sometime later, with the special intervention of God, the body of the male was formed from the "slime" of the earth and subsequently the body of the female was formed from the rib of the male. Does this process of formation suggest equality or subordination? Is there any justification for saying that one or the other is a lower order of being?

Augustine was convinced that both men and women are equally the "images of God" and that in both of them the perfection of this image is found in their souls more than in their bodies.[59] Both had souls which had been "breathed into them" by God, souls which were not made from "earth and water" as were the souls of the rest of the animal kingdom.[60] It could be said of the souls of both that "God alone is better, only the angel is equal, and everything else less."[61] In Eve and Adam, the soul was the vehicle through which their body received the form, order, and proportion of parts which made it also a reflection [but less brilliant] of God himself.[62] With respect to their rational souls, then, Augustine clearly believed that there was no basis for saying that one sex is inferior to the other either in the order of being or in the eyes of God.

However, when he comes to discuss the relationship between man and woman in the family, Augustine agrees with the common belief of the day that there is a quasi-natural subordination of wife to husband. He

defends such subordination somewhat laboriously by pointing out that
there are two sorts of wisdom in the world: speculative and practical. It is
speculative wisdom which enables a person to get a broad picture of reality, to see what is important and unimportant in the light of eternity, to
understand what needs to be done in order to achieve a life worthy of a
happy eternity. Practical wisdom, on the other hand, is not so much concerned about the future in some ideal world as it is in getting through the
troublesome "todays" of this world. Obviously both sorts of wisdom are
necessary for a person to live a somewhat balanced life. We need not only
ontology; we also need some common sense. Augustine interpreted the
scripture story of the two sisters, the practical Martha and the contempla-
tive Mary, as confirming the point that while both sorts of wisdom are
good, the speculative wisdom of Mary is more valuable since it will last
into eternity. No skills in "getting through the day" will be required in
heaven. The only activity there will be the joyful contemplation of God.[63]

Augustine recognized that practical and speculative wisdom can be
found in both men and women. Indeed, he demonstrated this truth in his
own life, spending most of his own days involved in practical concerns
while corresponding with a number of noble women who led contempla-
tive lives and who wrote to him knowingly about intensely abstruse issues. He still believed, however, that generally speaking women were
more gifted in practical wisdom and men more gifted in speculative wisdom. Since the latter is a higher order of wisdom, there is thus some justification for the view that it is appropriate for the husband to have the
final say in family matters when consensus is impossible.[64]

He is at pains to add that such subordination in society does not imply any special priority of male over female [or vice versa] in things that
really matter. Both are equally images and children of God. Both have
equal access to grace in this life. Both have an equal chance at happiness
in the next.[65] Neither woman nor man is stronger in "soul-power." Indeed, Augustine may even have recognized the fallacy of saying that the
male is more powerful in any sense. He points out that in the formation
of the first woman, she *gained* strength and he *lost* strength:

> . . . through him she became stronger, being strengthened by his bone,
> but he became weaker for the sake of her because only flesh was sub-
> stituted for his lost rib.[66]

Augustine would likely agree that the story was meant to teach
something about the ideal relationship between the sexes. Man and
woman are meant to be joined in a friendly compact whereby each is

strengthened by the other and each shares [or puts up with] the other's weakness.

The Origins of Later Generations

It seems clear that Augustine believed that the souls of the first man and woman were created fully formed at the beginning of time and were breathed into their bodies sometime later on. He rejected the theory that the soul of Adam was generated from the substance of God or from some pre-existing spiritual creature. He also rejected the view that Eve's soul was drawn out of the soul of Adam much as the bodies of future generations would be generated from the bodies of their parents. He was less certain about the origin of the souls of these future generations.

In his work *On the Freedom of the Will*, completed sometime before 395, he lists four possible explanations:

1. the souls are generated by the souls of their parents (traducianism);

2. they are created at the moment when they are "breathed into" the body;

3. they were created at the beginning of time and sent by God into the body of the individual at the appropriate time;

4. they were created at the beginning of time and freely chose to enter the body at the appropriate time.[67]

In a later work (*A Literal Commentary on Genesis*) completed in 415, he reduces the possible explanations to three:

1. all souls were created in the beginning in a "soul-making cause" [*generalis omnium animarum ratio*] analogous to the "body-making cause" contained in the procreative powers of the first humans;

2. all souls come from the soul of the first human being (traducianism);

3. individual souls are created directly by God at the moment of their infusion into the body.

All of the explanations on this final list posed problems for Augustine. The third option, *creation in time*, came into conflict with Augustine's conviction that nothing new was created after the first instant of creation. The first option, *creation at the beginning "in causa,"* gets around this objection by admitting that indeed all souls were created in the beginning but only in their causes. However this raises a new difficulty. Since the only creatures [excepting the souls of Adam and Eve] that existed fully formed from the beginning were the angels and the firmament, one holding that future souls were created "in their causes" would be forced to say that these future souls were either "children of angels" or [worse still] "children of the corporeal heavens." Such assertions seem improbable at best and impossible at worst.[68]

The second option, *traducianism*, encounters two difficulties. The first is similar to the objection brought up against the theory that Eve's soul came from the soul of Adam: namely, there is simply no mention of such an extraordinary event in the Genesis story, not even in Genesis 4:1ff which recounts the birth of the first children of Adam and Eve [Cain, Abel, and Seth]. The second problem is that it is difficult to conceive of such a process without falling into the error of believing that the soul is somehow material. How can one explain that a purely spiritual substance, one which by definition is simple and without parts, can give of itself to generate another purely spiritual, simple substance.[69]

It is somewhat interesting that the list of possible solutions from the *Commentary on Genesis* does not include the third solution [*creation fully formed at the beginning of time*] from Augustine's earlier listing in *On the Freedom of the Will*. It is especially puzzling since Augustine certainly maintains that this is precisely the way Adam's soul was formed and at least leans toward the opinion that the same process explains the origin of Eve's soul. Furthermore, in his discussion of Eve's soul he seems to extend the "silence of scripture" argument to include *all* souls that come into existence thereafter.[70] Of course, all "separate creation theories" [each individual's soul is created *ex nihilo*] share the common difficulty of offering no explanation for the transmission of original sin from Adam/Eve to later generations. If all human beings are separated in the formation of the rational soul [the source of sin and virtuous action] how is it that all of us are infected by the sin of the first humans? How can one explain a soul's being born in sin if the only one who had a hand in its making was the sinless God? There was an additional problem for Augustine in the theory that souls of future generations were created at that specific moment when the person began to exist. This contradicted what he considered to be the clear teaching of scripture that "in the beginning" God created and thereafter rested.

Augustine spent most of his life pondering the advantages and disadvantages of the competing solutions only to conclude that:

> I have not dared to make a firm decision for one or the other because I simply do not know which is the correct answer. . . . None are condemned by faith and none is imposed for certain by reason.[71]

The question of the origin of the human soul thus ended for him in a string of possibilities, but he did not seem to be too upset at this. He always felt that it was more important to know where he was going and how to avoid obstacles on the way than to know where he came from. As he said at the very beginning of his search for answers on the origin of the soul:

> The person who sails from Rome and then forgets from what shore he sailed is not in danger as long as he knows how to steer the correct course from where he is.[72]

This truth is especially important for one making a pilgrimage through this life. No one needs to worry about where his journey began as long as he knows where it is supposed to end. This is so because the place of beginning and ending is the same: namely, the heavenly city that is the land of God.

Notes

1. *DCD*, 10.13, PL 41, 291.

2. *ENN 41*, 6, PL 36, 467. In other places he admits that this process is difficult. We see creation but God speaks the "truth" about it deep within our being and often we cannot "see" that truth because our mind is clouded. See *DCD*, 11.2, PL 41, 317-18.

3. See *DCD*, 11.22, PL 41, 335-36.

4. Augustine has lengthy examinations of the story of creation in the following works: *C*, 11-13, PL 32, 659-868. *DGM*, PL 34, 173-220. *DGI* PL 35, 219-46. *DGL*, PL 34, 245-486. *DCD*, 11-14, PL 41, 315-436.

5. Thus, at the end of his life he makes the following comment on his *De Genesi ad litteram*: "In this work I have asked more questions than I have solved and, for those I have claimed to solve, most have not been answered in any conclusive way. Moreover some solutions have been proposed in a way that demands further investigation." *RET*, 2.24.1, PL 32, 640.

6. See *C*, 12.18.27, PL 32, 835-36; *DCD*, 12.19, PL 41, 368-69.

7. *C*, 11.4.6, PL 32, 835-36. See *DCD*, 11.4.2, PL 41, 319; *ENN 26*, PL 36, 205-06.

8. *C*, 11.7.9, PL 32, 812-13.

9. *CPO*, 1.3, PL 42, 671. On the history of the concept "creation *ex nihilo*," See Tarsicius Van Bavel, O.S.A., "The Creator and the Integrity of Creation in the Fathers of the Church especially in Saint Augustine," *Augustinian Studies*, 21 (1990), pp. 4-8. See also William A. Christian, "The Creation of the World," *A Companion to the Study of St. Augustine*, Roy Battenhouse (ed.) (New York: Oxford University Press, 1955), pp. 315-43.

10. *C*, 11.5.7, PL 32, 811-12; *DT*, 3.7-9, PL 42, 875-79; *DCD* 12, 24-26, PL 41, 373-76.

11. *DCD*, 12.25, PL 41, 374.

12. See *DGI*, 3.3.8, PL 34, 223; *DGL*, 8.23.44, PL 34, 389. Augustine maintains that the fact that the universe must have had a beginning can be demonstrated by reason. Aquinas later took an opposite view arguing that, granted that creation cannot have the quality of "being eternal" [which implies immutability], there is no coercive reason for saying that God could not have created and maintained creatures in time forever. See *Summa theologica*, I, q. 46, a. 2. See Portalié, *A Guide to the Thought of Saint Augustine* (Chicago: Henry Regnery, 1960), p. 136.

13. *DCD*, 11.21, PL 41, 334-35. See *DGM*, 1.3.4, PL 34, 175; *DDQ*, 1.28, PL 40, 18; *DGL*, 4.16.27, PL 34, 306-07. Augustine writes: "Whatever was created, God made not by any necessity nor by any need for his own use but by reason of his goodness alone." (*DCD*, 11.24, PL 41, 338). "Because God is good, we are!" (*DDC*, 1.1.32, PL 34, 32). "God does not create things the way humans build houses because they need shelter or make clothes because they need protection from the elements or raise crops because they need food. God made the universe not because he needed it, but because he wanted it" (*ENN 134,* 10, PL 37, 1745). See Christopher J. O'Toole, *The Philosophy of Creation in the Writings of St. Augustine* (Washington, D.C.: Catholic University of America Press, 1944), p. 4.

14. Augustine's conviction that the act of creation was instantaneous and never repeated was partially based on the description in Genesis (2:2) which states that after creation God "rested." He read this as meaning that now and from time immemorial we have existed in this period of God's "resting" where the changes in the world, especially the appearance of new species, is to be explained as the development of those primordial causes created "in the beginning" and inserted into the fabric of reality (See *DGL*, 4.33, PL 34, 318). Taylor notes that Augustine's conviction that creation was a unique act was also supported by his interpretation of a verse (18:1) from the book of Ecclesiasticus (Sirach). John Hammond Taylor, S.J. (trans.), *St. Augustine: The Literal Meaning of Genesis*, Ancient Christian Writers, vol. 41 (New York: Newman Press, 1982), p. 253, n. 67. See *DGL*, 6.6.11 (PL 34, 343), where Augustine uses the text to argue that the first human beings were created in the beginning but reached full development sometime later on.

15. *DGL*, 4.24.41, PL 34, 313.

16. See *C*, 13.2-3, PL 32, 845-46; *DGL*, 1.4.9, PL 34, 249; 1.5.10, PL 34, 249-50; 1.1.2, PL 34, 247.

17. *C*, 12.6.6, PL 32, 828; *DCD*, 12.5-6, PL 41, 352-53; *DNB*, 18, PL 42, 556-57; *DGM*, 1.5.9, PL 34, 177-78; *DFS*, 2, PL 40, 182. O'Toole comments that Augustine's "formless matter" is closer to the Greek concept of "chaos" than it is to the "prime matter" of Aristotle and St. Thomas. He admits, however, that it is

still a disputed conclusion among scholars. Christopher J. O'Toole, *op. cit.,* pp. 17 & 27. See W.J. Roche, "Measure, Number, Weight in Saint Augustine," *New Scholasticism*, 15 (1941), p. 359.

18. *DGL*, 1.15.29, PL 34, 257; 2.11.24, PL 34, 272. See *C*, 12.29, PL 32, 836-37; 13.33.48, PL 32, 866; *DGM*, 1.6.10, PL 34, 178; *CLP*, 1.9.12, PL 42, 610.

19. See *DGL*, 1.14.28, PL 34, 256. Augustine sees veiled references to "form-less matter" in various verses of the Genesis narrative. It is suggested in the phrase "heaven and earth" because it has the potentiality for being these. It is called "earth invisible and without order" and "darkness over the abyss" because it is formless and has no beauty that can be seen or touched. It is called "water" because it lies submissive and workable before the divine workman so that all things might be formed out of it. See *DGM*, 1.7.11-12, PL 34, 178-79; *DGL*, 1.1.3, PL 34, 247. On the concept of "spiritual" formless matter in Augustine, See Stanislaus J. Grabowski, *The All-Present God* (St. Louis: B. Herder, 1954), pp. 88-91.

20. *DVR*, 7.13, PL 34, 129. Rowan Williams makes the point that God is radically different from creation because creation is mutable. At the same time God is intimately involved in creation in that it becomes a coherent system be-cause of God's bringing each species and individual into existence with a specific way of being (measure), a formal structure (form) and a finality (order, number, weight) which draws each created being toward its own special state of equilib-rium or peace. See Rowan D. Williams, "Good for Nothing?': Augustine on Creation," *Augustinian Studies*, 25 (1994), pp. 11ff.

21. See *DGL*, 5.12.28, PL 34, 331. Augustine expresses this concept of crea-tion existing from all eternity in its exemplar in various texts. For example, "In God is to be found the archetypical species of all things, the absolute form of all, or the form of forms [*omnium speciossima species]"* (*DFS*, 2, PL 40, 182). "The Wisdom of God [that is, the Word], through which all things were created, knew them before they were made. The divine archetypes, unchangeable and eternal, are attested by scripture saying 'In the beginning was the Word . . .'" (Jn 1:1) (*DGL*, 5.13.29, PL 34, 331. See *DGL*, 2.6.12, PL 34, 267-68; 5.14.31, PL 34, 332; 5.15.33, PL 34, 332-33; *DDQ*, 46, PL 40, 29-31).

22. *DGL*, 4.18.34, PL 34, 309. In another place Augustine describes the three elements in the move from "formlessness" to "form" in the following words: "All created things that have been made by the divine skill show a certain unity and form and order. Each of them is *one specific thing*, as in the individualized natures of bodies and the special powers of souls. Each has its own *particular form* which [for example,] establishes the qualities of bodies and serves as the foundation for

the soul's scientific and artistic knowledge. Finally, each created being either pre-
serves or seeks an *order* special to itself, as [for example,] in the various weights
and structures of bodies and the various loves and delights of the spirit" (*DT*,
6.10.12, PL 42, 932).

23. See *DGL*, 4.3.7, PL 34, 299; 4.5.12, PL 34, 300-01. For a discussion of
the meaning of measure, number, and weight, See Roche, *op. cit.*, pp. 350-76, and
Taylor, *op. cit.*, notes 8-10, pp. 248-49.

24. *DT*, 6.10.12, PL 42, 932.

25. *DNB*, 3-4, PL 42, 553. There is no doubt that Augustine considered creation to be good. Indeed, its very goodness and beauty is a source of the temptation
in wounded human beings to love it too much. But this does not make it evil. As
Augustine says [speaking about corporeal creation]: "Every bodily creature is a
good thing [even though of the lowest order] and is beautiful in its own way. It
has an ordered unity that comes from its own specific form. If it is loved inordi-
nately by a soul who neglects God, even this does not make it evil in itself" (See
DVR, 20.40, PL 34, 138-39; *DCD*, 11.22, PL 41, 335-36; *C*, 7.15, PL 32, 744; 2.5,
PL 32, 679-80; *ENN 26/2*, 12, PL 36, 205-06). Of course Augustine recognized
that the world can be the source of both pleasant and disturbing events. He lists
the "good and bad" in three interesting chapters in the *City of God* (22.22-24, PL
41, 784-92). But all things considered, his attitude towards this world is perhaps
best summarized in his brief statement: "The world is a smiling place" (*Sermon
158*, 7.7, PL 38, 866. See Van Bavel, *op. cit.*, pp. 8-10).

26. *DGL*, 1.4.9, PL 34, 249. In another place Augustine writes: "All the good
things in creation would have remained in your Word [as their exemplar] but
would have stayed formless if that same Word had not recalled them to its unity
[with Father and Spirit] and given to them their form and being" (*C*, 13.2, PL 32,
845). See O'Toole, *op. cit.*, p. 22.

27. *DGL*, 4.18.34, PL 34, 309.

28. *DGL*, 1.18.36, PL 34, 260.

29. *C*, 11.12-13, PL 32, 815. See *DGL*, 5.5.12, PL 34, 325-26; 5.17.35, PL
34, 333-34.

30. *C*, 11.27.36, PL 32, 823-24. Augustine explains the difference between
time and eternity as follows: "Time does not exist without change or movement.
In eternity there is no change. It follows that there can be no time unless a creature
is made whose movement would cause some change" (*DCD*, 11.6, PL 41, 321-
22). In a letter to Proba Augustine says of the eternity of heaven: "There the days
do not come and go in succession and the beginning of one day does not mean the
end of another. All days are one simultaneously and without end and the life lived
out in these days has itself no end" (*E 130*, 8:15-17, PL 33, 499-501; 9.18, PL 33,

501). The following are helpful commentaries on Augustine's discussion of time: John M. Quinn, O.S.A., "The Concept of Time in St. Augustine," *Augustinianum*, vol. 5 (1965), pp. 5-57. John M. Quinn, O.S.A., "Four Faces of Time in St. Augustine," *Recherches Augustiniennes*, vol. 26 (1992), pp. 181-231. Gerard O'Daly, *Augustine's Philosophy of Mind* (Los Angeles, CA: University of California Press, 1987), pp. 152-161. Roland Teske, "The World-Soul and Time in St. Augustine," *Augustinian Studies*, 14 (1983), pp. 75-92. Donald Ross, "Time, the Heaven of Heavens, and Memory in Augustine's Confessions," *Augustinian Studies*, 22 (1991), pp. 191-206.

31. *C*, 11.14.17, PL 32, 815-16.

32. *C*, 11.15.18, PL 32, 816.

33. *C*, 11.21.27, PL 32, 819-20.

34. *C*, 11.29.39, PL 32, 825.

35. Augustine believed that the words recorded at the very beginning of Genesis (1:1-3) refer to the creation and illumination of the angels: "In the beginning . . . God created the heavens and the earth. . . . Then God said: 'Let there be light and there was light'." *DGL*, 1.9.15, PL 34, 251-52; 2.8.16-19, PL 34, 269-70.

36. Taylor, *op. cit.*, pp. 238-39. O'Toole *op. cit.*, pp. 44ff.

37. Speaking of the formation of angels, Augustine writes: "This was the intellectual light that [now] participates in the eternal and changeless Wisdom of God. First that light was created [that is, unformed spiritual matter] in which there was produced a knowledge of the divine Word by whom it was created and this knowledge consisted precisely in this creature's turning from its unformed state to the God who formed it and its [thereby] being created and formed." *DGL*, 3.20.31, PL 34, 292. See *DGL*, 1.1.2, PL 34, 247; 1.4.9, PL 34, 249; 1.5.10, PL 34, 249-50; *C*, 13.2-3.3-4, PL 32, 845-46.

38. On the fall of the angels See *DCG*, 10.27, PL 44, 932-33; *DCD*, 11.9-13, PL 41, 323-30; *DGL*, 11.23.30, PL 34, 441; 11.26.33, PL 34, 443.

39. *C*, 12.11.12, PL 32, 833.

40. See O'Toole, *op. cit.,* 41-44.

41. *DGL*, 4.32.50, PL 34, 317. See *DGL*, 4.24.41, PL 34, 313.

42. *DGL* 5.5.15, PL 34, 326. For an extensive description of the process See *DGL*, 4.31.48, PL 34, 316. Obviously there was a time sequence in the angelic knowledge of creatures as they existed fully formed since one cannot know an object that does not exist and most "fully formed" creatures began to exist only after a passage of some time. See *DGL*, 4.32.49, PL 34, 316; 4.21-24.38-41, PL 34, 311-13; 5.18.36, PL 34, 334.

43. *DGL*, 6.1.2, PL 34, 339. See *DGL*, 5.5.14, PL 34, 326. O'Toole notes [pp. 63-69] that Augustine followed the science of his day in believing that there were four basic elements in the physical universe: earth, air, water, and fire.

44. Augustine's conclusions on the possibility of a world-soul can be found in *RET*, 1.5.3, PL 32, 591; 1.11.4, PL 32, 602. Other texts on the matter include: *DIA*, 15.24, PL 32, 1033; *DMU* 6.14.43, PL 32, 1033; *DCE*, 1.23.35, PL 34, 1058. On the question of whether spirits guide the heavenly bodies, See *DGL*, 2.18, PL 34, 279; *ENC*, 15.58, PL 40, 259-60. On the continuing presence of the spirit of God intimately involved in the operations of the universe, See *DGI*, 4.17, PL 34, 226. For further discussion See O'Toole, *op. cit.*, 58-63; Etienne Gilson, *The Christian Philosophy of Saint Augustine* (New York: Random House, 1960), p. 209. Roland Teske, "The World-Soul . . .," *op. cit.*, pp. 76-80

45. See *DGL*, 6.10.17, PL 34, 346. Augustine remarks that creation is both already perfected and is yet just beginning. It is already perfected in that nothing will exist in its fully formed state that was not present from the beginning in its causes. It is just beginning because in its primordial causal state it contains the seeds of future fully formed perfections that will appear in their own due time (*DGL*, 6.11.18, PL 34, 346-47). See O'Toole, *op. cit.*, p. 50.

46. McKeough notes that for Augustine the *rationes seminales* were not principles of evolution [explaining how one species evolves into another]. Rather they are principles of stability explaining how each species was preserved in its identity from the very beginning until the time came for it to appear fully formed. Michael McKeough, *The Meaning of the Rationes Seminales in St. Augustine* (Washington, D.C.: Catholic University of America Press, 1926), p. 70. On page 71 he lists numerous texts where Augustine discusses the *rationes seminales*. See C. Boyer, "La théorie Augustinienne des raisons séminales," *Miscellanea Agostiniana*, II (Rome: 1931), pp. 795-819.

47. *DGL*, 5.4.11, PL 34, 325.

48. *DGL*, 6.1, PL 34, 339-40.

49. *DGL* 6.6.9-11, PL 34, 342-43. See *DGL*, 6.5.7, PL 34, 341-42.

50. *DGL*, 9.17-18.31-35, PL 34, 405-07. On the formation of Eve's body, Augustine writes: "The substance (nature) of the woman was not created by the activity of any creature already existing (for example, angels), although it was made from the substance of man (Adam) who was already existing. . . . To form or build a rib of a man into a woman could only have been done by God (*DGL*, 9.15.26, PL 34, 403-04).

51. See *DGL*, 6.13-14.23-24, PL 34, 348-49. See O'Toole, *op. cit.*, p. 86. See Eugène Portalié, *op. cit.*, pp. 139-41.

52. For a discussion of Augustine's position in his earlier commentaries on Genesis, See Roland Teske, S.J. (trans.), *St. Augustine on Genesis*, Fathers of the Church Series vol. 84 (Washington, D.C.: The Catholic University of America Press, 1991). See also Teske, "St. Augustine's View of the Original Human Condition in *De Genesi contra Manichaeos*," *Augustinian Studies*, 22 (1991), pp. 141-55; Robert J. O'Connell, "The 'De Genesi contra Manichaeos' and the Origin of the Soul," *Revue des Études Augustiniennes*, 39 (1993), pp. 129-41. In his later *Literal Commentary on Genesis*, Augustine phrases his conclusion on the soul of Adam in the following way: ". . . his soul in its *own proper being* was already created with the making of the first day. Once created it lay hidden in the works of God until the proper time came when God 'breathed it' into the body formed from the slime of the earth" (*DGL*, 7.24.35, PL 34, 368-69). It seems clear that the phrase "its own proper being" means that the soul was created in the beginning fully formed specifically as the soul of Adam rather than in spiritual seminal reasons which would eventually bloom into the soul of Adam. Much less does it mean that the soul was created in some sort of corporeal matter or spiritual being (for example, angels) that would eventually produce the soul as human parents produce the bodies of their children. For an extended analysis of Augustine's thinking on the origin of the soul See Robert J. O'Connell, S.J., *St. Augustine's Early Theory of Man, AD 386-391, (Cambridge: The Belknap Press of Harvard University Press, 1968); St. Augustine's Confessions: The Odyssey of Soul* (Cambridge: The Belknap Press of Harvard University Press, 1969); *The Origin of the Soul in St. Augustine's Later Works* (New York: Fordham University Press, 1987). The latter work contains an extensive bibliography of recent studies on the question.

53. *DGL*, 7.27.39, PL 34, 369-70. See *DGL*, 7.28.43, PL 34, 372.

54. *DGL*, 7.1.2, PL 34, 356.

55. *DCD*, 13.24.4, PL 41, 401.

56. *DGL*, 7.27.38, PL 34, 369.

57. *DGL*, 10.1.2, PL 34, 409.

58. In the same place Augustine summarizes his final position on the origin of Eve's soul in the following words: "Since it (the Genesis story) does not say that the soul of the woman was made from the soul of the man, it is reasonable to assume that the writer wished to instruct us not to suppose that the origin of her soul was in any way different from what we knew from scripture about the origin of Adam's soul: that is, that the woman received her soul in a similar fashion [*similiter datam esse mulieri*]" (*DGL*, 10.1.2, PL 34, 409). Augustine goes on to say that the explanation for Eve's soul is not obvious or certain, but still it remains for him [in his words] a "reasonable assumption."

59. *DGL*, 3.22.34, PL 34, 294. See *DT*, 12.7.12, PL 42, 1005. See also Richard J. McGowan, "Augustine's Spiritual Equality: The Allegory of Man and Woman with Regard to *Imago Dei*, " *Revue des Études Augustiniennes*, 33 (1987), pp. 259-60. Other helpful discussions on Augustine's view on man-woman relationships include the following: W. M. Alexander, "Sex and Philosophy in St. Augustine," *Augustinian Studies*, vol. 5, 1974. Gerald Bonner, "Augustine's Attitude to Women and 'Amicitia,'" *Homo Spiritalis: Festgabe für Luc Verheijen OSA*, Cornelius Mayer (ed.) (Würzburg: Augustinus-Verlag, 1987), pp. 259-75. Kari Elisabeth Borresen, *The Nature and Role of Woman in Augustine and Thomas Aquinas* (Lanham, Md, University Press of America: 1961); "Patristic Feminism: The Case of Augustine," *Augustinian Studies*, 25, (1994), pp. 139-52. Peter Brown, *The Body and Society: Men, Women and Sexual Renunciation in Early Christianity* (New York: Columbia University Press, 1988). Elizabeth A. Clark, "'Adam's Only Companion': Augustine and the Early Christian Debate on Marriage," *Recherches Augustiniennes* XXI (1986), pp. 139-62. David G. Hunter, "Augustinian Pessimism? A New Look at Augustine's Teaching on Sex, Marriage and Celibacy," *Augustinian Studies*, 25, 1994, pp. 153-77. R. J. O'Connell, "Sexuality in Saint Augustine," *Augustine Today*, ed. Richard John Neuhaus (Grand Rapids, Mich.: William B. Eerdmans, 1993), pp. 60-87. Tarsicius J. Van Bavel, O.S.A., "Augustine's View on Women," *Augustiniana*, vol. 39 (1989) Fasc. 1-2, pp. 6-53. F. Ellen Weaver and Jean Laporte, "Augustine and Women: Relationships and Teachings," *Augustinian Studies*, vol. 12, 1981.

60. *DCD*, 13.24.4, PL 41, 401.

61. *DQA*, 13.22, PL 32, 1048.

62. *DIA*, 15.24, PL 32, 1033.

63. Lk 10:42. See *SER 103*, 1-6, PL 38, 613-15. I have argued that the concept of "subordination" in Augustine was rooted in a relationship of friendship whereby the "superior" was in fact a servant of those governed. See Donald X. Burt, "Friendship and Subordination in Earthly Societies," *Augustinian Studies*, vol. 22 (1991), pp. 83-125.

64. *C*, 13.32.47, PL 32, 866. See *QH*, 1.153, PL 34, 590. Perhaps Augustine's views on the female gift for the practical was reinforced by his own experience. Both his mother and his wife seem to have been very practical women, the latter seeing to her household and her son while he wrestled with the problem of evil in the universe. Bonner (*op. cit.*, pp. 263-65) notes that Augustine was far from denying speculative wisdom to women nor asserting that all men had it. Thus, he will speak highly of his mother's gift for philosophical debate (for example, in *DO*, 1.11.31, PL 32 993-94 and in *DB*, 2.10, PL 32 964-65). Furthermore his later

letters indicate that he had many conversations with dedicated and intelligent women on ultimate questions. On the other hand, his often harsh language toward opponents in theological controversies (all of whom were male) suggests that he recognized that being a man was no protection from being a fool.

65. Some texts which bring out the essential equality of the sexes include the following. On being equally images of God: *CFM,* 24.2.2, PL 42, 476; *DAC,* 11.12, PL 40, 297-98; On being equally children of God: *ENN 26/2,* 23, PL 34, 211; *DSM,* 1.15.40, PL 34, 1249-50; *EEG,* 27-28, PL 35, 2124-25. On being equally able to receive the grace of God: See *DBC,* 12.14, PL 40, 383; *SER 51,* 13.21, PL 38, 344-45; *DGL,* 3.22.34, PL 34, 293-94.

66. *DGL,* 9.18.34, PL 34, 407.

67. *DLA,* 3.21.19, PL 32, 1299-1300.

68. *DGL,* 10.3.4, PL 34, 410. In a letter to St. Jerome written in 415, Augustine lists the four options of *De libero arbitrio* and humbly asks Jerome for instruction as to the best one. He then goes on to gently suggest to Jerome that the text he uses (John 5:17, "My Father works even until now") does not necessarily demand creation of souls through time. It can in fact be accommodated to the Genesis story [which Augustine believed clearly taught one act of creation after which God rested] in the following way . . . that individual souls were "formed" later on in time from "something" that had existed from the beginning. He then goes on to ask Jerome how he explains the transmission of original sin if all souls [except Eve's] were created sometime after the beginning of time. *E 166,* 3-5.7-12, PL 33, 723-26.

69. *DGL,* 10.24.40, PL 34, 409.

70. Thus, he writes: "If God makes all the souls of humans who will exist as he made the first one [*omnes animas hominum nascentium sicut primam*], scripture understandably will say nothing about the others because it can be reasonably assumed that what was said of the first one (Adam) applies also to all the rest" (*DGL,* 10.1.2, PL 34, 409).

71. *DA* 4.2.2., PL 44, 524. See *DA,* 4.11.15-16, PL 44, 532-34. Looking back over thiry years of thinking about the matter, he writes "I did not know then and I still do not know the true answer" (*RET,* 1.1.3, PL 32, 587). Finally, just a few months before he died, he confessed to his last opponent in controversy, Julian, that he was still not sure how it comes to be [as it certainly does] that the whole human race is one in Adam's sin, that is, whether we are joined simply through the body or also through the soul (*OIJ,* 2.178, PL 45, 1219). O'Toole is of the opinion that Augustine was inclined toward traducianism with all its problems because [1] it fitted in with his conviction that every being that would exist was created in some way at the beginning of time and [2] it gave an understandable

solution to the transmission of original sin, a blemish more of the soul than of the body (O'Toole, *op. cit.*, p. 93). Fr. O'Connell agrees that in the end Augustine "leaned toward" traducianism but was repulsed by its materialistic interpretation common to his day. He was also comfortable with the interpretation of creationism which argued that indeed God created all *genera* of things simultaneously on the first day but that he continues to create "individual instances of those *genera* even now" (for example, souls of later generations). This explained how it is said that "God rested" after the initial creative act and yet is also said "to work even till now." It of course did little if anything to solve the mystery of the transmission of original sin. See O'Connell, *Origin . . . Later Works*, pp. 240-41. On the creation of all *genera* from the beginning, See Grabowski, *op. cit.*, p. 144. Texts in Augustine relevant to this issue include the following: *E 205*, 3.17, PL 33, 948; *DGL*, 4.12.22-23, PL 34, 304-05.

72. *DLA*, 3.21.61, PL 32, 1301-02.

Chapter 10

The Existence and Nature of God

Introduction

At the very beginning of his philosophical writings, Augustine remarked that there are only two central questions for a philosopher examining the real world. The first has to do with the human soul; the second has to do with God. The first is an examination of self; the second helps us to know the context of our existence. Knowing self we become capable of a happy life; knowing God we become happy. The study of one's self is open even to beginners; the study of God is reserved for the well-instructed and the well-intentioned. In knowing self and God, a person is able to grasp the true order of reality, not only the order contained in this world of created things, but more importantly how this world is ordered to its creator.[1]

Up to this point, our examination of "Augustine's World" has concentrated on ourselves . . . what we are, what we can do, where we came from, where we are going. The time has now come to speak about what Augustine considered to be (and what is) the most important element in the real world . . . that being whom humans call "God." Of course God's importance can be argued on a purely philosophical level (the most perfect "being" must necessarily be the most important too), but for Augustine the importance of God was primarily pragmatic and personal. Augustine (like the rest of the human race) wanted to be happy but seemed doomed to live an imperfect life in a world that was withering away. In such a world God was for him the only foundation for the hope that someday and somewhere he would find perfect happiness.

There is much truth in Dittes' insight that Augustine's whole life can be summed up as a search for a "fail-safe" God.[2] He desired much more than simply some power greater than himself. From his earliest years he experienced enough of such powers, forces that seemed "bigger and stronger" than anything he could control. In his adolescence and youth he was driven by his own passions. In his Manichaean days he seemed to be moved this way and that by an evil god within. In both cases uncontrollable and uncaring forces dominated his days, and he longed for something more than such indifferent gods. What he needed and wanted was a God who was both infinitely perfect and infinitely loving, a God who was far above and separate from this tarnished world but who was yet deeply concerned and deeply involved in every aspect of this life. Augustine wanted a supreme being who was yet lovable, a God who respected individual humans while providentially caring for them. He wanted a God who was both omnipotent and loving, fair and forgiving, transcendent and immanent, awesome but not frightening. He wanted a God whom he could trust from afar and embrace happily at the end of time. After thirty years of searching, he found this God in the God of Christianity. Thereafter he spent his life trying to understand that God and to discover the presence of that God in the world of his experience. The following pages will examine some of his conclusions on these important matters.

The Search for God: The Process

Augustine's various discussions of the ways in which a person can come to know God rested on his assumption that no one can be completely ignorant of the existence of God, at least in the sense of a really existing being who is superior to humans. He believed that such a "barebones" God could not be hidden from humans once they began to use their reason. Indeed, he went so far as to say that (apart from a few "perverted" people) the whole human race of his day recognized a God who is the author of the world. In Augustine's opinion atheism was a moral problem, not an intellectual one. The question of belief was not about whether one accepted the existence of God; it was about what sort of God one accepted. Was it the Jupiter of the pagan religions? Was it the Manichaean principle of "the good"? Was it the Yahweh of the Old Testament? Or was it the God who Christianity maintained had been incarnated in the person of Jesus Christ?[3]

Augustine recognized three ways of coming to know the existence and nature of God:

1. by direct vision (mystical experience);

2. by faith (belief in the testimony of others);

3. by reason (argument from perceived facts about the universe).

The order of this listing reflects an increasing universality. Although theoretically every human has the possibility of a mystical experience, in fact few have it and those who do have it achieve it rarely and maintain it only briefly. Apparently Augustine himself had only one such moment of ecstasy.[4] It happened when he was thirty-three years old, lasted but a moment, and was never repeated through the rest of his long life. This early "mystical" experience (if that is what it was) remained a pleasant memory but it did not add substantially to his knowledge of the nature of God. Like a brief meeting with a human "other," a meeting with a divine "other" reveals little about what that "other" is truly like. Indeed, such events cannot even be described in ways that others will understand. Like love, the vision of God must be personally experienced; it cannot be learned from others.

Faith, the second method of coming to knowledge of God, is also limited in its extent; but for those who have it, it gives the most complete information. Faith, in the sense of a belief in God as revealed through the person and teaching of Jesus Christ, was the source of most of Augustine's knowledge of God. As we have seen, he did not believe that it was given to all people. It was God's first gift to the predestined, completely unearned and bestowed in accordance with a divine plan that was forever hidden from the human mind.[5]

The method of discovering God most available to humans is the way of reason. Augustine believed that any good-willed and normally intelligent human, first contemplating the wonders of the world outside themselves and then turning to the wonders in their own person, could come to some knowledge of God. All that was needed was a good mind, sincere attention, and the ordinary illumination required for grasping any fundamental truth about reality. Just as one can come to know one's soul by looking at one's self, so too one can find at least the "hint" of God's presence by looking a bit deeper. Augustine's words to his friends were meant to apply to any human being:

> Look, I shall show you my God by showing you his works. I will not
> do this in any terribly complicated way. I will not ask you without faith

to accept something you cannot understand. . . . I will not demand that you look at a lot of different things. Indeed, all you need do is look at yourselves.[6]

The reason why such discovery through creation is possible is because every creature is modeled on the nature of God present in the Word, the second person of the Trinity. All of creation "reflects" God in some way, the most perfect reflection being the soul of every human being.[7] The mind discovers God especially in its perception of eternal and immutable truths, truths that will never change and are forever. It is the experience of such truths within oneself that is the basis for the uniquely "Augustinian" proof from reason for the existence of God, that is, a "being which has no being superior to it."[8]

The most expansive statement of this argument is found in the second book of Augustine's work on the *Freedom of the Will*. The argument begins with the assumption that the human being is the best of all creation, and then asks if reason can find something better. The direction the proof takes (over many chapters) is suggested in the following exchange between Evodius and Augustine:

Evodius: "I will admit that a particular being is God if it can be shown that there is nothing superior to it."

Augustine: "Good! Then all I need do is to prove that something superior to human beings exists. If I do this, you will be forced to admit that either this being is God or, if something even more superior is found, then that being is God. I will accomplish this by fulfilling my promise to show you that there is something superior to human reason (that faculty which makes humans the best of all creatures)."[9]

Following Kondoleon and Roberts, the full argument can be outlined as follows:

1. God is that to which nothing is superior, that is, God is the supreme being.

2. If there is anything superior to our minds, then that reality is either God or God is superior to it.

3. But eternal and immutable truth exists and is superior to our mind (which is temporal and changeable);

4. If this "superior" truth exists and is identical with God, then God exists.

5. If this "superior" truth exists and God is superior to this truth, then God exists.

6. Thus (on either alternative), God exists.[10]

Analyzing the expanded forms of the proof in the *De libero arbitrio* and the *De vera religione*, one finds the following assumptions and assertions:

1. The characteristics of supreme being (that being which is superior in all possible worlds) are *eternity* and *immutability*.

2. If these characteristics can be found in the world of my experience, I am either experiencing the supreme being itself or a reality that can only be explained by the existence of the supreme being.

3. By examining the content of my knowledge I perceive truths which are immutably and eternally true.

4. It is clear that these same truths are to be found in the minds of others. They are therefore universal, not proper to the private knowledge of one, but common to the knowledge of all.

5. The experiences in (3) and (4) testify to the existence of a being that is eternal, immutable, and more universal than the human race itself.

6. They therefore testify to the existence of supreme being.

Translating the argument into an analogy based on color, one can recast it as follows. If the changeable temporal world of our experience is represented by the color red and the immutable eternal truths discovered in our mind are represented by the color blue, there is no rational explanation for how we humans (changeable and therefore colored red too) can have these "blue" truths without asserting that they are caused by something blue, that is, something eternal and immutable that must be part of reality even though beyond our direct experience. It is simply impossible for a "red" being in a purely "red" world to produce such radically different realities as beings which are eternally and immutably "blue." Clearly the argument is *a posteriori* since it depends on some experience of the real world: namely, the experience of eternal and immutable truths contained in the mind. From this experienced fact one moves to a superior being (superior to changeable humans in that it is eternal and immutable) who is beyond our experience.[11]

The Nature of God

Augustine's argument for the existence of God gives only a broad description of the divine nature as a being superior to humans in this actual world and [perhaps] superior to every being in every possible world. Augustine believed that such general knowledge of God was open to all humans but he also believed that further knowledge of God's nature was difficult to achieve without revelation and was difficult to understand even when revealed. He agreed with St. Paul that "Now we see indistinctly as in a mirror" (1 Cor 13:12), and he interpreted the mirror to be every human being now warped and darkened by the shadow of sin. God and the illumination to see him is present to all, but humans cannot see clearly because the mirror that is themselves is defective. It can reveal only imperfect knowledge of "what God is like." But, even so, the effort to know anything about God is worthwhile. Imperfect knowledge of the creator is always of more value than the most perfect knowledge of creatures.[12]

Even with our darkened mirrors we can at least see that God is different from ourselves and the rest of creation. Of all that exists, God is the most radically "other" and, after careful consideration, we can see that this radical "otherness" is manifested most clearly in God's mode of existence. The world of our everyday experience is clearly contingent. Every part of it (including ourselves) hangs by a thread of dependence on powers outside our control. We are not sufficient to explain our existence. We are "inferiors" because we are "dependents." God on the other hand exists of himself. Just as he is the good against which all created good is measured, so too he is THE "is." Indeed, he is "EXISTENCE ITSELF" (ipsum esse). We exist because we participate in his existence, drawn into being by his will. He, on the other hand, is completely independent. God would exist even if there were nothing else, but all that exists beyond him would be reduced to nothing if left unsupported in its fragile reality. Thus, the first important fact distinguishing God from ourselves is simply this: "God IS and we are not necessarily so."[13]

This complete perfection in God's mode of existence (he "is" necessarily) implies equally complete perfection in his nature ("what he is"). Perfect being can be found only in one who is perfect and therefore does not change.[14] If God is perfect in his being, he cannot lack anything nor can he lose anything that he has. He is IMMUTABLE and this immutability is the second factor in God's radical "otherness" with respect to creation. The first phase of creation's coming to be was establishing it in a foundation of potentiality (spiritual or corporeal "unformed matter") which could provide continuity through its ever-changing existence. It is our destiny as creatures to move through space and time, rushing from "what we were" to "what we will be" through the fleeting moment of "what we are." God, on the other hand, is subject to no "here and there" or "then and now." God simply is, without beginning, end, or fluctuation.

We are imperfect in that we are moved by the tides of time; God is most perfect precisely because in him there is no ebb and flow.[15]

Immutability along with the correlative perfection of eternity most clearly distinguishes the nature of the creator from all created natures. Other divine perfections such as knowledge, goodness, and power are shared with creatures. They to a lesser degree but no less truthfully can be said to be good, to know, to have powers. But immutability and eternity admit of no degrees. One is either subject to time or not. There is no such thing as being a "little bit" immutable. Though creatures strive to bring some stability into their lives by existing in an orderly way, they remain ever-changing beings. No matter how long they exist they can never escape their time, that measure of their limited but ever-flowing existence.

From God's immutability and eternity one can deduce other perfections. His immutability implies that he is *INFINITELY PERFECT*, lacking nothing and unable to lose anything he has. Being simply perfect without limits, it follows that he is the *HIGHEST GOOD*.[16] He is the eternally supreme spirit, unchangeable in himself but yet the unseen creator of changeable things.[17] He is the most excellent being who can be conceived.[18] He is the "good of all good,"[19] not simply in the ontological sense of having the fullness of being, but also in the moral sense of being the "gift-giver" *par excellence*, creating the beauty of the universe and dealing with humans so lovingly that each can join in the happy song of Augustine:

> I was nothing and he made me to be something. I was wandering and he searched for me. He sought me out and found me imprisoned and put up my ransom. I was a slave, and he made me his brother.[20]

Because God is good, he wants the best for creation and he can bring about this good because he is also *OMNIPOTENT*. His power is such that he works his will easily in this visible universe, summoning the rains, calling forth the thunder and lightning, drawing sap through the vine to create grapes. He is the maker of all these things, ordering the earth to produce them, governing them, giving them life.[21] His power far exceeds ours. In us what we "are" and what we "can do" are two different things. Sometimes we can do what we want and at other times we cannot. It is not so with God. In him "to will" and "to do" are one and the same thing.[22] He is perfectly *SIMPLE*, that is, without separations or divisions. God is not fragmented as we are . . . divided within ourselves, divided in our being and our powers. He is absolute unity because he is absolute simplicity: What the divine substance *has*, it *is*.[23] God, the creator of the beauty we see around us and in us, is the most *BEAUTIFUL* of all. He is beauty itself, the epitome of the "splendor of order" that we see in this world.[24] Since he is immutable, he is beyond the measure of time. He is *ETERNAL*; ". . . just as he never will not be, so he never was not."[25] God is *OMNISCIENT*. His unlimited knowledge includes both what was/is/will be actual and all that is possible.[26] He knows himself and can see in his nature the reflections of an infinity of possible worlds, the innumerable ways in which he can be mirrored in creation. And, as far as this actually existing world is concerned, God knows the least of creatures even though they may exist for only a fraction of a second at the furthermost edge of the universe.[27] Creatures are established as individual entities by the walls of their time and place, but God is *PRESENT* in all places and times without being confined by any of them.[28]

One can go on and on with the list of God's perfections, but what it comes down to is this:

1. All that we perceive as imperfection does not belong to God.[29]

2. All that is a perfection does belong to God in a supereminent way, far beyond our powers to comprehend.[30]

God is simply the supreme spirit, without division, without limitations of place and time.[31] Looking at the limited perfection in creatures and measuring this against the infinite perfection of the creator, it follows that as the "greatest" being who does or could exist, God transcends every changeable creature. Though he is interior to everything in creation, he is yet radically exterior to it by his immutable, infinitely perfect existence.[32] Augustine warns those tempted by pantheism that even though the true God is intimately involved in the created universe, he is not part of that universe. In his mode of being and in his immutable and infinitely perfect nature, God is radically transcendent.[33] It is for this reason that humans cannot comprehend the nature of God. Without revelation there can be only ignorance; with revelation there is at best mystery, the greatest being that of the Trinity, the vital inner life of God.

God as Trinity

Augustine wrote his massive (fifteen book) examination of the Trinity over a period of two decades. There is a story (created and applied to Augustine many centuries later) that when he had finished his work, he took a walk along the shore of the Mediterranean Sea. There he came upon a boy busily digging three holes in the sand. When finished the young lad went down to the water's edge, filled his little bucket with the water from the sea, and ran back to pour the water into the three holes. Augustine watched him for a while and then asked:

"What are you doing?"

The boy answered:

"I am pouring the sea into these three holes in the sand."

Augustine laughed and said:

"Why, that's just silly!"

The boy responded:

"It's no sillier than trying to pour the Trinity into fifteen books."

Of course Augustine never heard this story (at least on earth), but if he had, he would probably have agreed with the boy's judgment. We find him saying almost the same thing in his *Confessions* where he asks:

> Who can understand the all-powerful Trinity? . . . Rare is the person, whatever they say of the triune God, who knows what they are talking about.[34]

Augustine frankly admitted that understanding the inner life of God as expressed through the mystery of the Trinity would always be beyond the power of the human mind. At the same time he had no doubt about the fact. The doctrine was clearly revealed in scripture and taught by the growing tradition of the young Christian church. Pelikan notes that Christians had pretty well "hammered out" the dogma of the Trinity by the third quarter of the fourth century, especially establishing that the Christ who had appeared on earth to bring salvation to the human race was identical with the God who was the ruler of heaven and earth.[35] By the time of Augustine it was generally accepted that God was one nature and three persons through the mutual relations of paternity (the person of the Father), generation (the person of the Son), and procession (the person of the Holy Spirit). It was also accepted that the Son is generated by the Father "seeing himself" and is the perfect reflection/image of the Father.[36] The Holy Spirit in turn "proceeds" from and is equal to both Father and Son as their mutual love for each other.[37]

An understanding of how God can be one and yet three is explained by Augustine by noting that when one speaks of God being one, one is speaking about the divine nature or essence. When one speaks about three persons, one is speaking about relations . . . entities which (in his mind) are neither substance nor accident.[38] Of course, that God can be one nature and three persons without contradiction depends on being able to distinguish between the concepts of "nature" and "person." There does seem to be some merit in the distinction. When I consider myself, for example, it is possible to distinguish between the "nature" that I have (rational animal) and the person that I am ("Donald"). Others may have a nature similar to mine, but no one can share my particular personhood. If it is thus possible to separate the ideas of "nature" and "person" because of their different content, saying "God is one and yet three" does not involve the contradiction of saying that God is "one" and "not one" in the same respect.

However, the analogy between nature-person in humans and nature-person in God cannot be pressed too far. It is true that I am a separate person from my six brothers and sisters and that we share a common human nature, but "my" human nature is distinct from the "human nature" that each of my siblings has. When we get together we are "many," not one. In God the unity of nature is absolute. The three persons have one and the same divine nature. They are one with an absolute immutable unity that cannot be approached (or even clearly understood) by such divided creatures as human beings.

Without making any claim to fully explain the inner life and mutual relationships of the triune God, Augustine makes his most original contribution to the understanding of the mystery by suggesting analogies from ordinary human experience. For example, when we come to consider our "self," that consideration leads to an "idea of self." Considering our image in this idea, we come to see that our "self" is good and we are drawn to it by an act of love. Put simply, we exist as "self," we know our "self," we love our "self," and yet there is no separation in these three activities. My existing, my thinking, my loving are all aspects of my one spiritual nature. In a somewhat similar way, one can describe the Word (the second person) as the thought proceeding from the Father (the first person) reflecting on himself, and the Spirit (the third person) as the mutual love generated from the Father and Son contemplating the infinite goodness of the divine nature.[39]

Obviously all analogies from creation must limp, but they do support the conviction that the idea of a triune God is not absurd. Moreover, if one can come to a belief in God as Trinity (and such faith is a great gift) one can get a better understanding of the diverse ways in which God is present to creation: as Father creator, as Son exemplar and savior, as Spirit the giver of love. God in three persons is thus "with us" in a multitude of wonderful ways as creation spins through its allotted time. It is to this hopeful and consoling fact that we now turn our attention.

"God With Us"

In studying Augustine's writings, it is easy to lose sight of the forest for the trees, to spend so much time "tearing apart" and "analyzing" some small piece of his thought that one loses sight of the main message he wanted to convey. To use an analogy he uses himself, we are sometimes like little bugs making our laborious way across a beautiful mosaic floor. We become so entranced by the little pebble before our eyes that we cannot see the enormity and glorious beauty that surrounds us. Like Sisyphus, our rock becomes our "thing" and we gradually lose sight of where we are and where we are going.[40] So too it sometimes happens that when we come to study the "World of Augustine," we become so immersed in one little piece of that world that we miss the overriding message that such a world proclaims: the message that "GOD IS WITH US," that God is everywhere present to us in the world that we face each day.[41]

Augustine was convinced of God's presence in creation even before he had a clear idea of either. In his *Confessions* he reports that when he was a young man still trying to get beyond the materialism of his Manichaean days, he saw the relationship between the world and God as something like a sponge immersed in a great sea. He develops this image in the following way:

> I imagined the whole of your creation, O God, as a vast mass made up of different kinds of bodies, some of them real, some of them only the bodies which in my imagination took the place of spirits. I thought of this mass as something huge. I could not, of course, know how big it really was, but I made it as large as need be, though finite in all directions. I pictured you, O Lord, as encompassing this mass on all sides and penetrating it in every part, yet yourself infinite in every dimension. It was as though there were a sea everywhere, nothing but an immense infinite sea, and somewhere within it a sponge, quite large but not infinite, filled through and through with the water of this boundless sea. In some such way as this I imagined that your finite creation was filled by you who were infinite. I said to myself, "Here is God and here is what he has created. God is good, utterly and entirely better than the things which he has made. But, since he is good, the things that he has made are also good and this is how he contains them all in himself and fills them all with his presence."[42]

This vision of God containing the universe and flooding each and every one of its parts through all time is the most important fact about the world as Augustine saw it. It is the reason why he insists again and again to anyone who would listen that no matter how terrible existence may sometimes be, there is always reason for hope because in good times and bad "God is with us."

Though God is eminently transcendent and therefore radically different from his creation both in his mode of existence and in his nature, he is not separated from it. At one and the same time creatures are "outside" God because of his infinite superiority and are "inside" him because they are totally contained in him.[43] Though Augustine never again uses the analogy of the sea and the sponge (perhaps because of its materialistic implications), the image of God "containing" creation (as an infinite sea contains a finite sponge) and "being contained" by it (as a sponge everywhere absorbs and is soaked by the wetness of a containing sea) is repeated again and again throughout his writings.

Thus, we find him saying in his final commentary on Genesis that creation once drawn from nothingness spends all of its time "resting" in God.[44] In a sense, God "embraces" creation and is absorbed into its every pore. He is as completely and wholly present in its totality as in its most insignificant part. He "fills" heaven and earth just as the overpowering sea "fills" every crevice of a receptive sponge.[45] God is even present in those who have turned away from him by sin. They may have turned their back on him, but he still floods their life with the energy of his presence. He has not abandoned them; it is they who have closed their eyes to him.[46] If they ever want to find God, all they need do is open their eyes and turn to the book of creation. There they will discover every page flooded and filled with the divine presence.[47]

As time went by, Augustine came to prefer the image of "God containing creation" rather than "creation containing God." He reacted against the latter description with vigorous proclamations, saying dramatically on one occasion: "God is not anywhere!"[48] What bothered him about saying "God is here" or "God is there" is that such phrasing implies that God is confined by a particular place. This is impossible given the simplicity and spirituality of the divine nature. Because God is spirit, he must be present in every part of reality totally and completely and never confined by any part. Place is a characteristic of material things and to say that God is *in* creation as in a place or that creation is *in* God as in a place is to suggest a "material" God. God is not confined by the material world nor is the world a "part" of God. This being understood, one can then begin the investigate the ways in which God *is* present in this world.

Augustine would be the first to admit that the search for traces of God in creation is not an easy task. His presence is a secret presence and the exercise of his power in the world remains mysterious. Even the most sincere and good-willed investigator will discover that the mode of God's presence is scarcely comprehensible.[49] For this reason it is sometimes easier to begin by listing the ways in which God is *not* present. For example, he clearly is not present as the sun and moon and stars are present. They are in place and God is not. Nor is God present in the universe as the builders of houses are said to be present in the design and workmanship of the buildings they construct. A builder can walk away from a completed project, leaving it to exist on its own. Not so with God. He must remain with his creation, continuing to support its existence and its operation by his omnipotent power.[50]

God's relation to creation is more like a "blower of balloons" than the builder of houses. With a balloon, it is not enough to fill it with air and then leave it to its own devices. Without continued pressure on the opening, the air quickly escapes reducing the container to a frazzled quasi-nothingness. In like manner creation depends on God not only to come into existence, but also to remain in existence. Created things come from nothing and they can never be anything more than fragile vessels of being floating above an abyss of nothingness. Before time creatures simply were not. They did not "have to be" and now that they "are" they still remain "not necessarily so." In the words of Augustine, God must continue to support creation in existence lest it disappear "in the twinkling of an eye" (*ictu oculi*).[51] Infinitely above creation, God is yet intimately present in creation through the exercise of his power holding it in existence. Without such support creatures could not continue to *be*, much less continue *to function*. God is thus not only the omnipotent (*omnipotens*) God who creates all things; he is also the "all-supporting" (*omnitenens*) God who "holds in existence" the things he has created.[52] There is thus an ontological truth as well as a moral truth in Augustine's proclamation: "If I do not abide in him, neither shall I abide in myself." To exist happily is to exist with God as friend. To exist at all is to exist within the embrace of his creative and conserving power. Every creature can say with Augustine:

I would not be, I would in no way *be*, unless you were in me. Or rather, I would not be unless I were in you, "from whom, by whom and in whom are all things." (Rom 11:36).[53]

God is not only immanent in creatures as the support of their exis-tence [*"that* they are"]; he is also immanent in the structure of their nature [*"what* they are"]. Each part of creation is a reflection of the perfect *rea-sons* (forms, ideas) in the infinite nature of God. Through the Word (the second person of the Trinity) every creature has God as its exemplary cause. Only the Word proceeds from the Father as a perfect image and likeness, but created things have at least an imperfect resemblance to the divine nature present in the Word.[54] No creature is God or is part of God; at most they are dull reflections of him. Even created spirits, though they are the "best" things in creation, are closer to nothing than they are to the infinite everything that is God. Compared to the creator, the "best" of creatures remains none too good.[55]

Even so, there are traces of God (indeed, traces of the Trinity itself) in fully formed creatures. The triune God is one nature manifested in three persons. Creatures too are in some sense triune. The fully formed nature of any created thing is the result of the threefold gift of measure, form, and order to the receptive formlessness at the root of all changeable being. From these "three" there is formed an order of parts which fabri-cates the quasi-unity that makes individual existence possible. Augustine believed that "being" was equivalent to "oneness," "unity," "perma-nence."[56] God is perfect being precisely because he is perfectly "one." Creation in its formless state is perfectly "many." It is pure potentiality, more a capacity for change than for being a "this" or "that." To move from nothing through potentiality to actuality, a creature must acquire some sort of unity, some sort of specificity, some sort of "thisness." It accomplishes this by acquiring measure, form, and order from its triune creator. I *am* because I have received these three gifts from the divine three persons.[57]

Without these three elements in its nature, a creature could not have identity. It needs a particular "measure" which establishes it in its own space and time. It needs a "form," an internal definition which places it in a specific genus and species. It needs an "ordering," a purpose for its existence and a coordinated ability to function so as to achieve that pur-pose. Just as it is impossible for God to exist in any way other than three persons and one nature, so it is impossible for creatures to separate their individual existence from the three factors which together bind their fluctuating changeable roots into one unified being.[58] Creatures exist only because they have a unity coming from the three characteristics at the root of their nature. The hand of God is thus evident not only in "that they are" (their existence) but also in "what they are" (their nature).

The "plan" that is given to every creature is a sign that God does not simply supply them with the power to exist and the model for their nature. He is present in their every activity through his knowledge, concern, and love. He "knows" what each creature is, makes plans for its future, and is concerned that the best future be realized by each one. By his *creation* God made the first "now" for creatures. By his *concurrence* he supports their being and activity in their subsequent "nows." Through his *providence* he foresees and acts to bring them to their proper "future," that state of being where finally they can be at rest.[59]

Augustine sees evidence of God's planning in the structure of even the simplest creature. This providential plan establishes the internal order of individuals whereby their many parts are able to operate as one whole. It also brings order to creation at large so that creatures are subordinate to God, the corporeal is subordinate to the spiritual, the irrational is subordinate to the rational.[60] The present status and future of creation is thus not the result of chance (a haphazard coming together of unknown causes) nor is it the result of fate (a destiny fixed by blind and uncaring powers). To the contrary, the course of the universe is set by the will of an infinite being whose essence is identified with goodness, whose wisdom easily devises the best plan for creation, and whose omnipotence can bring it about that this plan is accomplished for the good of all concerned.[61]

The first step in effecting this plan was to make finality or direction part of the essence of every creature. Each being cannot merely be established in a subsisting individuality (a "measured" existence) and given a specific nature (a "formed" existence) and then set loose to ramble in any and every direction. It must also be given a specific finality, a "drive" or "weight" which pushes and pulls it toward its proper goal. The generation of new species and new members of existing species gives evidence of such finality. The unswerving and orderly direction of these everyday natural processes suggests a divine provident control.[62] It is through the energies placed in creation at the beginning that new species develop out of their "primordial seeds." God created once and then rested but he remains involved in nurturing the "seeds" of species that will appear fully formed through the course of time, driven by the energy placed in them at the beginning.[63]

Once individuals of a fully formed species begin to exist God continues to be involved in the day by day processes which carry them toward their proper perfection.[64] He does this by supporting their own powers, both the natural and/or instinctual movements of material creation and the voluntary movements of spiritual creation (angels and humans).[65] It is through such powers embedded in creation and supported by God that stars shine, night follows day, the earth is washed by waters, winds blow, and living things are generated and born, develop, grow old, and die. Through voluntary actions "natural" to free beings education takes place, fields are cultivated, societies are governed and the arts are practiced.[66] Sometimes God uses outside agents to aid the internal energies of a creature. Thus he provides farmers to cultivate crops and teachers to instruct the young.[67] Such outside aides include both material causes (for example, the earth, water, and sun needed for a plant to flourish), and good free will decisions of human beings accomplished through grace illuminating the mind and moving the will.[68]

The God of creation gave to all creatures their purpose and their powers. He holds in his hands the causes of creation's activity. He is the source of the energy of the seed and plant, of fire and water, of sun and stars. No aspect of creation is unworthy of his attention. He reaches down to the simplest creature, giving fertility to the sea and earth so that they may produce food for fish and animal. Reflecting on the words of Jesus that no sparrow falls to earth without God willing it (Mt 10:29) and that God himself covers the fields with the green grass that flourishes briefly only to be consigned to the oven (Mt 6:30), Augustine asks:

> In saying this, does not our Lord assure us that not only this whole region of the world which has been assigned to mortal and corruptible beings but also the least and lowliest parts of it are ruled by divine providence?[69]

Moved by the energy given by God, stars move in their courses, winds blow, waterfalls shrouded in mist disappear into deep pools, meadows come to life, animals are born and live out their lives guided by instinct.[70] Nothing is left to chance. All is foreseen by the knowledge of God, executed with the help of his supporting power, and accomplished by working through and respecting the natural powers which he placed in creation from its beginning.[71]

At times (though rarely) God accomplishes his purpose through miracles, direct divine interventions which override the natural processes of creation.[72] Some of these are quite extraordinary (for example, communication with humans through angelic messengers), but many are simply the "speeding up" of a natural process. Augustine suggests that when something occurs frequently in an accustomed fashion (for example, making water into wine through the usual productivity of the grapevine) we call it natural. When the same process occurs on rare occasions in an unusual way (for example, the making of wine out of water at Cana) we call it a miracle. Our amazement at the unusual blinds us to the wondrous activity that is occurring daily all around us and (perhaps even more) inside us.[73]

The human being is the greatest miracle of creation and it is in the human that the immanent power of God is most dramatic. In a thought-provoking interpretation of Genesis 2:15, Augustine suggests that one of the reasons why God created Eden and then placed the first humans there was because he wanted to guard and cultivate *them*. And so too today. "The same God who creates and makes human beings to be human also cultivates and guards them in order that they may be good and happy humans."[74] God created humans with the highest gifts of all creation, gifts shared only with angels: the gift of being able to "know" who they were and where they were going and the gift of being able to freely choose to follow their goal. Humans could choose not to seek their goal, and this unfortunately they did, choosing against the order of the universe whereby they were "subordinates" to the one who had created them. The consequence was that they were blocked from achieving that goal whose need had been built into their being at the moment of creation. They experienced the truth of the famous proclamation made by Augustine in his *Confessions*, "You have made us for yourself, O God, and our hearts are restless till they rest in you."[75]

After Eden such rest was impossible for humans because they had turned their back and walked away from the only one who could give them rest. No longer were humans able to see clearly and easily the ultimate truths about themselves and God. No longer were they able to effectively choose the good. Given this desperate state, it is no wonder that Augustine considered the coming of God in the person of Jesus Christ as the most dramatic evidence of God's desire to be involved in creation's history. Through the sacrifice of Christ humans once again had the possibility of reaching that goal for which they had been made: to be happy in the arms of their creator for all eternity.[76]

On a day by day basis, the redemption of humanity meant that once again God was deeply involved in each individual's history, the Father giving the law and the gift of faith for their direction, the Son illuminating their mind that they might see the way to their goal, the Spirit giving them the power to love and choose the good and, through the final great grace of perseverance, to do so till the very end of their time.[77] This human need for God is ever present. God's *continuous* help is necessary for humans to be just, faithful, and wise. The human weakness is not one that can be cured by a therapist coming once in a while to turn them in the right direction. Our good actions depend on our being constantly "turned to God" but we cannot accomplish that on our own. We must be constantly "cultivated and guarded" by God lest we fall away. A field cultivated by a skilled farmer is still cultivated even when the farmer goes about other business, but our cultivation must be a continuous process. Our situation is more like air that is illuminated by a brilliant light. If the light is ever removed, the hapless air becomes dark. In like fashion:

> When God is present to them, humans are illuminated; but when God is absent, darkness is immediately upon them and they are separated from God not by a distance in space but by a turning away of their will.[78]

The fact of the matter is that God has created all beings by his goodness and rules them by his power. No creature exists without the support of that power and no good will exists without its assistance.[79]

Believing in creation, Augustine became convinced of the infinite transcendence of God. Believing in the incarnation, he came to see that this ineffable infinite being was close by, indeed that he was a neighbor. As he said to his friends one day:

> What is more different, more distant, than God and the human being? They are separated not by space, but by their dissimilarity. Since this immortal and just God was so far distant from us who are sinners and mortal, God traveled over a great expanse to become our neighbor, Jesus Christ. . . . Jesus-God became our neighbor so that we might not worry so much anymore. And even though afterward he returned bodily to his home beyond the heavens, his majesty stays with us. Indeed, that God who made everything we see is still everywhere present to us.[80]

Jesus-God is truly in heaven but he continues to be present on earth through his divinity and his power and his love.[81] Indeed, Augustine suggests that God is so intimately present to and in every human being that it can truly be said that he is closer to us than most things in creation since "in him we live and move and have our being" (Acts 17:28).[82] He goes even further. Remembering his condition while still searching for God in the world beyond God, Augustine says him: "All the while you were more inside me than my most inmost part; you were higher than my highest powers."[83] Put simply, Augustine is saying, "God is closer to us than we are to ourselves."

God then is close by, but what is he like? The favorite analogies used by Augustine to answer that question are the stories of the prodigal son and the good Samaritan. God is like the loving father of the prodigal, always willing to open the doors of his house to any of his children who wish to return. God is like the Good Samaritan, always ready to come to the aid of even the most foreign of humans and help them to heal.[84] God is a divine doctor who comes again and again to heal the wounds reopened by our constant sins, giving the medicines that will strengthen us for the challenges that lie ahead.[85] God comes to us not as a stranger but as a parent, as both mother and father. He is father because he created us, calls us to his service, directs us and governs us. He is mother in that he cherishes us and feeds us and suckles us and nurses us. Commenting on the words of the psalmist "Though my father and mother forsake me, yet will the Lord receive me" (Ps 27:10) Augustine says:

> Mortal parents procreate; the children take their place. Mortals give place to mortals. Children are born to succeed those who begot them and those who begot the children depart. But the God who created me shall never depart nor shall I ever be separated from him.[86]

"I shall never be separated from him" . . . this was for Augustine the most important fact about the world that he discovered inside and outside himself. It is a beautiful world of land and sea and sky in which each individual is most precious. It is a world, in truth made from nothing, but created by a being who is everything and who wants everything good for the fragile beings who continue to depend on him for their existence. It is a world in which humans are made with a thirst for everything, a thirst that drives them to go beyond this or that good to the infinite good that is their goal. It is a world in which that terrifying transcendent omnipotence that is God walks the streets with human beings as their neighbor, friend, doctor, and parent. It is no wonder that Augustine, believing all this, heard trumpeted throughout his world this consoling message to a struggling humanity:

> Wherever you go on earth, however long you remain, the Lord is close to you. So don't worry about anything. The Lord is nearby.[87]

Notes

1. *DO*, 2.18.47, PL 32, 1017.

2. James E. Dittes, "Augustine's Search for a Fail-Safe God to Trust," *Journal for the Scientific Study of Religion*, vol. 25, #1 (1986), pp. 57-63.

3. *IJE*, 106.4, PL 35, 1909-10. "God is hidden everywhere; he is manifest everywhere. No one can know him as he is, but no one is permitted not to know him" (*ENN 74*, 9, PL 36, 613). "Atheists are few and far between" (*ENN 52*, 2, PL 36, 613). "They (atheists) refuse to believe only because of the passion in their hearts" (*ENN 13*, 2, PL 36, 141).

4. The experience occurred at Ostia in the midst of a conversation with his mother Monica about the search for God. See *C*, 9.10, PL 32, 773-75.

5. See *IJE*, 27.7, PL 35, 1618-19; 3.10, PL 35, 1400-01. The ordinary condition for receiving this grace of faith was to learn from others the life and teaching of Christ. There were (in Augustine's view) very few who received the grace without "having the gospel preached to them." See *DDP*, 19.48, PL 45, 1023.

6. *Sermon 223A [Verbraken]*, (Denis, 2), #4, *Miscellanea Agostiniana*, I, p. 15. For a description of the traces of God in the world of nature See *C*, 10.6, PL 32, 782-83; *SER 241*, 2-3, PL 38, 776; *DCD*, 11.4.22, PL 41, 317-18; 11.2.1, PL 41, 319.

7. "The human mind is not the same as the essence of God and yet it is possible for us to seek and find in ourselves the image of that divine being who is the most perfect of all possible beings. . . . Our mind is a reflection of God because it is able to receive him and to participate in him. This wonderful gift would be impossible if we were not the very image of God." *DT*, 14.8.11, PL 42, 1044; 6.10.12, PL 42, 932.

8. *DLA*, 2.6.14, PL 32, 1248. Kondoleon argues that by this broad description of God Augustine "intended *God* to mean not merely 'that to which nothing in reality is superior,' the definition he actually accepts, but also 'that being which

(if it exists) is supreme and to which no other being *could* be superior.' " In sum, God is the supreme being in every possible world. See Theodore Kondoleon, "Augustine's Argument for God's Existence: De Libero Arbitrio, Book II," *Augustinian Studies*, 14 (1983), p. 108.

9. *DLA*, 2.6.14, PL 32, 1248-49. The entire argument is spread over book 2, chapters 3-15 of the *De libero arbitrio.* A somewhat briefer statement of the proof can be found in *De vera religione,* chapters 27-30. See also *DDQ*, 54, PL 40, 38; *C*, 7.10.16, PL 32, 742.

10. See Kondoleon, *op. cit.*, p. 107; Lawrence D. Roberts, "Augustine's Version of the Ontological Argument and Platonism," *Augustinian Studies*, 9 (1978), p. 94.

11. Both Augustine and Anselm argue from what humans find in their minds to the existence of God, but there is this difference in their argument. Anselm argues from the content of the idea of a "most perfect being" to its real existence. Augustine argues from the existence of eternal and immutable truths to an eternal and immutable (and therefore, "superior") being who through exemplarity and illumination is their cause. I would agree with Portalié that Augustine's proof concludes only *that* God exists, not that God *ought to* exist. Indeed, Augustine suggests that to assert that God *ought to exist* is an improper use of language. When we say something "ought to be x," we suggest that it could be otherwise. Thus it is more proper to say that God "exists" and leave it at that. If one must go further in describing the mode of God's existence, it would seem better to say that God exists "necessarily" rather than to say that God "ought to exist." See Eugène Portalié, *A Guide to the Thought of Saint Augustine* (Chicago: Henry Regnery, 1960), p. 126. See also *E 162*, 2, PL 33, 705; *DVR*, 31.58, PL 34, 147-48.

12. See *DT*, 15.23.44, PL 42, 1091; 15.27.50, PL 42, 1096-97; *DGL*, 5.16.34, PL 34, 333. Augustine expresses the difficulty in knowing the nature of God in various places in various ways. For example: "It is easier to know what God is not than what he is" (*ENN 85,* 12, PL 37, 1090; *DT*, 5.1.2, PL 42, 911-12). "Everything can be said of God, yet nothing can be said worthily. . . . You seek a name to fit God and find none. He cannot be put into a category because he is everything" (*IJE*, 13.5, PL 35, 1495). "To reach to God by the mind in any measure is a great blessedness but to comprehend him is altogether impossible" (*SER 117*, 3.5, PL 38, 663-64). "If it is God (you claim to know), you do not understand; if you understand, it is not God" (*SER 52*, 16, PL 38, 360). For examinations of "What God is not" See *IJE*, 23.9, PL 35, 1587-88; *SER 4*, 4.5, PL 38, 35. Augustine notes that knowledge of "what God is not" is not insignificant information as a beginning of the search for "what he is." See *DT*, 8.2.3, PL 42, 948

13. Some relevant texts include the following: "God would exist even if nothing else did" (*E 187*, 6.18, PL 33, 839). "God is THE is. Other things that are, when compared to God, are not" (*ENN 134* 4, PL 37, 1741; *C*, 13.31.46, PL 32, 865). "God is *ipsum esse*" (*DMC*, 1.14.24, PL 32, 1321; *DT*, 5.2.3, PL 42, 912; *DCD* 11.10.3, PL 41, 327). "God alone has being in the highest sense" (*DGL* 5.16.34, PL 34, 333; *DT*, 5.10.11, PL 42, 918). See Stanislaus J. Grabowski, *The All-Present God*, (St. Louis: B. Herder, 1954), pp. 169ff.

14. *DCD*, 7.30, PL 41, 219. Grabowski (*op. cit.*, p. 225) remarks that the central perfections in the order of essence that separate the creator from creatures are immutability, simplicity, and spirituality. All of these contribute to the absolute "oneness" that is God, a being who has no divisions.

15. Augustine states the relationship between perfect "being" and "immutability" as follows: "No matter how excellent a thing is, if it is changeable it does not have true being. This is so because true being is not found where there is also non-being. When that which has the possibility of change actually does change, it ceases to be what it was before the change. If that which once was *is not* now, a kind of death has occurred. Something that had been there and is now no longer has been destroyed. . . . Examine the changes of things and you will everywhere find 'has been' and 'will be.' Think about God and you will find 'is' where 'has been' and 'will be' cannot be" (*IJE*, 38.10, PL 35, 1679-81). See *IJE*, 19.11, PL 35, 1548; *SER 7*, 7, PL 38 66-67; *DT*, 5.2.3, PL 42, 912; *ENN 121*, 5-12, PL 37, 1621-29; *DMC*, 2.1.1, PL 32, 1345; *C*, 13.16, PL 32, 853.

16. *DNB*, 22, PL 42, 558; *C*, 7.5.7, PL 32, 736.

17. *IJE*, 19.6, PL 35, 1545-46.

18. *DDC*, 1.7.7, PL 34, 22.

19. *DT*, 8.3.4, PL 42, 949.

20. *SER 254*, 6, PL 38, 1185. "When I turn my attention to God I can think of no better way to describe him than to say simply 'The Good'. . . . There is no good to be found which does not derive its goodness from him. Since he is the good which makes all things good, he is properly called 'The Good'" (*ENN 134*, 4, PL 37, 1740-41).

21. *DT*, 3.4.10 - 3.5.11, PL 42, 873-74.

22. *IJE*, 20.4, PL 35, 1558; *C*, 7.4.6, PL 32, 735-36.

23. *IJE*, 99.4, PL 35, 1887-88. See *DT*, 6.7.8, PL 42, 928-29; 6.10.11, PL 42, 931; 5.10.11, PL 42, 918.

24. *C.*, 11.4.6, PL 32, 811.

25. *DT*, 14.15.21, PL 42, 1051-52. See *ENN 101/2*, 10, PL 37, 1310.

26. *SER 70*, 2.3, PL 38, 44.

27. *DCD*, 16.5, PL 41, 483.

28. *IJE,* 31.9, PL 35, 1640-41; 34.6, PL 35, 1654; 35.5, PL 35, 1659. Grabowski (*op cit.*, p. 163) notes that Augustine, following earlier traditions, emphasized the "dynamic" presence of God in the universe rather than stressing the presence of the divine essence. However, since Augustine identifies the powers of God with his essence, there is reason for saying that God not only "works" everywhere; he "is" everywhere.

29. *DNB*, 22, PL 42, 558.

30. *C*, 22, PL 42, 558. See *DDC*, 1.7.7, PL 34, 22.

31. *IJE*, 13.6, PL 35, 1546.

32. *DGL*, 8.26.48, PL 34, 391.

33. *IJE*, 38.4, PL 35, 1677. On the pantheistic currents existing in Augustine's day, See Grabowski, *op. cit.*, 211-38.

34. *C*, 13.11, PL 32, 849-50. Augustine was well aware of the difficulty in understanding the mystery of the Trinity. As he began his attempt, he warned his readers: "I now begin to talk about topics which are beyond the powers of any person (including myself) to express in words that accurately reflect what is in the mind. Our mind realizes the distance even between its thinking and the God about whom it is thinking. . . . The human mind simply cannot comprehend God as he is; it can only see him as the apostle Paul said: 'through a darkened mirror' [1 Cor 12:12]" (*DT*, 5.1.1, PL 42, 911). In another place Augustine describes his mental anxiety, admitting that in facing the project he was troubled and felt the need to "sweat over the task" and perhaps thereby free himself of the troublesome venture by completing it (See *IJE*, 21.12, PL 35, 1570-71). One of the earliest recountings of the story of Augustine's conversation with the young boy on the beach appeared toward the end of the fifteenth century in John Caxton's English translation of and addition to James of Voragine's biography of Augustine, the *Legenda aurea*. On this See Edmund Colledge, O.S.A., "Caxton's Addition to the *Legenda sancti Augustini*," *Augustiniana*, vol. 34 (1984), pp. 198-212. See by the same author "James of Voragine's *Legenda sancti Augustini* and Its Sources," *Augustiniana*, vol. 35 (1985), pp. 281-313. As Colledge points out, this story was not unique to Augustine. It appeared in the legends of other saints from the same period, perhaps demonstrating the principle that a good story is worth repeating whether it is true or not.

35. Jaroslav Pelikan, *The Christian Tradition* (Chicago: The University of Chicago Press, 1971), I, pp. 211 & 171. Richardson writes: "Augustine wrote at a time when the main lines of the doctrine of the Trinity had been settled. The Council of Constantinople in A.D. 381 had witnessed the final triumph of the Nicene cause . . . (that) the one essence or *ousia* of the Godhead expressed itself in three modes of being to which they (the Cappadocian fathers) applied the term

hypostaseis" (Cyril C. Richardson, "The Enigma of the Trinity," *A Companion to the Study of St. Augustine*, Roy W. Battenhouse, ed. [New York: Oxford University Press, 1955], p. 237). Teselle adds that when Augustine came to write write his own lengthy work on the Trinity (400-416), the problem was not to explain how one God could yet be three but rather to show (against the Arians) how God being three could yet be one. Eugene Teselle, *Augustine the Theologian* (New York: Herder & Herder, 1970), p. 122.

36. *DT* 2.1.3, PL 42, 846-47; 6.10.11, PL 42, 931-32. See Teselle, *op. cit.*, pp. 298-99.

37. *DT*, 15.17.27 - 15.18.32, PL 42, 1079-83. Teselle summarizes the following important aspects of Augustine's position. "Person" refers to one divine being insofar as it is related to itself in three ways. (*DT*, 7.4.9, PL 42, 941-42; 7.5.10, PL 42, 942-43). Each person possesses the divine nature in its fullness and is not anything less in itself that what it is together with the other persons (*DT*, 7.6.11, PL 42, 943-45; 14.7.9, PL 42, 1042-43). Teselle, *op. cit.*, pp. 298-99.

38. See Teselle, *op. cit.*, pp. 294-97.

39. *DT*, 14.7.9-10, PL 42, 1042-44. Portalié (*op. cit.*, pp. 132-33) lists three special Augustinian contributions to the development of the Christian doctrine of the Trinity:

1. emphasis on one divine nature more than on the three persons while yet emphasizing the equality of the three persons;

2. insisting that all actions *ad extra* (creation, redemption, sanctification) are the work of all three persons;

3. establishing the foundation for the psychological theory of the processions where the Son processes from the mind of the Father as "Word" (or "Thought"), and the Spirit processes from the will of the Father and Word (that is, Son) as "Love."

40. *See DO*, 1.1.2, PL 32, 979.

41. Augustine writes: "When humans think of a particular substance as something which is alive, everlasting, all-powerful, infinite, present everywhere in its entirety but confined in no place . . . when they combine all these perfections in one concept, then they are thinking of God" (*IJE*, 1.8, PL 35, 1383). Grabowski remarks (*op. cit.*, p. 61) that being "present" in creation is one of the central characteristics of Augustine's idea of God.

42. *C*, 7.5.7, PL 32, 736-37. Translated by R. S. Pine-Coffin, *Saint Augustine: Confessions* (Baltimore: Penguin Books, 1961, p. 138.

43. *DGL*, 8.26.48, PL 34, 391.

44. *DGL*, 4.18.32, PL 34, 308.

45. See *IJE*, 38.4, PL 35, 1677; *SER 277*, 13.13, PL 38, 1264.

46. *E 187*, ("On the Presence of God" to Dardanus), 5.17, PL 33, 838.

47. *Sermon 68 (Verbraken)* (Mai 126), 6, *Miscellanea Agostiniana*, I, p. 360.

48. "God is not anywhere. For what is somewhere is contained in a place, and what is contained in a place is body. But God is not body, so he is not anywhere. Nevertheless, since he is and yet is not in a place, all things are in him rather than he himself being anywhere" *DDQ*, q. 20, PL 40, 15-16. "God is spread throughout all things, not as a characteristic or quality of the world but as the creator of the substance of the world, ruling creation without work and filling it without effort." See *E 187*, 4.14, PL 33, 837. See *C*, 1.2.2, PL 32, 661-62; 7.15, PL 32, 744; *DGL*, 4.12.23, PL 34, 304; 8.26, PL 34, 391.

49. *ENN 81*, 2, PL 37, 1047; *C*, 6.3.4, PL 32, 721; *DQA*, 1.34.77, PL 32, 1077; *DGL*, 5.20.40, PL 34, 335.

50. *IJE*, 2.10, PL 35, 1393. See *DGL*, 4.12.22, PL 34, 304; 8.26.48, PL 34, 391.

51. *DGL*, 4.12.22, PL 34, 304.

52. See *DGL*, 4.12.22, PL 34, 304; 8.26.48, PL 34, 391; *DCD*, 22.24, PL 41, 788-92; *E 187*, 4.14, PL 33, 837.

53. *C*, 7.11.17, PL 32, 742; 1.2.2, PL 32, 661.

54. See *DGI.*, 16, 57, PL 34, 242; *DCD*, 12.2, PL 41, 350; *IJE*, 1.17, PL 35, 1387. "Individual things are created in accord with "reasons" (models, forms) which are unique to them . . . These "reasons" cannot be thought to exist anywhere but in the mind of the creator. . . . By participating in these exemplars, whatever *is* exists in whatever fashion it does exist." *DDQ*, 46.2, PL 40, 30-31.

55. *DGM*, 1.2.4, PL 35, 1677; *DCD*, 12.15.3, PL 41, 365. See Grabowski, *op. cit.*, pp. 221-22. Teselle (*op. cit.*, p. 115) explains the difference between the procession of the "Word" (the second person of Trinity) and formation of creatures as follows: "The Word is the only proper image and likeness of God . . . *likeness* because he is in no way unlike the Father; *image* because he is derived directly from or expressed by the Father. Therefore, it cannot be said that man is the image and likeness of God (in the sense above). . . . However, (in the words of Augustine) 'Because man is able to participate in Wisdom through the inward man, it is according to the latter that he is said to be created *ad imaginem* in order that he might be fully formed by this image (that is, the Word) with nothing intervening and in such a fashion that nothing could be closer to God. Thus he would truly know and live and be. No created thing could be greater" (*DDQ*, 51.2, PL 40, 32-33; *DDQ*, 74, PL 40, 85-86). Teselle (*op. cit.*, p. 225) sums up the comparison between Word and creature by saying: "The Word is the image or likeness of the Father, whereas the creatures are unlike him and gain their similarity to God through participation in the Word."

56. *DMC*, 2.4.6, PL 32, 1347.

57. "I cannot observe the body and members of any living thing without finding that measure, number, and order contribute to its harmonious unity. I cannot understand where these perfections come from if they do not come from the highest measure, number, and order which are to be found only in the unchanging and everlasting sublimity of God" *DGM*, 1.16.26, PL 34, 186.

58. See Teselle, *op. cit.*, pp. 117-22.

59. "Everything reaches the perfection determined by its nature when it is in a state of rest. This comes about through the direction established through its natural tendencies, not simply in the universe of which it is a part, but more especially in the God to whom it owes its being and in whom the universe itself exists." *DGL*, 4.18.34, PL 34, 309. See Grabowski, *op. cit.*, pp. 156-57.

60. See *DGL*, 5.22.43, PL 34, 337; 8.23.44, PL 34, 389.

61. For the influence of providence in the development of the Roman empire, See *DCD*, 5.1, PL 41, 141-42.

62. "God moves [*movet*] all of creation by a hidden power and all things are subject to that force: angels follow out his commands, the stars move across the sky, the winds blow now one way and then another, deep pools at the base of waterfalls seethe and explode in mist, meadows spring to life as seeds produce the grass, animals are born and live out their lives following their natural instincts, and evil humans are permitted to harass the just." *DGL*, 5.20.41, PL 34, 336.

63. *DGL*, 4.12.22-23, PL 34, 304-05; *E 205*, 3.17, PL 33, 948.

64. *DGL*, 8.25.46, PL 34, 390.

65. See *DGL* 8.9.17, PL 34, 379.

66. *Ibid.*

67. *DGL*, 8.9.18, PL 34, 380.

68. See *DGL*, 8.26.48, PL 34, 391; 5.23.46, PL 34, 338; 5.4.10, PL 34, 325; *C*, 7.1.2, PL 32, 733-34.

69. *DGL*, 5.21.42, PL 34, 336.

70. See *DGL*, 5.20.41, PL 34, 336.

71. *DGL*, 5.21.42, PL 34, 336. In another place Augustine says: "It is the God we worship who constituted, for each of the natures he created, an origin and purpose of its being and powers of action. He holds in his hands the causes of things, knowing them all and connecting them all. It is he who is the source of all energy in seeds, and he who put rational souls, or spirits, into the living beings. It was he who selected and gave us the gifts of speech and language." *DCD*, 7.30, PL 41, 219-20.

72. See *DGL*, 9.17-18.32-33, PL 34, 406-07.

73. See *Enn 43*, 4, PL 36, 484; *DT*, 3.5-6.11, PL 42, 874-75.

74. *DGL*, 8.10.23, PL 34, 381.

75. *C*, 1.1.1, PL 32 661.

76. On God's gifts to fallen humanity, See *DCD*, 7.31, PL 41, 220-21.

77. *E 194*, 4.16, PL 33, 880.

78. *DGL*, 8.12.25-27, PL 34 382-83.

79. *DGL*, 8.23.44, PL 34, 389-90.

80. *SER 171*, 3.3, PL 38, 934.

81. *Sermon 263a [Verbraken]*, (Mai 98), 1, *Miscellanea Agostiniana*, I, p. 348.

82. *DGL*, 5.16.34, PL 34, 333.

83. *C*, 3.6.11, PL 32, 688.

84. On the story of the prodigal son, See *QE*, 2.33, PL 35, 1344-48. On the story of the good Samaritan, See *SER 131*, 6.6, PL 38, 732.

85. See *ENN 102*, 5-6, PL 37, 1319-21.

86. *ENN 26/2*, 18, PL 36, 208.

87. *SER 171*, 5, PL 38, 935.

Bibliography

A. Latin Texts

Patrologia Latina, J. P. Migne, vols. 32-47 (Paris: 1844-64) (abbreviation: PL).

Corpus Scriptorum Ecclesiasticorum, (Vienna: Tempsky, 1866 -   ) (abbreviation: CSEL).

Corpus Christianorum, series latina (The Hague: Nijhoff, 1953 -   ), (abbreviation: CC).

B. English Translations

The Works of Saint Augustine: A Translation for the 21st Century, J. Rotelle (ed.), Hyde Park, N.Y.: New City Press, 1990-.

Ancient Christian Writers, J. Quasten et al. (ed.), Westminster, Md.: Newman Press: 1946-.

Fathers of the Church, R. Deferrari et al. (ed.), Washington, D.C.: Catholic University of America Press, 1948-.

The Works of Aurelius Augustinus, Marcus Dods (ed.), Edinburgh: T. & T. Clark Co., 1871-1876.

A Select Library of the Nicene and Post-Nicene Fathers, Philip Schaff (ed.), New York: Scribners, 1892.

C. Secondary Sources

Alexander, W. M., "Sex and Philosophy in St. Augustine," *Augustinian Studies* 5 (1974), 197-208.

Alfeche, M., "The Basis of Hope in the Resurrection of the Body according to Augustine," *Augustiniana*, 36 (1986), 240-96.

Babcock, William S., "Augustine on Sin and Moral Agency," *The Journal of Religious Ethics*, 16 (1988), 28-55.

Battenhouse, Roy W. (ed.), *A Companion to the Study of St. Augustine*, New York: Oxford Univ. Press, 1955.

Bonner, Gerald, *St. Augustine of Hippo: Life and Controversies*, Philadelphia: Westminster Press, 1963.

—— *Augustine and Modern Research on Pelagianism*, Villanova, Pa.: Villanova Univ. Press, 1970.

—— *God's Decree and Man's Destiny*, London: Variorum Reprints, 1987.

—— "Augustine's Doctrine of Man," *Louvain Studies*, 13 (1988), 41-57.

—— "Pelagianism and Augustine," *Augustinian Studies*, 23 (1992), 33-52.

—— "Augustine and Pelagianism," *Augustinian Studies*, 24 (1993), 27-48

Bourke, Vernon, *Augustine's Quest of Wisdom*, Milwaukee: Bruce Publishing, 1945.

—— *Augustine's View of Reality*, Villanova, Pa.: Villanova University Press, 1963.

—— "The Body-Soul Relation in the Early Augustine," *Augustine: Second Founder of the Faith: Collectanea Augustiniana I*, eds. J. Schnaubelt & F. Van Fleteren, New York, Peter Lang, 1990, 435-450.

Borresen, Kari E., "Patristic Feminism: The Case of Augustine," *Augustinian Studies*, 25 (1994), 139-52.

Boyer, C., "La théorie Augustinienne des raisons séminales," *Miscellanea Agostiniana*, 2, Rome: Vatican City Press, 1931, 795-819.

Brown, Peter, *Augustine of Hippo*, Los Angeles: University of California Press, 1967.

—— *The Body and Society: Men, Women and Sexual Renunciation in Early Christianity*, New York: Columbia Univ. Press, 1988.

Bubacz, Bruce S., "Augustine's Account of Factual Memory," *Augustinian Studies*, 6 (1975), 181-92.

—— "St. Augustine's *Si fallor, sum*," *Augustinian Studies*, 9 (1978), 35-44.

—— "Augustine's Illumination Theory and Epistemic Structuring," *Augustinian Studies*, 11, (1980), 35-48.

—— *St. Augustine's Theory of Knowledge: A Contemporary Analysis*, New York: Edwin Mellen Press, 1981.

Burnaby, John, *Amor Dei*, London: Hodder and Stoughton, 1938.

Burns, J. Patout, *The Development of Augustine's Doctrine of Operative Grace*, Paris: Études Augustiniennes, 1980.

—— "Augustine on the Origin and Progress of Evil," *The Journal of Religious Ethics*, 16 (1988), 9-27.

Burt, Donald, "Augustine on the Authentic Approach to Death," *Augustinianum* 28 (1988), 527-63.

—— "Friendship and Subordination in Earthly Societies," *Augustinian Studies*, 22 (1991), 83-125.

Cavadini, John, "The Structure and Intention of Augustine's *De Trinitate*," *Augustinian Studies*, 23 (1992), 103-23.

Chadwick, Henry, "The Ascetic Ideal," *Studies in Church History*, 22 (1985).

—— *Augustine*, New York: Oxford Univ. Press, 1986.

—— "Providence and the Problem of Evil in Augustine," *Studia Ephemeridis "Augustinianum,"* 24, Rome: Augustinian Patristic Institute *(Augustinianum)*, 1987.

Christian, William, "The Creation of the World," *A Companion to the Study of St. Augustine*, Roy Battenhouse (ed.), New York: Oxford Univ. Press, 1955, pp. 315-43.

Clark, Elizabeth A., "'Adam's Only Companion': Augustine and the Early Christian Debate on Marriage," *Recherches Augustiniennes*, 21 (1986) 139-62.

Colledge, Edmund, "Caxton's Addition to the *Legenda sancti Augustini*," *Augustiniana*, 34 (1984), 198-212.

—— "James of Voragine's *Legenda sancti Augustini* and its Sources," *Augustiniana* 35 (1985), 281-313.

Coughlan, M.J., "*Si Fallor, Sum* Revisted," *Augustinian Studies*, 13 (1982), 145-50.

Cress, Donald, "Augustine's Privation Account of Evil," *Augustinian Studies*, 20 (1989), 129-42.

Dittes, James E., "Augustine's Search for a Fail-Safe God to Trust," *Journal for the Scientific Study of Religion*, 25, #1 (1986), 57-63.

Duffy, Stephen J., "Our Hearts of Darkness: Original Sin Revisited," *Theological Studies*, 49 (1988), 597-622.

Evans, Gillian R., *Augustine on Evil*, Cambridge: Cambridge Univ. Press, 1982.

—— "Augustine on the Soul: The Legacy of the Unanswered Questions," *Augustinianum*, 25, (1985).

Gannon, M. Ann Ida, "The Active Theory of Sensation in St. Augustine," *New Scholasticism*, 30 (1956), 154-80.

Gilson, Etienne, *The Christian Philosophy of St. Augustine*, New York: Random House, 1960.

Gousmett, Chris, "Creation, Order, and Miracle according to Augustine," *Evangelical Quarterly*, 60 (1988), 217-40.

Grabowski, Stanislaus J., *The All-Present God*, St. Louis: B. Herder, 1954.

Harrison, C., "Measure, Number and Weight in Saint Augustine's Aesthetics," *Augustinianum*, 28 (1988), 591-602.

Hölscher, Ludwig, *The Reality of Mind: Augustine's Philosophical Arguments for the Human Soul as a Spiritual Substance*, London: Routledge & Kegan Paul, 1986.

Hopkins, Jasper, *Augustine on Foreknowledge and Free Will*, Minneapolis: The Arthur J. Banning Press, 1994.

Hunter, David G., "Augustinian Pessimism? A New Look at Augustine's Teaching on Sex, Marriage and Celibacy," *Augustinian Studies*, 25 (1994), 153-77.

Kaufman, Peter I., "Augustine, Evil, and Donatism: Sin and Sanctity before the Pelagian Controversy," *Theological Studies*, 51 (1990), 115-26.

Kirwan, Christopher, *Augustine*, London: Routledge & Kegan Paul, 1989.

Kondoleon, Theodore J., "Augustine's Argument for God's Existence: *De libero arbitrio*, Book II," *Augustinian Studies*, 14 (1983), 105-16.

—— "Augustine and the Problem of Divine Foreknowledge and Free Will," *Augustinian Studies*, 18 (1987), 166-89.

K. Kono, "On *Materia Spiritualis* in Augustine, According to his Exposition of the Beginning of Genesis," *Studies in Medieval Thought,* 33 (1991), 98-109.

Kristo, Jure G., *Looking for God in Time and Memory: Psychology, Theology, and Spirituality in Augustine's Confessions*, Lanham Md.: University Press of America, 1991.

Kuntz, Paul G., "St. Augustine's Quest for Truth: The Adequacy of a Christian Philosophy," *Augustinian Studies*, 13 (1982), 1-22.

Lane, Craig W., "Augustine on Foreknowledge and Free Will," *Augustinian Studies*, 15 (1984), 41-63.

Lehmann, Paul, "The Anti-Pelagian Writings," *A Companion to the Study of St. Augustine*, Roy W. Battenhouse (ed.), New York: Oxford Univ. Press, 1955.

Lousousky, Mary, *De Dono Perseverantiae*, Patristic Studies 91, Washington, D.C.: Catholic University of America Press, 1956.

MacDonald, Scott, "Augustine's Christian-Platonist Account of Goodness," *New Scholasticism*, 63, pp. 485-510.

McGowan, Richard J., "Augustine's Spiritual Equality: The Allegory of Man and Woman with Regard to *Imago Dei,*" *Revue des Études Augustiniennes*, 33 (1987), 255-64.

McKeough, M. J., *The Meaning of the Rationes Seminales in St. Augustine*, Washington, D.C.: Catholic University of America Press, 1926.

Miethe, Terry L., "St. Augustine and Sense Knowledge," *Augustinian Studies*, 8 (1977), 11-20.

Miles, Margaret R., *Augustine on the Body*, Missoula, Montana: Scholars Press, 1979.

Mosher, David L., "The Argument of St. Augustine's *Contra Academicos*," *Augustinian Studies*, 12 (1981), 89-114.

Mourant, John A., "The *Cogitos*: Augustinian and Cartesian," *Augustinian Studies*, 10 (1979), 27-42.

—— *Augustine on Immortality*, Villanova, Pa.: Villanova Univ. Press, 1969.

Nash, Ronald H., *The Light of the Mind: St. Augustine's Theory of Knowledge*, Lexington: University Press of Kentucky, 1969.

—— "Some Philosophic Sources of Augustine's Illumination Theory," *Augustinian Studies*, 2 (1971), 47-66.

O'Connell, Robert J., *St. Augustine's Early Theory of Man, AD 386-391*, Cambridge, Mass.: Harvard University Press, 1968.

—— *St Augustine's Confessions: The Odyssey of Soul*, Cambridge, Mass.: Harvard University Press, 1969.

—— *St. Augustine's Platonism*, Villanova, Pa.: Villanova Univ. Press, 1984.

—— *Imagination and Metaphysics in St. Augustine*, Milwaukee: Marquette Univ. Press, 1986.

—— *The Origin of the Soul in St. Augustine's Later Works*, New York: Fordham University Press, 1987.

—— "Peter Brown on the Soul's Fall," *Augustinian Studies*, 24 (1993), 103-31.

—— "Sexuality in Saint Augustine," *Augustine Today*, ed. Richard John Neuhaus, Grand Rapids, Mich.: William B. Eerdmans, 1993, 60-87.

—— "The *De Genesi contra Manichaeos* and the Origin of the Soul," *Revue des Études Augustiniennes*, 39 (1993), 129-41.

O'Daly, Gerard, *Augustine's Philosophy of Mind*, Los Angeles: University of California Press, 1987.

—— "Predestination and Freedom in Augustine's Ethics," *The Philosophy in Christianity*, Godfrey Vesey (ed.), Cambridge: Cambridge Univ. Press, 1989, 85-97.

O'Donnell, James J., *Augustine*, Boston: Twayne Publishers, 1985.

—— "Augustine's Idea of God," *Augustinian Studies*, 25 (1994), 25-35.

O'Meara, John J., *The Creation of Man in De Genesi ad litteram*, Villanova, Pa.: Villanova Univ. Press, 1977.

—— *The Young Augustine*, New York: Longman, 1980.

—— "Saint Augustine's Understanding of the Creation and the Fall," *Maynooth Review* 10 (1984), 52-62.

O'Toole, Christopher J., *The Philosophy of Creation in the Writings of St. Augustine*, Washington, D.C.: Catholic University of America Press, 1944.

Pagels, Elaine, "The Politics of Paradise: Augustine's Exegesis of Genesis 1-3 versus that of John Chrysostom," *The Harvard Theological Review*, 1985, 67-100.

—— *Adam, Eve, and the Serpent*, New York: Random House, 1988.

Pelikan, Jaroslav, *The Christian Tradition*, vol. 1, Chicago: The University of Chicago Press, 1971, 278-331.

—— *The Mystery of Continuity: Time and History, Memory and Eternity in the Thought of Saint Augustine*, Charlottesville, Va.: The University Press of Virginia, 1986.

—— "An Augustinian Dilemma: Augustine's Doctrine of Grace versus Augustine's Doctrine of the Church?" *Augustinian Studies* 18 (1987), 1-30.

Portalié, Eugène, *A Guide to the Thought of Saint Augustine*, Chicago: Henry Regnery, 1960.

Quinn, John M., "The Concept of Time in St. Augustine," *Augustinianum* 5 (1965), 5-57.

—— "Four Faces of Time in St. Augustine," *Recherches Augustiniennes*, 26 (1992), 181-231.

Ramirez, J. Roland, "The Priority of Reason over Faith in Augustine," *Augustinian Studies*, 13 (1982), 123-32.

Richardson, Cyril C., "The Enigma of the Trinity," *A Companion to the Study of St. Augustine*, Roy W. Battenhouse, ed., New York: Oxford University Press, 1955, 235-56.

Rist, John M., "Augustine on Free Will and Predestination," *Journal of Theological Studies*, 20, 2 (1969), 420-47.

Roberts, Lawrence D., "Augustine's Version of the Ontological Argument and Platonism," *Augustinian Studies* 9 (1978), 93-102.

Roche, W. "Measure, Number and Weight in St. Augustine," *New Scholasticism* 15 (1941), 350-76.

Ross, Donald, "Time, the Heaven of Heavens, and Memory in Augustine's *Confessions*," *Augustinian Studies* 22 (1991), 191-206.

Russell, Frederick, "Only Something Good Can Be Evil," *Theological Studies*, 51 (1990), 698-717.

Sachs, John R., "Current Eschatology: Universal Salvation and the Problem of Hell," *Theological Studies*, 52, 2, (1991), 233-41.

Taylor, John H., "The Meaning of *Spiritus* in St. Augustine's *De Genesi XII*," *Modern Schoolman*, 26 (1948-49), 211-18.

Teselle, Eugene, *Augustine the Theologian* New York: Herder & Herder, 1970.

Teske, Roland J., "The World-Soul and Time in St. Augustine," *Augustinian Studies*, 14 (1983), 75-92.

—— "Augustine's Use of *Substantia* in Speaking about God," *The Modern Schoolman*, 62 (1985), 147-63.

——— "Divine Immutability in Saint Augustine," *The Modern Schoolman*, 63 (1986), 233-49.

——— "The Aim of Augustine's Proof that God Truly Is," *International Philosophical Quarterly*, 26 (1986), 253-68.

——— "The Image and Likeness of God in St. Augustine's *De Genesi ad litteram liber imperfectus*," *Augustinianum*, 30 (1990), 451-51.

——— "St. Augustine's View of the Original Human Condition in *De Genesi contra Manichaeos*," *Augustinian Studies* 22 (1991), 141-55.

Tremmel, William C., "The Converting Choice," *Journal for the Scientific Study of Religion* 10, 1 (1971).

Van Bavel, Tarsicius, "The Creator and the Integrity of Creation in the Fathers of the Church especially in Saint Augustine," *Augustinian Studies* 21 (1990), 1-34.

——— "Augustine's View on Women," *Augustiniana* 39 (1989), 6-53.

Van Der Meer, F., *Augustine the Bishop*, London: Sheed & Ward, 1961.

Van Fleteren, Frederick E., "Authority and Reason, Faith and Understanding in the Thought of St. Augustine," *Augustinian Studies* 4 (1973), 33-72.

Verbraken, Pierre-Patrick, *Études Critiques Sur Les Sermons Authentiques De Saint Augustin*, The Hague: Martin Nijhoff, 1976.

Weaver, F. Ellen and Laporte, Jean, "Augustine and Women: Relationships and Teachings," *Augustinian Studies* 12 (1981), 115-32.

Weismann, F.J., "The Problematic of Freedom in St. Augustine: Towards a New Hermeneutics," *Revue des Études Augustiniennes,* 35 (1989), 104-19.

Williams, Rowan D., "'Good for Nothing?': Augustine on Creation," *Augustinian Studies*, 25 (1994), 9-24.

Index